HAND BOOK OF LUBRICANTS, GREASES AND PETROCHEMICALS TECHNOLOGY

Written By :
EIRI Board of Consultants &

ENGINEERS INDIA RESEARCH INSTITUTE
4449, Nai Sarak, Main Road, Delhi-110 006 (India)
Ph.: 91-11-23918117, 23916431, 23840361, 9811437895
Fax :91-11-23916431, 23918117
* **E-Mail**: eirisidi@bol.net.in
* **Website**: www.eiriindia.org
Also at : 4/54 Roop Nagar, Opp. Kamla Nagar, Delhi—110007

Printed and Published by :

ENGINEERS INDIA RESEARCH INSTITUTE

4449, Nai Sarak, Main Road, Delhi-110 006 (India)
Ph.: 91-11-23918117, 23916431, 23840361, 9811437895
Fax :91-11-23916431, 23918117
✶ **E-Mail**: eirisidi@bol.net.in
✶ **Website**: www.eiriindia.org

ISBN : 978-81-89765-21-7
Printed in New Delhi (India)

Rs. 750/-

Printed and Published by Sudhir Gupta for "Engineers India Research Institute", 4449, Nai Sarak, Main Road, Delhi-110 006 and Printed at Swastik Offset, Delhi

Preface

The Book **Hand Book of Lubricants, Greases and Petrochemicals Technology** covers almost all the basic and advanced details to setup own Product Introduction, Lubricating Base Stocks, Oxidative Degradation and Stabilisation of Mineral Oil Based Lubricants, Lubricating Oils Classification, Synthetic Fluids, Speciality Oils, Miscellaneous Additives and Vegetable Oils, Various Formulations of Lubricants and Grease, Asphalt Technology, Speciality Products, Treatment of Lubes, The Formulation of Automotive Lubricant, Industrial Lubricants, Lubricating Greases, Manufacture of Lubricating Greases, Lubricant and Their Environmental Impact, Jatropha (Bio Diesel) Cultivation & Extraction, Crude Oil Bleaching for Petroleum Jelly, Soluble Cutting Oil, Emulsifiers for Cutting Oils, Peroleum Jelly, Toluene and SBP from Crude Naphtha, White Oil from Kerosene Oil, Transformer Oil, Biodiesel Project Report.

The book has been written for the benefit and to prove an asset and a handy reference guide in the hands of new entrepreneurs & well established industrialists.

ENGINEERS INDIA RESEARCH INSTITUTE

4449, Nai Sarak, Main Road, Delhi-110 006 (INDIA)
E-mail : eirisidi@bol.net.in

Contents

4

Lubricating Oils Classification 27–38

5

Synthetic Fluids 39–54

1

Product Introduction

The recorded *use* of lubricant dates back almost to the birth of civilisation with, early historical development being concerned with the use of lubricant of animals or vegetable origin in transportation of machinery. During the Middle Ages there was a steady development in the use of lubricant, but it is not until AD 1600-1850 that the value of lubricant in decreasing fraction and wear was recongised.

The classical studies of friction suggested that surface roughness played a major role in determining the resistance to sliding between two surface, it was therefore thought that lubricant were effective because they filled by the hollows in surfaces and reduced the roughness. This view was widespread and long sustained, but the classical experimental investigations by Tower (1883) and Petrov (1883). clearly indicated that in successful bearing the rotating journal was completely separated from the bearing by a coherent film of lubricant. The principle of fluid film lubrication was fully recognised when Reynods (1886) analysed the , viscous flow of lubricants in plain bearing and derived the differential equation for pressure that underpins bearing design procedures to the present day.

When the principle of fluid film lubrication had been established for almost 40 years. Hardy (1922) drew attention to another form of protection now known as boundary lubrication. In this condition normally associated with high loads, low speeds and low viscosity's the surface cannot be separated by coherent fluid films that exceed in considerable measure the composite surface roughness. The friction and wear characteristics in this regime are thus determined by the properties of surface films, often of molecular preparation formed on the solids, or generated by adsorption or by chemical reaction between constitutes of the lubricant and the solids. The recognition of this major mode of lubrication provide a sound base for the spectacular development of certain forms of additives later in the 20th century.

Mineral oil was first produced commercially in the 18th and early 19th centuries, but it really established itself towards the end of the 19th century.

Mineral oil rapidly overtook oil of animal and vegetable origin in as the essential lubricant of the 20th century. The disparate nature of the mineral oil derived from different source of crude oil is outlined. Mineral oils readily oxidise at temperature above about 100° C and are reluctant to flow at temperatures lower than about 20°C. As the aerospace industry developed in the 20th century it became necessary to introduce alternative, synthetic base oils. Synthetics still represent a small volume proportion of the base oil used today, but their range of application is extending steadily and they have been accommodated by mineral oil.

Fluid film lubrication is associated with the physical rather than the chemical nature of lubricants, for separating sliding solids. However all this exceptional mechanism for separating sliding solids come into bearing start with stop and the surface of the sliding solids come into contact with each interruption of movement. Furthermore, the major economic pressure for improved efficiency in most form of machinery in the latter year of the 20th century has caused designers to adopt higher mean bearing pressure and lower viscosity fluids, thus reducing the effective minimum film thickness in bearing. In many dynamically loaded bearing and most severally tasted, lubricated machine element such as gears, cams and piston rings, the friction and life for the machine are gears, cams and piston rings, the friction and life of the machine are greatly influenced by the protected afforded by films of molecular proportions formed on the solid by additive. Such substances, added to mineral oil, have contributed in a major way to the spectacular development of lubricant in the second half of the 20th century. Additives. also added to oils to restrict oxidation of the lubricant, to act as rust inhibitors and to perform a role as detergents. Furthermore, they can be used to modify the viscosity temperature characteristics of lubricant and used to modify the viscosity temperature characteristics of lubricant and use to depress the pour point.

The greatly improved ability to analyse and design lubricated machine elements in the latter stages of the 20th Century has progressed along side the formulation of additive containing mineral oil and the introduction of synthetic lubricants. The response of equipment, for machinery to operate in severe environment is quite remarkable. If the engineer or tribologist can draw some satisfaction from the fact that improved analysis, design and manufacture have films or thickness of *0.1-1.* um the chemist or lubricant technologist can certainly claim that none of the would have been possible if additive packages had not produced thin protective layers of molecular proportion of the surface of the bearing solids.

2

Lubricating Base Stocks

Introduction

The bulk of commercial lubricants consist of refined petroleum oils. Crude petroleum consists of very complex mixture of saturated and unsaturated hydrocarbons with minor amount of non-hydrocarbons. Trace amounts of metals are also present in petroleum in the form of suspended inorganic compounds. The hydrocarbons vary in molecular size from methane (CH_4) to compounds of such high molecular weight and low volatility that they cannot be distilled even under high vacuum. Saturated hydrocarbons consists straight chain saturates, branched chain saturates and cycloparallins. The cycloparaffins are also called napthenes in petroleum terminology and consists of rings having five, six or seven carbon atoms with paraffinic side chains. Among the unsaturated hydrocarbons, some crude do contain olefins but mostly the unsaturated compounds are in the form of aromatics. The aromatics may be in aromatics upto seven rings with various alkyl and cycloalkyl groups or biphenyl and its higher homologues.

The sulphur present in crude oils occurs as numerous types of organic compounds and also as hydrogen sulfide and elemental boiling fractions. Nitrogen compounds in various forms, occur in petroleum in smaller concentrations than sulfur compounds. Like sulphur compounds they are usually more concentrated in the higher boiling fraction. Oxygen compounds found in petroleum include carboxylic acid, phenols, ketones, dibenzofurants, lactons and possible esters and alcohols. The most important and varied groups is carboxylic acid.

The low boiling factions of crude petroleum consist of gasoline naptha, kerosene, diesel fuel and gas oil. The higher boiling fractions consist of lubricating oil stocks and wax.

The residue from the distillation consist mostly of asphalt and wax with some viscous lubricating oil.

Some crudes consist predominantly of gasoline and napthas, while others contain asphalt as the principal and constituent. Still other contain lubricating oil distillate as major constitents together with gasoline, naptha gas oil, wax and asphalt in varying proportions.

Classification

It is customary to classify the crude oil into three broad groups of bases the paraffinic base, the napthenic base and mixed base or intermediate base.

This classification has many limitation but is indicating the probable method of processing. The paraffinic base but the oil contains appreciable wax and give lubricating oils of high viscosity index contains appreciable wax.. The naphthene base stock often contain *no* wax and they usually contain high asphalt content. The lubricating oils obtained from napthenic stocks have low viscosity index. Mixed base oils contain both wax and asphalt. Most of the crude oils are mixed base. A further group aromatic base may be made if the crude contains significant amounts of aromatic hydrocardons.

Each of the groups includes a large variety of oils and it sometimes becomes difficult to classify an oil, especially if it is a borderline case. The US Bureau of Mines has concluded that a crude may be classified as one base in low boiling range and another in the high boiling (lubricating oil) range.

The crude petroleum may also be classified into non lubricating and lubricating types. All crude oils can be converted into fuels by various process but not all of them are satisfactory for the production of lubricating oils. Processing of crude petroleum depends on whether we want to produce gasoline and other light fractions or the heavier fractions suitable for lubricating oils. In both cases light fractions are removed by distillation but the yield of light fractions can be increased by the breakdown of heavier fractions by cracking, coking and viscosity breaking process. The yield of fuels, may also be increased by rebuilding process such as alkylation and polymerization from gaseous breakdown products. Thus any crude can be used for the production of fuels. In case of the production of lubricating oil stocks the crude should be inherently rich in heavier fractions and also these fractions have *good* lubricating properties. The lubricating properties of heavier fractions depend on their chemical composition.

Composition and properties of lubricating oil fractions

The petroleum fractions used as lubricants generally contain compounds containing 18 or more carbon atoms. The lubricating paraffinic and aromatic compounds together with hetrocyclic compounds containing sulphure and nitrogen atoms of the thinaphthene indole, quinoline and carbazoles and various most of the chemically bounds oxygen in petroleum fractions. The sulphur, nitrogen and oxygen compounds are removed during refining of petroleum fractions.

The molecules in the lubricating oil fractions consist essentially of the long carbons atom chain attached at both ends a ring system or short branch. Monocycloalkanes and monoaromatics usually have several short branches on cycloparffine ring attached to paraffinic chain. Aromatic along with long paraffinic chains. Polyaromatic usually have all their rings a single condensed nucleus which also might have short branches attached. Polyclic saturates may have all the rings in a single condensed system or two or more ring system may be separated by alkyl chains. Aromatic compounds may also be in the form of biphenyls and their derivaties. Thus the lubes are composed primarily for five characteristic classes; paraffin napthenes, condensed napthenes, aromatic napthenes, napthalenes (two ring aromatic) and multriing aromatic. All molecules in lubricating oil in the range C_{40} C_{25} contain at least one napthene ring whether or not aromatic rings are present. In the lower range upto 12 carbon atoms simple aromatics that is hydrocarbons containing benzene or napthalene rings structure with paraffinic side chains, are present.

Approximate average analysis with respect to kind of molecules of middle part of lubricant fractions, containing 25 to 35 carbon atoms :

Analysis of lubricating oil fraction

Type of Hydrocarbon		Volume % of Lubricant Fractions
Normal Paraffins		13.7
Branched paraffins		8.3
Monocycloparaffins	18.4	
Dicycloparaffins	9.9	→ 44.8
Tri and higher cycloparaffins	16.5	
Mononuclear aromatics with cycloparaffin rings		10.5
Dinuclear aromatics with cycloparaffin rings		8.1
Trinuclear aromatics with cycloparaffin rings		6.6
Multiring aromatics very low in hydrogen with bulk of non hydrocarbon material		8.0

Including as appropriate necessary paraffinic side or connecting groups.

The effect of different type of compounds on the properties of the lubricating oil can be seen as under which gives the composition and viscosity indexes (VI) of two oils one a Raw Coastal medium motor cut oil and the other a mid continent raw medium motor cut oil.

From table we see that paraffinic naphthenes and single ring aromatics are premium oils as far as viscosity index is concerned. The viscosity index of condensed (polycyclic) naphthenes is quite low as the index in the for the condensed aromatic fractions, particularly for the highly condensed aromatic and naphthenic fraction of raw coastal oil. The table also shows that the viscosity index of various types of compounds is also dependent on the source of oil.

Table

Composition of lubricating oil fraction

Compound class	Raw Vol.%	Coastal V.I	mid Vol.%	Continent V.I
Paraffinic	52	102	60	124
napthenes Polycyclic	14	-60	10	47
napthenes Single ring	7	41	8	95
aromatic Naphthalenes (twa ring aromatics)			12	38
Higher condensed aromatics	27	-85	10	-81

Effects of solvent refining

Yield on treatment Vol.% compounds class	Feed 100	Extract 17.8	Raffinate 89		Estimated removal % based on extract
	Average	App. distribution			
	V.I.	Vol%	Vol.%	Vol.%	
Paraffinic	124	60	21	69	6
napthenes Polycyclic	47	10	9	11	16
napthenes Single ring	95	8	10	7	22
aromatics Naphthalenes	38	12	14	13	21
Higher codensed aromatics	-81	10	48	0 approx.	82

This extract was of ~4 viscosity index, produced at a yield 17.8% on extraction viscosity index of raffinate was 1.2. this raffinate was of 99.3 viscosity index produced at an estimated yield of 89% n extraction; viscosity index of extract was about 72.

The higher aromatics and condensed napthenic compounds which give lower viscosity indexes are removed by solvent refining. The effect of solvent refining on the proportion of various compounds. A wax free mid continent medium motor oil was extracted with phenol and the extract and raffinate were separated from phenol by distillation. The raw oil and extracts and raffinate are composed.

From the table it can be observed that phenol preferentially, extracts higher condensed aromatics. Other solvent may extract polycyclic napthenes and bicycle aromatic also. Modern refining methods generally remove most of the polycyclic aromatics and diaromatics and their analogous nonhydrocarbons so that the final lubricant consist chiefly of saturates and monocyclic aromatics fractions. Thus the properties of oil when depend upon the bulk composition such as viscosity index are controlled by the properties of saturates and monocyclic aromatics the properties of saturate (paraffinic naphthene and polyecyclic naophthenes) and monocyclic aromatic fractions of lubricating oil fraction of various type of oils are shown below:

Viscosity index of lubricating oil fractions

Oil type	Viscosity index of saturates	Viscosity index monocyclic aromatic
Paraffinic	120+	80
Mixed base	100	30
Napthenic	70	Negative

From the above table we can see that high viscosity index (HVI) oils can be produced from the paraffinic base or mixed base oils. Even if all the aromatics were removed from the napthenic oils it would still have viscosity index of 70. Typical values from HVI oils are greater than 70. The monocyclic aromatics in naphthenic base condensed napththenic rings which are have seen before give low viscosity indexes. The saturates of napththeic base oil also give relatively low viscosity indexes because of the same reason of condensed naphthenic rings being attached to paraffinic chain. Monocyclic aromatics in paraffinic base oil have higher viscosity indexes because they are attached with paraffinic chains. From the viscosity index point of view paraffins with single ring cycloparaffins and monocylic aromatics with single ring cycloparaffins are the most suitable.

Paraffinic oils have higher viscosity index, flash point and boiling range than naphthenic oils. But paraffinic oils are not suitable at low temperature and increase the pour point (the temperature at which the oil just barely pours). For the reasons naphthenic oils are preferred at low temperature. Napthenic oils have lower viscosity index but their viscosity index and high temperature stability may be increased by the use of solvent refining techniques.

Aromatic especially condensed ring aromatics cause excessive sludging and carbonization during high temperature operation. Condensed the ring napthenes also suffer from the above disadvantage. A paraffinic type was formerly preferred to napthenic type oil because of its superior lubricating quality at than temperature. Modern refining methods can produce good quality lubricant form any type of crude. When lubricating qualities are equal, napthenic oil have the advantage that when carbon residue do from inside the engine, the carbon residue from napthenic oil is less hard then from paraffinic oil. However the carbon residue should not be excessive this is avoided by removing polycyclic compounds through solvent refining.

Although compounds sulphur, nitrogen and oxygen in their structure are present in only trace amounts, these substance being chemically more reactive may have a significant effect on important lubricating properties such as sludging tendency and thermal and oxidative stability. These compounds are usually removed during refining processes.

In addition to normally liquid hydrocarbons and trace quantities of nitrogen, sulphur and oxygen compounds lubricating oil fraction may contain asphalt, wax and resins which have high molecular weight and are solid at normal temperature and pressures. Wax crystallizers at low temperature from oils, and asphalt and resins cause sluding and have serious effect on colour and carbon residue. The substances are also removed during refining.

A fully saturated oil free from all nonhydrocarbons is not necessarily the best lubricating oil, some of the natural compounds in petroleum may be beneficial, for example by acting as oxidation inhibitors. In actual practice a compromise is made between various properties by making compositional analysis and actual testing. Modern refining process make it possible to use many crude oils, for the production of lubricating base stocks, which are not inherently suitable for the purpose.

Production of lub stocks

The low boiling fractions must be removed from crude petroleum, before the production of lubricating oil base stock or lub stocks. This is done by distillation of crude petroleum at 300 -360 °C at atmospheric pressure usually with stream injection in a fractionator. The light fractions are separated into various fractions and are further stripped with stream in another smaller fractionator. The light fractions obtained are light gasoline, naptha, kerosene or "skimming" the undistiled residue left in the first fractionator is commonly called 'topped crude' the topped crude is topped from the bottom of the fractionator and is further fractionated to produced the various lub stocks.

The lubricating oil fractions are too higher boiling (about 350 °C and the higher) to be distilled at atmospheric pressure without decomposition. They are distilled at reduced pressure either by using a vacuum or steam or a combination of the two. The reduced oil is preheated and fed to a vacuum tower. Some gas oil, especially in parffinic crude, tends to remain in reduced crude during topping operation. This gas oil is removed from top of vacuum tower. Two low viscosity waxy distillates and a high viscosity distilled 'cylinder stock' are usually produced as sidestream products. Each stream is further stripped with vacuum to meet flash point requirements.

There are slight variations in the production of bottom product of the vacuum tower depending on the type of crude oil. In a third method a compromise is made between the above two methods. In this method some cylinder stock is left with the asphalt in the bottom. The short residue is further treated with propane to remove the asphalt. The third method allows lower temperature or less vacuum to be used in the tower than when asphalt is the bottom product and also yields more heavy oils.

In the early days of petroleum processing the reduced stock was separated into distillate by steam refining. The distillate was then dewaxed or pressed and filtered through clay to produce neutrals of 60-300SSU viscosity at 50 °C. the neutrals were further fractionated into light or medium non viscous neutrals and the residue was called viscous neutral. The residue from original steam refining was called stream cylinder stock and after deasphalting, viscous neutral was also sometimes mixed with the bright stock. The viscous neutral also sometimes mixed with bright stock. Now a days 'cylinder stock' refers to any high viscosity stock left after lighter parts have been distilled. Sometimes the topped crude was first pressed to remove the wax and then fire distilled without stream at atmospheric pressure. The over head fractions were called pale oil and the residue red oil. Now a days red and pale refer to the colour of oil without referring to the method of manufacture.

Wax distillated contain wax which crystallizes at low temperature and thus increase the pour point. Heavy fraction of crude contain asphalt and resinous materials which are undersiable because they cause excessive sluding in service. Asphalt materials also have a serious effect on colour and carbon residue at high temperature. Aromatics especially condensed ring aromatics cause operation and effect the viscosity index adversely. Sulpher, nitrogen and thermal and oxidative stability. These compounds, must be removed before the oils can be used as lubricants. Various refining process are used to remove these compounds. The processes are discussed below in brief :

Deasphalting

Deasphalting may be done by vacuum distillation in which asphalt is obtained as a residue after distillation of light ends. This process has the disadvantage that is leaves a good deals of desirable material in the asphaltic residue. This process does not produce a residual lube oil which are necessary in the heavier grades of lubricating oil.

Propane deasphalting has grained prominence in recent years because it eliminates a very hard, oil free asphalt without the use of high temperature required in vacuum distillation. This result in relatively light coloured heavy lube stocks because very little decomposition occurs. Another method of deasphalting is treatment with concentrated sulphuric acid but this method gives high loss of hydrocarbons and also the disposal of acid sludge is a problem. Acid treatment is not employed in deasphalting of reduced crude and residual stocks containing appreciable matter but it can be used to remove the final traces of asphaltic and unstable compounds.

Near its critical temperature propane dissolves hydrocarbons while rejecting asphaltic materials. Also it dissolves smaller molecules in preference to larger ones. The process consist of a countercurrent liquid extraction. The charge stock is introduced near the top of an extraction lower and liquid propane near the botton using solvent oil ratios from 4:1 to 10:1 pressure is 300-500 psi, process using propane and cresylic acid may also be sued cresylic acid is selective process is used for reduced crudes or residual stocks of high asphalt or aromatic content.

Solvent refining

Solvent refining process is used to improve the viscosity index and paraffinicity of lube stocks. The solvent used are such that they preferentially dissolve aromatic naphthenic and unsaturated hydrocarobons as well as large amounts of the sulphur and other undesirable element found in petroleum. Thus solvent extraction make it possible to produce lubricant from many crude which do not contain inherently good lubricants.

Many solvent such as furfural, phenol, liquid sulphur dioxide, dichloroethyl ether, nitrobenzene can be used in solvent refining. A mixture of liquid sulphur dioxide and benzene is employed for refining stocks to yields lubricating oils with improved oxidation stability and viscosity index, under proper condition of treatment dewaxing is simultaneously effect. Duo Sol process as described above removes asphalt along with aromatic and naphthenic constituents.

Dewaxing

Raw oil fractions containing appreciable quantities of paraffin wax are dewaxed to obtain oils of low pour point. Wax crystallizes out at low temperature and hence wax containing oils are underabe for low temperature applications. The wax oil mixture that distill from petroleum below about 440 °C contain crystalline wax that can be filtered from oil in simple filter presses. The wax distillates are first chilled by refrigeration to crystallize the wax and the wax is then filtered. The wax oil mixture that distills at temperature above 440°C contains was which is microcystalline and hence cannot be filtered. Such a wax is removed by chilling and centrifuging in naptha solution. Raw petroleum was oil stocks that boil at temperatures above 440°C are dark coloured materials that may contain significant amounts of asphalt. In such cases the high boiling charge stock (called cylinder stock) is diluted with 60-80% naptha, treated with sulphuric acid to remove asphaltic sludge, neutralized and then decolourized by heating it with finely powdered fuller earth. The deasphalted decolorised and dewaxed cylinder stocks which are not dewaxed are called straight run cylinder stocks.

The above methods have now been superseded by solvent dewaxing which remove both crystalline and macrocrystalline waxes. The solvent used in such they it dissolves preferentially the at low temperatures. The solvents usually employed are methyl ethyl ketones, propane, mixture of liquid sulpher dioxide and benzene, mixture of ethylene dishloride and benzens, and trichlorethlene. Methyl ethyl ketone is the most widely and trichlorthlene. Methyl ethyl ketone is the most widely used solvent. The solvent is added to the oil mixed and chilled when the wax separates out. The solution is separated from wax by filtration or centrifuging and distilled to recover the solvent. Dewaxing with propane is carried out at high pressures to maintain propane gas in the liquid state; chilling is affected by the evaporation of a part of the propane is solution.

Decolourizing

Nearly all lubricating oils must be decolourised even those that are produced by the solvent refining process. The main bulk of dark coloured materials is eliminated by vacuum distillation by deasphalting, by solvent extraction or in older practice by acid treating but the last traces of coloured materials are removed by hydrogen treating, by acid treating and clay contacting and to a limited extend by percolation through a bed of absorbent clay.

Hydrogen treating is the newest and the rapidly growing method of decolouring. The operation is usually a mild hydrogenation, termed hydrofinishing conducted at a relatively low pressure and a relatively low temperature. However by introducing some cracking function to the catalyst, more severe treatment, approaching hydrocracking, can be conducted resulting in extensive saturation of aromatic rings and almost complete elimination of sulphur and nitrogen compounds. Hydrogen treatment result in improved oxidation stability colour, and viscosity index, and reduced tendency to form carbon redidue. Oils with very high viscosity index can be produced by hydrocarking . the hydrogen treated oils do not need further decolouizing. hydrogen treatment is usually done before dewaxing.

Acid treatment is one of the oldest decolouring methods. Today acid treatment is generally limited to the production of medicinal and technical white oils. Acids treatment removes primarily unsaturated, asphaltic and unstable compounds which would case the oil to darken when exposed to air. The acid treatment reduces the tendency of oil to form sludge and also improves specific gravity, viscosity index and flash and fire points. In the case of heavy distillates and residual oil stocks it improves colour and decrease carbon residue. The oil is intimately mixed with 66c be sulphuric acid and the asphatic and aromatic sludge is removed by settling or centrifuging. The acidic oil is settle which is removed by settling or centrifuging. The acidic oil is neutralized with casutic soda, ammonia or in some cases by treatment with absorbent clays.

The clay contacting method consist of intimately mixing the oil with finely divided clay and then filtering. It is usually practiced on acid stage oil, that is acid treated but not neutralized. The oil is usually heated to a temperature about 50F below the flash point of the oil. Activated fuller earth bauxite or benton it, is used for this purpose. Resinous, asphaltic, carbonaceous and sulphure bearing constituent are removed by clays through preferential absorption.

In percolating filtration the oil is usually neutralized acid treated oil, but certain light coloured stocks do not requires acid treatments. The heated oil is poured from the top of a tower packed with activated clay and the percolated oil is collected. The spent clay may be regenerated in a kiln. This treatment also removes traces of organic acids, mineral acids, selected solvent from previous treatment apart from the usual colouring asphaltic, sulphur bearing and carboneous constituents.

The light and medium viscosity, solvent refined, dewaxed and decolourized distillate oil are called neutral stocks while deasphlated dewaxed and decolourized heavy or cylinder stocks are called bright stocks.

White oils are oils in the lubricating oil range that have been drastically refined usually with fuming sulphuric acid. These oils are used in specially products such as transforming oils, cable oils and medicinal oils.

Yield and properties of lubricating oil base stocks

The products derived from distillation and refining processes vary widely in composition and characteristic depending upon the type of source of crude oil charged to the distillation still and the nature of refining process. The naphthenic crude produce oils with viscosities varying from 40 to 150 SSU at 210 °F and asphaltic residues of viscosities up to 1000SSU at 210°F which may be useful for the lubrication of crude machinery such as wire ropes and open gears. Paraffinic and mixed base crude produce lubricating stocks with viscosity's in the range of 40-700 SSU at *50°C.*

Yield

The mixed base or paraffinic crudes usually contain considerable amount of wax while naphthenic base crudes give high amount of asphalt. The table give the yield of asphalt, wax and dewazed oil from various reduced crudes. The table also gives the yield of 60,80 and 100 viscosity index oils from dewaxed oils.

Properties

Table 2.1 gives the typical properties of lubricating case stocks of American origin.

Table 2.1 gives the properties of base stocks obtained from Indian refineries.

Table 3.1 gives the properties of various base stocks produced in Haldia refinery from Light Iranian (aghajari)crude oil.

Base stocks are usually divided into spindle or light, medium or intermediate, heavy and extra heavy or bright stocks, according to increasing viscosity. These stock may further be divided into light viscosity index (LVI) and high viscosity index (HVI) stocks according to viscosity index. These different petroleum lubricating base stocks are blending with each other compounded with other animals, vegetable or synthetic oils to meet the different specifications of density, viscosity, viscosity index, pour point etc. additives are also added to obtain special properties.

Table 2.1

Yield of various crudes

	Asphalt %	Wax %	Dewaxed oil		Percentage of dewazed oil		
			%	V. I.	60 V.I.	80 V.I.	100 V.L
California Waxt crude A	32.8	11.0	56.2	+30	46.2	36.2	22
California Naphthenic A	52.9	2.4	44.7	+27	29.9	20.6	9.5
Taxas Crude B	17.6	4.3	78.1	+103			78
Arabic Crude B	26.0	9.0	65.0	+72		61.4	50
Iron crude A	24.8	11.7	64.5	+58		52.3	38
Borneo Crude A	10.6	3.0	59.4	-142	25.7	19.6	13
Sumatra Crude A	21.6	41.8	36.6	+68		28.0	20
Venezuela A	19.5	3.2	77.3	-171	30.8	18.6	8

Table 2.2

Typical properties of lubricating base stocks

	Carbon residue wt%	Colour	Flash point	Gravity deg. API	Pour point	Viscosity SSU 100°F	Viscosity SSU 210°F	VI
Asphatic or naphthenic residue	12.0	Black	530	10.0	(+)50		1050	
Paraffinic or mixed base bright stocks, solvent processed	1.1	Green	535	27	(+) 10	1700	160	96
Paraffinic or mixed base stream refined	1.3	7.0*	520	22.0	(+)25		160	
Paraffinic cylinder stock steam processed	2.2	Green	580	23	(+) 15		330	
Distilled stock								
Asphaltic or napthenic acid treated, neutral	0.02	2.0*	365	22	(-20)	300	47.5	40
Asphaltic or napthenic acid treated, heavy stock	0.02	6.0*	470	2	(+_10)	3600	120	10

Asphatic or naphthenic solvent	0.02	2.0*	400	26.0	(~)25	300	49.8	65
Paraffinic or mixed base neutral	0.03	2.0*	410	27.5	(+)20	190	46	100
paraffinic Neutral	0.02	2.5*	425	29.5	(+)20	190	46	100
Paraffinic or mixed base acid treated, neutral	0.03	3.0*	410	27	(+)5	200	45.1	175
Paraffinic or mixed base 98 VI, heavy neutral	0.04	2.5*	490	28	(+)10	650	72	98

** Viscosity in second saybolt universal (SSUO

*Expressed in NPA (National Petroleum Association) Colour.

Table 2.3

Typical properties of lubricating Base stocks

Base oil	Pour point °C	Viscosity in Centistocks		Viscosity index
From Madras Refinery Ltd.				
HVI Light Neutral	(~)6	10.75	2.70	92
HVI 150, neutral	(~)6	32.15	5.36	107
LVI	(~)6	35.50	5.13	71
HVI Intermediate neutral	(~)6	70.28	8.28	94
SAE30	(~)6	118.74	11.56	92
HVI Heavy neutral	(~)3	173.20	14.97	93
From lube India Ltd.				
LVI	(-)6	30.26	4.85	85
150 Neutral	(~)6	35.34	5.47	98
500 Neutral	(~)6	107.90	11.32	99
1300 Neutral	(~)3	276.60	21.18	99

Table 2.4

Typical properties of Base Stocks from Aghajari Crude

Base oil	**Carbon conradson % max.**	**Viscosity SSU at 100°F**	**VI Min.**	**Colour ASTM Max.**	***Pour* Point °C**	**Flash point °C min.**
Neutral oil						
Spindle	0.01	60	95	0-0.5	(~)12	150
Intermediate	0.05	300	95	1-1.5	(~)7	243
Heavy	0.1	700	90	3.5-4	(~)7	266
Bright stock	0.6	2500	90	4-4.5	(~)7	300
Pale oils						
Spindle		70	60		(~)12	
Intermediate		500	70		(~)7	
Heavy		1300	70		(~)7	
Bright stock		5500	60		(~)7	

Development in processing in India

In India, the Digboi Refinery (Assam oil company) still uses conventional technology, starting with vacuum distillation followed by acid treatment, clay contacting and dewaxing by chilling (sweating process). The Brauni refinery (IOC) uses phenol extraction instead of acid treatment followed by dewaxing and clay contacting. The Madras Refinery (MRL) employs furfural extraction for most stocks and uses modern hydrofinishing techniques followed by dewaxing instead of dewaxing and clay contacting. The Lube refinery (LIL) uses phenol extraction instead of furfural extraction followed by hydrofinishing and dewaxing, it also employ acid treatment of some stock. The Haldia refinery also employs solvent extraction and hydrofinishing.

Thus is evident that the trend is towards use of latest technology. The latest techniques of manufacturing lube oils by hydro cracking eliminates the needs of solvent extraction for viscosity index improvement and will enable the manufacturing of very high viscosity index lube oils. However the suitability of this process for adaptation *in* our refineries to be established.

3

Oxidative Degradation and Stabilisation of Mineral Oil Based Lubricants

Introduction

The reaction of atmospheric oxygen with hydrocarbon polymer and liquid hydrocarbons (lubricants) as well as with certain biological systems, under varying conditions of temperature and oxygen pressure are undesirable processes. Such reactions lead to a deterioration of these materials. All oxidative process with oxygen have a common reaction pattern attributable to the biradical status of oxygen.

The aim of this contribution is to present the reaction mechanisms of the degradation process of lubricants and the factors influencing them. In addition, the mechanism by which antioxidants inhibits lubricant oxidation with respect to specific industrial and engine oil applications are suggested.

Autoxidation of hydrocarbons

Oxidation of hydrocarbons at low temperature (30-120°C)

The self accelerating oxidation of hydrocarbons is called autoxidation. The initial stage is characterised by a slow reactions with oxygen followed by a phase of increased conversion until the process comes to a standstill. The degradation is driven by an autocatalytic reaction which can be described by the well established free radical mechanism. It consists of four distinct stages:

- initiation of radical chain reaction
- propagation of the radical chain reaction
- chain branching
- termination of the radical chain reaction

Initiation of the radical chain reaction .

Under moderate temperature and oxygen partial pressure greater than 50 tor, the first step is a process which a catalysed by traces of transition metalions.

R refers to a long chain alkyl substitutent and the catalyst M is a transition metal such as *Co,* Fe, Cr, Cu or Mn. The rate of initiation is very slow.

The site of the oxygen attack is determined by the strength of the C~H bond and the reactivity for hydrogen abstraction increase in the following order:

$$RCH_2\sim H<R_2CH\sim H<R_3C\sim H<RCH=CH(R)HC\sim H<C_6H_5(R)HC\sim H$$

Hence oxidation of an n~paraffin normally commences by abstraction of a hydrogen at the second carbon atom (alpha -position to the CH_3 group).

Propagation of the radical chain reaction.

Once an alkyl radical has been formed this reacts irreversibly with oxygen to form an alkyl peroxy radical:

$$R(CH_3)CH+0_2 \xrightarrow{k_3} R(CH_3)CH\sim OO$$

Reaction is extremely fast and has a very low activation energy. The rate of reaction of carbon centered radical with oxygen depends the type of substitutents attached to the C atom and increase in the following order

$$H_3C<C_6H_5(R)CH<RCH=CH(R)CH<R_2CH<R_3C$$

For instance, a tertiary alkyl radical reacts 10 times faster with oxygen than a methyl radical. This difference in reactivity explains why hydrocarbons with tertiary hydrogen (iso~paraffins)are oxidised faster than n~paraffins.

The next step in the chain propagation scheme is the hydrogen abstraction by a peroxy radical from another hydrocarbon:

$$R(CH3)CHOO+RH \xrightarrow{k3} R(CH3)CHOOH+R$$

Since peroxy radical process in low energy status they react selectively and abstract tertiary hydrogen atoms in preference to secondary and primary hydrogen atoms (C~H primary :C~H Secondary :C~H tertiary- *1:30:300* as relative rates; primary and secondary peroxy radicals shows a three to five times higher reactivity than tertiary peroxy radicals.

A more favourable route of hydrogen abstraction by a peroxy radical occurs via an intramolecular propagation.

The hydroperoxide peroxy radical reacts with hydrocarbons through intermolecular hydrogen radical abstraction resulting in an alkyl dihydroperoxide and a chain initiating alkyl radical. Radical may also intramolecularly abstract a hydrogen radical.

The occurrence *of* these intramolecular reaction sequence leads to an increased rate of formation of hydroperoxide, which result *in* a reinforced autocatalytic degradation of the hydrocarbons.

Chain branching.

During the early stage of autoxidation various types of hydroperoxides are generated. At low concentrations they may be cleaved homolytically to yield an alkoxy and a hydroxy radical:

However this process is thwarted because of a high activation energy, hence reaction only plays a significant role at higher temperatures or under catalysed conditions. Once formed hydroxy and especially primary alkoxy radicals are so active that they abstracts hydrogen atoms in non selective reactions;

As a consequence of hydroxide accumulation and subsequent cleavage, the concentration of reactive free radicals initiating new chains increases. The time from the beginning of the oxidation to the autocatalytic phase of the autoxidation is called the induction period.

Termination of the radical chain reaction.

Autoxidation is followed by an autoretardation stage resulting in a standstill before the hydrocarbon is completely consumed. This autotermination is called the chain termination reaction and dominates in this final phase of the oxidation process such that degradation comes to a halt. Termination may be effected by the combination of radical species such as peroxy radicals yield ketones and alcohols:

The primary and secondary peroxy radicals form intermediates which disproportionate to non radical degradation products. In contrast, tertiary peroxy radicals may either combine to give di-tertiary alkyl peroxides or undergo a cleavage reaction leading to ketones and alkyl radicals

Oxidation of hydrocarbons at high temperature (>120°C)

Above 120 °C the degradation process can dived into a primary and a secondary oxidation phase.

Primary oxidation phase initiation and propagation of the radical chain reaction are the same as discussed under low temperature conditions, but the selectivity is reduced and the reaction rate is increased. At high temperature the cleavage of hydroperoxide plays the most important role.

Secondary oxidation phase.

At higher temperature the viscosity of the bulk medium increases as result of the polycondensation of the diffunctional oxygenated products formed in the primary oxidation phase. Further polycondensation and polymerisation reactions of these high molecular weight intermediates result in products which are no longer soluble in the hydrocarbon. The resulting precipitate is called sludge; under thin film oxidation conditions, as in the case of lubricant film on a metal surface, varnish like deposit are formed.

Metal catalysed autooxidation of hydrocarbons

The decomposition of an alkyl hydroperoxide molecule occurs at temperatures of about 150°C. transition metal ions having two ionic valence states, such as Fe^{2+3+},$Pb^{2+/4+}$ and Cu l+/2+, reduce the activation energy of this decomposition process, these ions must be present as metal soaps otherwise they are not catalytically active.

Chain braching under the influence of a catalyst at a given temperature proceeds faster when compared with the uncatalysed reaction. The consequence is a high rate of hydroperoxide formation (and hence oxidation).

Oxidation stability of base oils

The base stocks used for lubricants are a mixture of C_{20}—C_{45} hydrocarbons which can be subdivided into three main groups, paraffins, napthenes and aromatics. In addition, intermolecular combinations of these three groups also comprise a part of the base stock composition. Traces of nitrogen sulfur and oxygen containing heterocycle, together with mercaptans (RSH) thioethers (R~S~R) and disulfides (R~ S-S-R) are an integral part of the complex composition of lubricating base, oil. some of these compounds may act as natural antioxidants, other as pro oxidants.

The compositions of base stocks are greatly influenced by the refining processes, their oxidation stability shows a maximum when the aromatic content is between 10 and 20%.

This reason for the strong increase in oxidation stability at the optimum aromatic sulfur ratio is the result of synergistic interaction pattern between phenols and certain thioethers. These phenols are formed by an acid catalysed decompositions of hydroperoxides, where the peroxide groups is in the side chain at the alpha position to the aromatic nucleus. The necessary catalytic traces of acids arise from a thermal cleavage of certain oxidised sulfides and disulfides together with further oxidation of the cleavage products of SO3/ H2SO4. The rates of transformation of these aromatic hydroperoxides depns on the types of aromatic compounds . alkylated polynuclear aromatics reacts much faster than alklbenzenes as they are energetically favoured to undergo acid catalysed decomposition's.

The polynuclear aromatics, toghet with the appropriate sulfure compounds, retorted the rate of oxidation in the post induction phase when sufficient hydroperoxides have formed. However, they also contribute to sludge formation via polycondensation reactions especially when the aromatic sulfur ratio falls outsides the optimum value according to the fuchs concept.

Inhibition of oxidation degradation of lubricants

The use of additives to control lubricant degradation requires a focus on alkyl radical; (R) alkylperoy radical (R) and hydroperoxide (ROOH). Primary alkoxy radicals (RCH2O*) and hydroxy radicals (HO*) rapidly abstract hydrogen from the substrate. It is therefore very unlikely that they can be deactivated by nature or synthetic antioxidants. In practice three additive type have proven to be successful in controlling the degradation of lubricating oils.

- Radical scavengers
- hydroperoxide decomposers
- synergistic mixtures of these

Radical scavengers

The most widely used types of radical scavengers are phenolic and aminic antioxidants. Organo copper salts have been introduced to control the oxidative degradation of engine oils.

Sterically hindered phenols

Phenols which are substituted in the 2 and 6 positions with tertiary alkyl groups are called sterically hindered phenols. The most common substituents is the tertiary butyl groups.

Reaction mechanism

Sterically hindered phenols like (VII) compete successfully with the rate determining step of the propagation reaction.

Aromatic amines

Secondary aromatic amines are another important class of antioxidants used in lubricants. The principal substituents of the nitrogen atom are either two aryl or one aryl and a naphthyl group.

Reaction mechanism

The reaction mechanism of diphenylamines is dependent on the temperature, under low temperature conditions (< 120°C) the interaction with peroxy radicals predominates.

Organocopper antioxidants

A breakthrough in terms of controlling the oxidation of automotive oils have been achieved with the introduction of organocopper salts, they can also act as pro oxidant and several bench oxidation test use copper or copper salt as a catalyst in order to make test conditions more severs and so shorten test duration, the catalytic activity of copper ions dominates up to 40ppm of copper but in the range of *100-200* ppm in combination with ZnDTP or dthio thadiazoles organcopper salts control the oxidation of engine oil.

Organosulfur Compounds

Reactions mechanism of organosulfur compounds. The most important reaction melamine to elimiate hydroiperoxides is the acid catalysed decomposition. The catalysts are protic (RS)2H) or Lewis (S)2) acids.

Zinc dialkyi dithicarbamates.

These compounds are mainly used as antioxidants although, like the ZnDTP, they also have extreme pressure activity.

Multifunctional additives

Zinc dithiophosphates.

The dominating position of ZnDTP as additives for lubricating oils is due to their multifunctional performance. Not only do they act as antioxidants, but they also improve the wear inhibition of the lubricant, and project metals against corrosion. ZnDTPs are mainly used to formulate anti wear hydraulic fluids and engine oils.

organomolybdenum compounds.

Recent patent literature shows that these compounds are of general interest in the engine oil areas. They are antioxidants and in addition improve the frictional and anti wear characteristics of the lubricants.

phenates and salicylates.

Both phenates and slaiculates of magnesium or calcium behave as antioxidants at high temperature . the antioxidant activity may be related to hydroperoxide decomposition by the sulfure in structure and peroxy radical scavenging by the OH groups in structure.

sulfur nitrogen and sulfur./ phoshours compounds.

Other multifunctional sulfur/ nitrogen., sulfur/ phosphorus based additives have antioxidant and antiwear properties. Syntheses and generalised chemical structures.

Synergism between antioxidants

The effectiveness of one class of antioxidant may be enhanced by combining it with another type of stabiliser. Hence, combining two different peroxy radical scavengers, in a lubricant gives improved oxidation stability compared with either alone. This form of additive response is called synergism or, more specifically, homosynergism because they operated by the same stabilisation mechanism.

Application of antioxidants

Industrial lubricant in service have to prevent damage to the machinery which arise from friction between moving parts. Oxidation stability is one of the key requirement if the lubricant because the oxidation degration products, e.g, peroxy radicals hydroperoxide and organic acids as well as sludge and deposits, are detrimental to the equipment. The well as sludge and deposits, are detrimental to.the equipment. The important role of antioxidants, to protect the various types of base oil under different operation conditions, is outlined in the following sections.

Anti wear hydraulic fluids

Requirements . increased severity of pump operations and the trend to move universally applicable hydraulic fluid lead to the following requirement:

- improved oxidation stability
- reduced sludge formation (better filterability)
- higher thermal stability
- less internal friction (energy conservation)
- good hydrolytic stability
- excellent filterability

Two classes of lubricant have emerged with fulfil these stringent requirement

- premium grade ashless (ZnDTP free)lubricants
- premium grade ZnDTP based lubricants containing calcium detergents for improved thermal and hydrolytic stability of the ZnDTP.

Antioxidant technology. In order to give an indication of the oxidation and thermal stability of a variety of ZnDTP containing and ashless antiwear hydraulic fluids.

In order to boost the oxidation stability of fluids formulated with stabilised ZnDTP(in most cases zinc di 2 ethylhexydithiophosphate) phenolic or aminic antioxidantsim often in combination are added. In a similar waty to the ashless antioxidants, the response pattern of the ZnDTP used in these fluids is strongly influenced by the degree of raffination of the base stock.

Future antioxidant technology

ZnDTP sterically hindered phenols and alkylated diphenylamines are the groups of products fulfilling the present need of the lubricant industry concerning protection of lubricant against oxidation. There are important driving forces leading to future antioxidants:

- environmental concerns
- higher performance standards
- base stock variability

Antiodidants for industrial lubricants

Presently, there is a strong demand for environmentally acceptable fluids. These bio lubes needs to satisfy biodegradation and bioaccumulation standards, which mineral oils based for many industrial applications will develop. Not only the base fluid but also the antioxidants used in them will have to fulfil certain specifications for aquatic toxicity, biodegradation and bioaccumulation. Because the antioxidant response in these new fluids is different from mineral oil based lubricant, new classes of ashless bio antioxidants may be developed.

Due to environmental concerns, the majority of ZnDTP based antiwear hydraulic fluids will be gradually replaced by asheless formulations using antioxidant technology which is environmentally acceptable, in this connection, the Blue angle specification in Germany for biodegradable hydraulic fluids represent a milestones in terms of toxicity and ecotoxicity requirements for the additives, including antioxidants, used to formulate them, currently no biodegradable hydraulic fluid meets these criteria.

There is general trend to reduce the size of industrial equipment without reducing power output. This lead to increased thermo oxidative stress on the lubricant, which has to be met with more effective antioxidant substituting existing antioxidant with lower volatility, higher molecular weight products. Also, poorer quality base stocks will lead to higher treat levels of antioxidants.

Antioxidants for engine oils

Lubricant for the next generation of passenger engine will have to cope with increased power out put from smaller engines, longer drain intervals and reduced oil consumption. Thus the oil will be exposed to increase temperature for longer times and to higher NO concentration. Ceramic parts will lead to even higher temperatures. Thus a new antioxidant types will be requried which has low volatility high thermal stability, the ability to control future higher NO level in the blow by and piston cleanliness.

The limitation of particulate emissions, especially in the US from 1994 onwards, and their strong impact on future engine design raise from question of how future diesel engine oil will be formulated. Ashles antioxidant, leading to improved deposit control and therefore via reduced oil consumption to less particulate emission, could be an important building block.

Biodegradable engine oils are controversially discussed in the literature nevertheless, the industry is developing proprietary technology, based on ashless antioxidants and antiwear additives, and seek to establish a market position.

4

Lubricating Oils Classification

Introduction

Lubricating oils are generally classified according to the use they are put. Lubricating oils are used in a wide variety of application under varying conditions of temperature, pressure and speed. Each application requires a specific performance characteristics from the lubricating oil. In some purpose lubricating oil may be used for purpose other than strict lubricating, for example the transformer oil is used for the double purpose of electric insulation and cooling. Thus, it is clear that a thorough classification based on uses would requires as many types of lubricating oils as there are application. Such as classification would be too cumbersome and not of much practical purpose, however a broad classification based on use is possible, such as classification is not perfect and there may be overlapping in some case but this is unavoidable in view of many uses to which a lubricating oil may be put.

Classification

There may be many ways of classifying lubricating oils based on use. A simple classification is given below. Lubricating oil may be classified into following board groups.

A. Automotive oils
B. Industrial oils
C. Speciality oils

Automotive oils

These oil are used for the lubrication of internal combustion engine parts such as crankcase, gear, antifrication bear in and chassis. The engine may be either aircraft engine, automobile engine or diesel engine. Automobile oils may be further divided into following three subgroups:

1. Crankcase Oils
2. Axle and Transmission oils
3. Automatic Transmission oils

Crankcase Oils

These oils are used for the engine lubricating of passenger cars, trucks, buses, motorcycles, military motorized vehicles, tractors, marine and railroad diesel engines and aircraft engines. Their other purpose are sealing of the combustion chambers and partial cooling of engines.

These oils are manufactured by blending well fractionated and refined lubricating cuts from paraffin base mixed base or naphthemixed base crudes. These oils contain antioxidants to prevent or reduce deposition of sludge in engine parts and also detergenting easily removable colloidal suspensions. Other additives added are rust inhibitors, VI improves, pour pound depressants, antiwear agents and form inhibitors.

The oil used for engine lubrication vary in viscosity from approximately 39 to 110 SUS (Saybolt Universal seconds) at 210°F. These oils must have good viscosity index for easy starring at low temperature and for proper lubrication at the high wall temperature of engine crankcases. VI of 90-100 is usually sufficient.

Axle and Transmission oils

These oil are used for the lubrication of transmission and rear axles (differentials) in automotive equipments. The lubricating stocks required for these oils should be well refine heavy stock of viscosity approximately 40-200SUS at 210°F. extreme pressure agents (EP Agents) are added in these oils particularly for hypoid gear service oxidation and rust inhibitors, pour point depressants and antifoam agents are also added.

Automatic Transmission Oils

These oil are a special types of hydraulic oils used for the automatic transmission in automobiles. They are used in hydraulic torque converters and fluid coupling. These oil are produced from well refined paraffin base or solvent refined mixed base stocks and contain rust inhibitors, antioxidants foam inhibitors VI improves and pour point depressants. Their viscosity is around 185 SUS at 100°F , VI 140 and pour point 55°F.

Industrial lubricating oils

A wide variety of lubricating oils are used in industrial application both in power plant and production shop. Industrial lubricant may be divided into following broad groups:

1. Machine and engine oils
2. Steam cylinder oils
3. Stream turbine oils
4. diesel engine oils
5. Compressor oils
6. Spindle oils
7. Gear oils

8. Hydraulic oils
9. Circulating oils
10. Electric motor bearing oils
11. Wire rope lubricants

Machine and engine oils

These oils are used for the external lubrication of engines and general machinery. These oils are intended mainly for those machines or parts of machines in which the oils I not recirculated or where the leakage rate is so heavy that the oil remains in the machines for relatively short time, these oils are generally used for the lubrication of sleeve and line shaft bearing and rocker arm bearings.

Since these oils do not remain in contact with the machine for a long time and since the operating conditions are not severe where they are used, these oils needs not be particularly stable towards heat and oxidation. Hence they are refined to lesser degree than more specialised turbine or circulating oils. Mostly straight run refined, medium viscosity oil from paraffin, mixed based naphthenic crude's are used for the preparation of these oils. These oils may contain additives in special application but are usually without additives.

These oil usually have viscosities of 300-800 SUS at 100°F or 50-80 SUS at 210°F. the viscosity index is usually 80 or below.

Steam Cylinder oils

These oils are used for the lubrication of cylinder wall, piston and valve of stream engines. The base stock used for the manufacture of these oils are steam refined straight cylinder stocks, dewaxed cylinder stocks and bright stocks of high viscosity mostly obtained from paraffin base crudes. Stream cylinder oils are usually compounded with *2-5%* fat, such as degrees, tallow and lard oil for use in saturated and superheated steam. Compounding is avoided when completely dry stream is used or when steam is condensed and recycled.

Steam turbine oils

These oil are used as lubricants, coolants, and rust preventives in the oil circulating system of steam turbines. Since these oils are required to function without trouble for a long period they must be very stable. Hence these oils are manufactured from to highly refined paraffin base or mixed base neutral stocks. These oil contain oxidation inhibitors, rust preventives and antiwear additives. Oils used for steam turbines should resist emulsification of oil with water which usually comes from leakage's of steam into oils. Hence additives with emulsifying properties are avoided. These oil usually are medium viscosity oils, 150 -450 SUS at 100° F with high viscosity index (100-110).

Steam turbine oils are also used for the lubrication of bearings of electric motors and steel mills and in the other industrial circulating systems.

Diesel Engine Oils

These oils are used for the internal lubrication of diesel engines in power plants. These oils are similar to automotive crankcase oil which have been discussed in previous section.

Compressor oils

Compressor oils as the name implies are used for the lubrication of air, gas or refrigeration compressors. The oils for refrigeration compressor requires special properties and will be discussed under speciality oil.

The compressor oils are usually naphthenic oils as these breakdown to a fluffy soot at high temperatures which prevail in cylinders of the compressors. Paraffin oils though more stable are undesirable because they tend to form a hard deposit on decomposition which clogs the values.

The compressor oils may be compounded as in many application relatively heavy contamination with water is almost certain. The oils used may have viscosity in the range of 150-550 SUS at 100° F but mostly 150 350 SUS 100°F. these oils contain oxidation inhibitors, rust inhibitors and antifoam agents.

Spindle Oils

These oils are used for the lubrication of high speed shaft in plain bearing running at very small clearances. These oils are mostly used in modern high speed oil bath spindles used in spinning operations in textiles mills. These spindles rotates at speeds varying between 45000 rpm and 14,000 rpm and may run for period upto 400 hours on the initial charge of oil.

Highly refined low viscosity *(60-200* SUS at 100°F) light coloured paraffin base or solvent refined stocks are used for the manufacture of spindle oils. Sometimes antiwear and rust preventives are used with the oil. the oil must have marked resistance to oxidation and thickening in service.

Gear oils

These oils are used for the lubrication of closed and open gear of all types such as bevel gear, spur gear, worm gear and hypoid gears. A variety of oils from highly refined bright stocks (90 150 SUS at 21°F) to black residual oils or mixture of black residual oils with volatiles oils are used for the lubricating of gears. Worm and hypoid gears requires extreme pressure additives for proper functioning. Other additives used in gear oils are oxidation inhibitors, rust inhibitors, pour point depressants and antifoam agents, the viscosity of gear oils may vary from 50 10 220 at 210°F and the viscosity index is usually in the range of 80-120.

Hydraulic oils

These oils are used in hydraulic system e.g., as power transmitting fluids in hydraulic drives and controls fluid media in shock absorbers and recoil mechanisms and lubricant coolant for moving parts of the hydraulic power transmissions.

These oils are similar to turbine oil but may be less refined. They are manufactured from predominately paraffin base or solvent refined mixed base stocks of viscosity from 100-900 SUS at 100F. they usually have viscosity index 60-70. These oils should have low pour points compared to turbine oils. Rust inhibitors oxidation inhibitors and antiwear additives are usually added to these oils. Antifoam agents, pour point depressants and VI improves are also added in some cases.

Hydraulic fluids may be non petroleum origin also. Water glycol hydraulic fluids are used in aircraft. Synthetic fluid are also used in aircraft's.

Circulating oils

Any lubricating system in which the toil is pumped under pressure through some form of distributing system, to the parts to be lubricated and then returned to a sump or central base for circulation is regarded as circulating oil system. The crankcases, turbine and hydraulic oils are also circulating oil. however here we are connected with circulating oil is steel rolling machinery paper machinery, gyratory crusher and certain types of machine tools. Tubine type of oils the various additives depending on the requirement are used for circulating system oils. These oils will be discussed in detail later.

Electric Motor Bearing oils

These oil are used in sleeve type and ball and roller bearing of electric motor. Turbine type of oils are used in electric motor bearings.

Wire Rope Lubricants

These oils are used for the lubrication of wire ropes in cranes, hoists, and elevator, straight mineral petroleum residual oils especially prepared from adhesive and penetrating ability are used for the lubrication of wire ropes.

Speciality oils

A number of oils are manufactured which are used for special purpose, generally not directly connected with lubrication. These oils are called speciality oils and may be dived into following broad subgroups

1. Insulating oils
2. white oils
3. instrument oils

4. spray oils
5. textiles oils
6. rubber oils
7. vacuum pump oils
8. refrigerator oils
9. metal working oils
10. heat treatment oils
11. heat transmission oils.

Insulating oils

These oils are intended for use as an insulting agent in electic equipments. These oils are divided into following classes.

a. Transformer oils
b. Switchgear oils
c. cable oils
d. capicitor oils

Transformer oils

When an electric transformer is in operation heat is developed in the core and winding and must be effectively dissipated. In large Transformers adequate cooling be maintained by air cooling and the cores and winding are placed in the bath of oil which serves the double purpose of electric insulation and cooling by convection current set up in the oil. transformer oils must posses high electrical resistance for effective insulation, low viscosity for effective heat removal and great stability so that it remains unaffected by heated and atmospheric oxidation. Transformer oils are made from highly refined low viscosity naphthalene base oils. These oils are produced from non waxy type distillates by solvent extraction followed by more or less intense treatment with sulfuric acid or alkali and careful purification for the removal or moisture and mechanical contaminants. These oils usually have viscosities below 65 SUS at 100F.

Switchgear oils

Oil filled switchgear is widely used, particularly for high voltage, the function of oil is to quench the arc formed between the contact when the switch is operated and to prevent the tendency of the arc to persist or are stick. The oil should possess good mobility and high dielectric properties. Transformer oil fulfil these requirement and is used also to fill switchgear's.

Cable oils

The insulation of solid cables is commonly effected by winding them with paper impregnated with material of high dialectic strength. The oils used for impregnation is usually conventionally reined naphthene base oil of fairly high viscosity, about 1000 SUS at 100F containing 25% to 35% rosin. The VI of these oils should be low so that the oil is thin liquid at the temperature of impregnation.

Hollow cables are oil filled. Oils that have been refined to such a degree that they are virtually strutted are not satisfactory for this purpose, for this purpose naphthenic oils containing a proportion of unsaurates are preferred. These oils are non gassing, that is, that do not evolve gas at high electrical stresses.

Capicitor oils

These oils are used in the capicitor to impregnate the insulating paper between metallic foils which form the conduction surfaces of the capicitor. Normally oxidizing conditions in the capicitor are mild because of low operating temperature and almost complete exclusion of air. Consequently oxidation stability is less essential than in the case of transformer oils. The chief long term factor or consider is that effect of the high electrical stress on the impregnation for example the tendency for the gas to be formed under these condition. Special non gassing oil containing a portion of unsaturated have been developed for use in capacitors as in case of hollow cable oil.

White oils

White oils are mineral oils which have been so refined that unsaturated constituents and those which impart colour to the oil have been removed. Usually such oils are solvent extracted and then treated with strong sulfuric acid and alkalis. White oils divided into two classes, medicinal and technical.

Medicinal white oils

These oils are drastically refined colourless, tasteless and nearly odourless naphthene base hydrocarbon oils. Various grades or medicinal oils are manufactured to meet the specification drawn up by the Pharmacopoeia authorities in different countries. The main requirement of such specification is that oil shall be free from all harmful component. Medical white oils arc ingredients of medical preparations for internal and external use. Medicinal white oil is used as mild laxative.

Technical white oils

These oils are less drastically refined than the medicinal white oils. Their main use lies in the manufactures of hair oils and cosmetics but they also find use in horticultural spray oils, for egg preserving as a substitute for waterfalls and for imparting a polished appearance to currant, raisin and other fruits. Technical white oils are also used for the lubrication of self acting mules in the textile industry and for the lubrication of machinery handling food e.g. bacon shears and machinery making containers.

These oils are made from spindle oil by treatment with strong sulfuric acid and alkali.

Instrument oils

Instrument oils are used for special and delicate parts of light machinery like sewing machines, clocks and fine instruments. These oils should be of such a viscosity that only a very thin layer about 0.1 micron or less averse to the mechanism to which I it applied solidification while it is at low temperature condition as it should not fuel oxidized or polymerized at high temperature, since accuracy is of prime important in instrument these oil should heave least variation in properties over operating condition and over the length of their use. These oils should also gave tackiness to prevent spreading over other parts and have low volatility to prevent evaporation.

The mineral oil used for light instrument lubrication are obtained from naphthenic or aromatic type crude and refined by fuming sulfuric acid and clay treatment. Animals oils are used in combination with mineral oils. Synthetic lubricant are finding increasing use in instrument oils. They are used as such or in combination with minerals or fatty oils. Antioxidants are frequently added to these oils.

Spray oils

These oils are use for the spraying of trees and for the spraying of large buildings. These can be divided in two classes.

(a) Plant spray oils and

(b) Dust allaying oils

Plant spray oils

These oils are used for insect control on trees. These are two types (i) dormant spray oils (ii) verdant spray oils.

(i) Dormant Spray oils are used for insect control on trees whose leaves have fallen (in winter), these oils are conventionally refined paraffin base or mixed base oils of viscosity 80-123 SUS at 100°F. ,

(ii) verdant spray oils are used for insect control on green trees in summer. These oils are highly refined oils from paraffin-based or solvent refined mixed base stocks of viscosity 40-80 SUS at 100°F.

Dust allaying oils

Oil is frequently used for spraying the floors of large buildings in order to absorb the dust and allow it to be removed without spreading into the atmosphere. Thin spindle oil is generally use for this purpose.

Emulsified white oils are used for treating bed lines and blankets in hospitals to prevent the dissemination of fluf and so reduce risk of air borne infections.

Textile oils

Spindle oils are used for the lubrication of high speed oil bath spindles used in textile industry.

For the general lubricant of textile machinery it is an advantage of use high quality oils which can be applied sparingly, thereby reducing any tendency towards splashing, a condition which may lead to the staining of the yarn or fabric. For these application oil with stringiness and non drip properties are required.

Where contamination of textile product with lubricant cannot be avoided, such as in the drafting roller, ring travellers, the overhead mechanism fitted to certain type of loom in weaving and in knitting and stitching machines, oils containing emulsifies are used so that the oil can be easily washed in subsequent scouring operation. Where it is not possible to scour the fabric a highly refined colourless oil which will not discolour on exposure to air is very often used.

Oils are also used for lubricating textile fibres, particuly wood during the manufacturing process and such oils must be easily removed in the subsequent scouring process, in the production or rayon goods the main function of lubricant is to prevent the breaking of fine filament during the processing operation. Emulsifiable oils based on low viscosity technical white or pale oils are normally used.

Rubber oils

These oils are used in the following applications:

(a) For the procesing natural, synthetic or reclaim rubber

(b) For the manufacture of oil extended rubber

(c) For the manufacture of reclaim rubber

(d) As a secondary plasticizer in the manufacture of PVC leather cloth.

The rubber oils be aromatic, naphthenic or paraffinic depending upon their end use.

Vacuum pump oils

These oils are used in provide an oil film between the casing and the rotating vanes of rotary vacuum pumps. The function of the oil film is two fold to reduce friction between the vanes and the casing and to form a seal to prevent leakage back of the gas past the vanes.

For normal, low vacuum, rotary pump and blowers a highly refined oil of medium viscosity is normally used, although when temperatures are unusually high (above 180°C) it may be desirable to use refined cylinder stock for the purpose.

When high vacuum of the order 10 mm or less are required oil immersed multistage pumps are used, special oil with very low vapour pressures are required in high vacuum pumps. Stable oil with medium to light viscosity are most suitable for this purpose and they are generally selected from solvent refined lubricating oils.

To obtain still higher vacua, diffusion pumps are used in connection with rotary backing pumps. These diffusion pumps originally operated with mercury as the working fluid. Now it is possible to substitute for mercury, specially prepared hydrocarbon oil made by a very high vacuum process, these oil posses extremely low vapour pressures.

Refrigerator oils

These oils are used for the lubricating of refrigerator machines in direct contact with refrigerants such as fluro chemical and ammonia.

The most commonly used refrigerating media fall into two classes those which are immiscible with lubricating oil and those which are miscible. The first class which includes ammonia, carbon dioxide and sulfur dioxide, necessiate the use of oil to low pour point which will not solidify and be deposited in the colder part of the system, in case of ammonia and sulfur dioxide it is also important to use highly refined oil, as these gases will react with chemically unstable elements prevent in mineral oil and cause the formation of disports.

The second class of which methyl chloride and certain of freon series of refrigerants are common example, mix dreely in all proportions which mineral oil and consequently a mixture of oil and refrigerant is always present in the system, the effect of this are two fold the refrigerant dilutes the oils and reduces is viscosity so that thicker must be used than would be required with a nonmiscible refrigerant and it bestows on the mixture a low pour point so that it is not so necessary for the oil itself to posses the property.

Highly refined, solvent extracted naphthenic type oils of medium viscosity (150~450) SUS at 100°F) are commonly used in refrigerator compressors and for low temperature applications. These oils should be wax free.

Metal working oils

These oil are used in cutting, forming and deforming of metal and function both as lubricant and coolant. They may be further divided into two divisions

(a) Cutting oils,

(b) Metal forming oils.

Cutting oils

When steel or other metal are being turned, drilled, bored, ground or given any other type of machining operation a fluid medium is usually required to carry away the heat generated by friction and to lubricate the surface of the tool as the metal cutting pass over it. Such media are called cutting fluids. They may be divided into two classes:-

(i) Soluble cutting oils

(ii) straight cutting oils

Soluble cutting oils

These oils are emulsions of oil in water, these cutting oils are marketed in the form of concentrates consisting of mixture of mineral oils and emulsifiers which can be diluted with water for form stable emulsions over a wide range of concentrations. The dilute emulsions are circulated over the site of the cutting operation and beside causing effective cooling carry away the metal particle formed.

The soluble cutting oil are conventionally refined lubricant oils stocks containing emulsifying agents, chief among the emulsifies used for this type of oil are naphtha sulfornates and sulfornated fatty oils. Soluble cutting oil have greater cooling but less lubricating power and are consequate used for light operation.

Straight cutting oils

These are used when conditions of cutting are more sever making lubrication more important than cooling. These conditions are encountered when cutting speeds are low and pressures high.

Straight cutting oils are made from conventionally refined lubricating oil. Blends of mineral oils and lard oil or other fatty oils were the standard type of cutting fluid in the past. However now lubricating oils containing film strength additives such as sulfur or chlorine compounds are preferred. Sulfurized napthene base oils are widely used as cutting fluids. However oils used for cutting copper and its alloys should be free from sulfur.

These cutting oil usually have viscosities in the range of 100-150 SUS at 100°F.

Metal forming oils

Rollingoils

These are used in the manufacture of metal sheets and plates. The billets of the metal pass through a succession of rolls to reduce the thickness to the required dimensions. These oils are used to lubricants the metal during its passage through the rolls, spindles oils containing about *3%* olein (a fatty oil contained *in* olive oils, beef fat and other vegetable and animal oils) or oleci acid are usually used for the purpose, white oils containing 1% olein are used when bright annealing is to be carried out after rolling operation so that no deposits or lacquers are formed on the metal during the annealing process.

Drawing oils

For the manufacture of many metal articles, metal sheets are pressed into the required shape in suitable dies. Wires, rods and tibes on the other hand are produced by drawing through special dies. These processes which often need to be carried out in several stages must have adequate lubrication so as to reduce friction, prevent wear of the formers or dies, and assist in the production of good surface finish. A variety oils is used for these operations ranging from heavy mineral oils and compounded oil to aqueous emulsion of partly saponified fats, with or without mineral oils. A non petroleum lubricant is dry powdered soap which is particularly effective for steel wire. Oils or aqueous emuisions are preferred however, for no ferrous wire daring and many ferrous wire drawing operations are similarly done with emulsions.

Heat treatment oils

These oils are used in the manufacture of metal parts for imparting certain qualities such as hardness, toughness and freedom from stress. They may be divided into two classes:-

Quenching oils

These oils are used as a quenching medium for case hardening of metal, especially steel, parts the heated (760C-950C) metal part is plunged into a bath of cold oil and becomes hard on cooling. The oil used for quenching operation should be of a low viscosity of facilitate heat transfer and should obviously have as low a volatility as possible, specially refined high flash spindle oils either alone or blended with viscous residual oils are used for quenching purposes. Antioxidants and detergents are added to quenching oils.

Tempering oils

During the quenching operation dangerous stresses are set up in the metal and the metal becomes harder than desirable for certain application. Tempering process is designed to soften and toughen the steel and to remove the stresses.

The temperature oils should have a high flash point and also have high oxidation stability so that slugging and thickness is used as retarded as much as possible, mineral oil can be used upto 320°C only and other methods must be used for tempering higher than this. Non volatile oils of steam cylinder types are used for tempering process.

It is essential that the oils selected for this application should be stable to heat so that deposits are not formed in the feed lines or furnace tubes. They should also have as low a viscosity as is compatible with low volatility so that there is no difficulty in pumping around the circuit when the plant is started up from cold.

The oil used as heat transfer oils are refined mineral cylinder oils, 150-300 SUS at 2I0°F; bright stocks, 90-150 SUS at 21 OF, and refined aromatic oils, 230-300 SUS at 100°F.

5

Synthetic Fluids

Introduction

Synthetic lubricants have been for many years, in general, the improved properties of lubricants achieved with the early synthetic base stocks could be obtained more cost effectively by improved formulation based on mineral oils. However, the desire for lubricants to perform over increasing temperature ranges, led by military and aero engine requirements, has stimulated the continuing developing of synthetic lubricant technology. Synthetic lubricant are now found in all areas of lubricant such as automobiles, trucks, marine diesels, transmissions and industrial lubricants as well as aviation and aerospace lubricants.

Many compounds have been investigated as possible base stock for synthetic lubricants . seven types of major importance:

- polyaphaolefins
- alkylated aromatics
- polybutenes
- aliphatic diesters
- polyolesters
- polyalkyleneglycols
- phosphate esters

Other materials such as silicones, borate esters, are also of importance, but their applications, are restricted due either to high cost or to performances limitations

Polyalphaolefins

PAO, when used for lubricant based stocks, refers to hydrogenated oligomers of an olefin, usually decene. Several methods have been investigated for the oligomerisaion of olefins for use as lubricant base stocks, the most important being free radical processes, Ziegler catalysis, and cationic, Frieldel Crafts catalysis. Following oligomerisation, the unsaturated products are separated from the reaction mixture, then hydrogenated using supported nickel or palladium catalysis after removal of unwanted monomer. Fractionation may then be used to obtain the required viscosity grades, commonly 2,4 6 or 8cSt at 100°C

Properties and applications

The higher than expected degree of branching in the final product gives very good low temperature properties especially as the product are wax free. In additions the molecular rearrangements are intermolecular and molecular weights are therefore predictable. Thus, the volatilities of FAOs are intermolecular and molecular weight are therefore predictable. Thus, the volatilities of PAOs are lower than those of equiviscous mineral derived products whether solvent refined, hydro cracked or hydro isomerised. Overall, PAOs are able to be operated effectively over a very wide temperature range. Table compares typical viscosities of at 100C pour point and volatilities for solvent refined (SN150), hydro isomerised and PAO base fluids.

Table base fluid comparisons

	SN 150	hydo-isomerised	PAO
viscosity at lOOC(cSt)	5.43	5.64	5.98
pour point (C)	-12	-15	-64
NOACK(%loss)	15	7.8	6.1

In addition to control of the temperature viscosity properties to give base oils with low pour point and high viscosity indices, the oligomerisation process also gives rise to high purity base fluids. These can be used to formulate lubricant with very good thermal and oxidative stability. Interestingly, in some oxidative tests on base oils without additives, mineral base oil appear to be superior to PAOs, eg. the onset of oxidation as measured by differential scanning calorimetry (DSC). This observation is ascribed to the presence of naturally occuring antioxidant in mineral oils which have survived the refining process, however, PAOs, are more responsive to added antioxidants thus leading tio the superiority of fully formulated lubricants based on PAOs.

The purity of composition of PAOs and hence their low polarity lead to poor solvency for polar compounds such as the additives required for fully formulated engine lubricants. The very low polarity of PAOs can also give rise to problem with seal performance. Therefore PAO base fluids tend to be used in combination with other, more polar, base fluids such as aliphatic esters and solvent refined mineral oils.

The wide range of temperatures over which PAO based lubricants can perform, together with their excellent physical, chemical and thermooxidative stabilities, has lead to an increased use of PAOs in a wide variety of applications, traditional areas of application such as aerospace, transmissions and hydraulic system continue to require the lubricant performance benefits of PAOs. In additions, the increasing stresses placed on automative and marine lubricants, in terms of both performance and longer lifetimes, have led to growth in the use of PAO based synthetic lubricants in these applications.

Alkylated aromatics

Introduction

Three types of alkyl benzenes are available for use as or in lubricant

(i) dialkyl benezenes produced as a by product in the manufacture of liner dodecyl or tridecyl benzene a sulphonation feedstock for anionic detergent manufacture

(ii) dialkyl benzenes produced from these detergent alkylates by reacting further with olefins and

(iii) synthesised alkyl aromatics purpose built from benzens and short chain olefins such as propylene.

Characteristics of the materials which either individually or in combination make them suitable for particular application include sulphur free chemistry, low pour point., good thermal stability (when compared with mineral oils), and good solvency. Furthermore, sulphonated alkyl aromatics, particularly those derived from the purpose made material are used as emulsified in metal working fluids (as the sodium salts) and as detergents in automotive crankcase lubricant (as calcium and magnesium salts).

Production and general properties

The lowest cost (di)alkyl benzenes are produced as a by product in the manufacture of linear monalkylates used extensively in detergent manufacture. Synthesis is usually by Friedel Crafts, type reactions, either by the reaction of the alkyl benezes are synthesised from benezens and proylene, with catlyst and conditions elected to give some control over the molecular weight and structure and hence the physical and chemical properties of the alkyl component.

Applications

The lower cost dialkyl benxenes are used in a wide variety of industrial and metalworking product. In particular, their sulphur free chemistry has led to their extensive use in rolling and drawing oils for copper. The synthesised alkyl benezene, even through optimised for their chemistry, generally exhibit poorer properties than PAOs. However their excellent solvency and low pour point make them suitable for lubricant designed to operate in extremely low temperature conditions, such as greases, gear oils, hydraulic and power transmission fluids. The most widespread use of the tailored alkylates, is however as refrigerator oils. When carefully designed the oils are fully compatible with flurorienated refrigerants (such as R22 and R5~2) whereas mineral oils suffer from wax precipitation and PAOs give phasing problems. The oil may be carried through the entire refrigeration circuit and can experience extremes of temperature, good thermal stability is therefore essential. The natural solvency of the alkylates is also of benefit in minimising the formation of sledges varnishes and other deposits.

Polybutenes

Introduction

Polybutenes used in lubricant are composed mainly of isobutene and are also often referred to as polyisobutenes or PIBs. Amongst polyolefin fluids of equal viscosity, polybutene show different properties compared with PAOs, which are generally made from higher molecular weight straight chain alpha olefins. Low molecular weight polytbutenes are used when the ability to depolymerise and burn completely without leaving deposits is advantageous. Being hydrocarbons, polybutenes are compatible with mineral oils and have good metal wetting properties and improved film strength. Polytbutenes are commonly used in a very wide variety of applications, for lubricant applications they are used as viscosity index improviser as well as base fluids and in the manufacture of dispersants.

Markets

Polybutene is an extremely versatile class of and can be used either in deviated from as oil and gasoline additives or in applications that makes use of its physical properties. World wide production of polybutene is estimate at around 650 *000* tonnes. Of this, about 60-70% is derivatised to poltybutenyl succinimide for use as dispersant additives to combat sludge in crankcase engine oils and as detergent additives in gasoline to prevent carbutrettor fouling and engine deposits. Between 5 and 10% of polybutene is used in cable application for impregnating paper used for power cables and as non draining, filling, compounds to gurad against water pentration of telecommunication and fibre optic cables. Industrial applications exploit the physical properties of polybutene and account for 20-25% of total production. Polybutenes are widely used in oils, and lubricant, adhesive and sealants, tackified polyethylene, bitumen and rubber modification concrete mould oils and in putties, anticorrosion coatings, masonry coatings, paint inks and dispersion aids it is estimate that 30% of polybutene sold for industrial applications is for oils and lubricants.

Properties

polybutenes are non polar and soluble in aliphatic and aromatic hydrocarbons, chlorinated hydrocarbons and certain oxygenated solvent such as tetrahydrofuran and diethyl ether. They are insoluble in simple alcohols, ester and ketones, in lubricant applications, polybutenes are normally combined with other based fluids and compatibility is found with all types of mineral oils, polyalaolefins (PAO), alkyl benzenes and most types of synthetic esters. In compatibility is found with polyalkylene glycols and with few exceptionms, silicons oils. Fluoroelastomers, polychloroprene and nitriole rubbers are unaffected polybutenes and are most suitable for pump seal and Packings used handling equipments. Grasses of polybutene are defined by the viscosity measured in SSU at 100C divided by 100 or by direct reference to molecular weight.

Lubricant applications

If comparing on an equal viscosity basis the properties of polybutene with a PAO and ester, polybutene is more volatile, less resistant to oxidation and has a lower viscosity index. This illustrates the limitation of polybutene as a true synthetic base oils. For example, it would be inappropriate to use a low viscosity polybutene as the base oil for crankcase engine oils. Polybutenes used as a major base fluid for two stroke oils, high pressure polyethylene compressor lubricants, metal working lubricant and speciality greases. In these applications the prime desire is for low smoke low deposits, or low toxicity, with volatility and oxidation resistance being less critical.

Polybutene key properties for lubricant sectors

applications	key property
general	control of viscosity
two stroke oil	low smoke, low blocking good lubricity, clean burning
metal working lubricant	non staining, low deposits, low toxicity low biodegradability
gear oil	shear stable, viscosity index improper abhesiveness additive
compressor lubricant	good lubricity, inertness, low toxicity good electrical properties
grease/wire rope	ahesiveness, hydrophobic, inertness, good lubricity.

Polybutene grades of interest for use in oils and lubricants

Applications	Grade										
	03	04	07	3	5	10	30	150	200	600	2000
viscosity adjustment						X	X	X	X	X	X
two strokc oils		X	X	X	X	X	X	X			

metal working		X	X			X	X		X	X	X
lubricants LDPE			X				X	X	X		
compressor oils											
gear/ hydraulic oil					X		X	X	X	X	X
greases	X	X		X		X	X			X	X
wire rope protectives						X	X				X

Synthetic esters

Introduction

Prior to the early 19th century, the main lubricants were natural esters contained in animals fats such as sperm oil and lard oils, or in vegetable oils such as rape seed and castor oils. During world war II a range of synthetic oils was developed. Amongst these, ester of long chain alcohols and acid proved to be excellent for low temperature lubricants. Following world war II the further development of esters was closely linked to that of the aviation gas turbine. In the early 1960s neopoyol esters were used in this application because of their low volatility, high flash point and good thermal stabilities, esters are now used in many application including automotive and marine engine oils, compressor oils, hydraulic fluids, gear oils and grease formulations. The inherent biodegradability of ester molecular offer added benefits to those of performance.

Ester types

The direct effect of the ester group on the physical properties of a lubricant is to lower the volatility and raise the flash point. This is due to strong dipole moment, binding the lubricant together. The presence of the ester group also affects other properties such as:

- thermal stability
- hydrolytic stability
- solvency
- lubricity
- biodegradability

Manufacture of esters

The manufacture process of esters consists of three distinct processes: esterification, filtration and distillation, the fundamental reaction process is that of acid + alcohol ester +water. this reaction is reversible but is driven to the completion by the use of excess alcohol and removal of water as it forms. The use of an azeotropping agent, e.g. toluene, to aid water removal is optical.

The acid and alcohol can be reacted thermally, usually in the presence of a catalyst in the esterification reactor. Possible catalysts include sulphuric acid, p toluene sulphonic acid, tetra alkyl titanate, anhydrous sodium hydrogen sulphate, phosphorus oxides and stannours octanoate. After the ester has been formed, unreacted acid is neutalised using sodium carbonate or calcium hydroxide and removed by filtration.

Typical reaction conditions 230°C and 50-760 mmHg pressure, a significant amount of alcohol vapories along with the water and must be recovered. This is accomplished by condensing the reactor vapour and separating the resulting two phase liquid mixture. The alcohol is then returned to the reactor.

Polyol ester are made by reacting a polyhydric alcohol, such as neopentyl glycol (NPG) timethylol propane (TMP) or pentaerthritol (PE), with a monobasic acid to give the desired ester. When making neopolyol esters, excess acid is used because the acid is more volatile than the neopolyol and is therefore easy to therefore easy to recover from the ester product.

Physicochemical properties of ester lubricant

Mineral oil base stocks are derived from crude oil and consist of complex mixture of naturally occurring hydrocarbons. Synthetic ester lubricants, on the other hand, are prepared from man made base stock having uniform molecular structures, and therefore well defined properties that can be tailored to specific applications.

Many lubricant requirements are translated into specific properties of an oil measurable by conventional laboratory test e.g. viscosity evaporation,. Flash point, etc. other more critical requirement are related to the chemical properties of the lubricant and many of these can only be measured satisfactorily be elaborate and expensive rigs specially developed to simulate performance.

A wide variety of raw material can be used for the preparation of ester type base fluids and this can affect a number of lubricant properties including:

- viscosity
- flow properties
- lubricity
- thermal stability
- hydrolytic stability
- solvency
- biodegradability

Viscosity The viscosity of an ester lubricant can be altered by :

- increasing the molecular weight of the molecule by
  -increasing the carbon chain length of the acid
  -increasing the carbon chain length of the alcohol
  -increasing the number of ester groups

- increasing the size of degree of branching
- including cyclic groups in the molecular backbone
- maximising dipolar interactions

one disadvantages of very long chain molecules is their tendency to shear into smaller fragment under stress.

Flow properties . the viscosity index (VI) Of an ester lubricant can be increased by:

- increasing the acid chain length
- increasing the alcohol chain length
- increasing the linearity of the molecular
- not using cyclic groups in the backdone which lowers the VI even more than aliphatic branches
- molecular configuration- viscosity indices of polyol esters to tend to be somewhat lower than their diester analogues due to more compact configuration of the polyol molecule

The pour point of the lubricant can be decreased by:

- increasing the amount of branching
- the positioning of the branch branching in the centre of the molecular gives better pour point than branches near the end
- decreasing the acid chain length
- decreasing the internal symmetry of the molecule

As can be seen from the above lists, there is a natural trade off between viscosity index and pour point. For instance by increasing the linearity of the ester the viscosity index improves but the pour point increases . Esters made from mixtures of normal and branched acid (having the same carbon number) have viscosity indices between those of the normal and branched acid ester, but have lower pour point than esters used from either branched or normal acids.

Lubricity . ester groups are polar and will therefore affect the efficiency of anti wear additives. When a too polar base fluid is used it, and not the anti wear additives, will cover the metal surfaces. This can result in higher wear characteristics. Consequently although esters have superior lubricity properties compared to mineral oils, they are less efficiently than anti wear additives.

Ester can be classified in terms of their polarity, or non polarity by using the following formula

$$\text{Non polarity index} = \frac{\text{Total number of C atom x molecular weight}}{\text{Number of carboxylic groups x 100}}$$

Generally, the higher the non polarity index, the lower the affinity for the metal surface. Using the above formula it can be seen that as a general rule, increasing molecular weight improves overall lubricity. Esters terminated by normal acids or alcohols have better lubricities than those made from branched acids alcohols, while esters made from mixed acids / alcohols have lubricities intermediate between esters or normal acids/ alcohols and esters of branched acids/ alcohols.

Thermal stability. The ester linkage is an exceptionally stable one; bond energy determinations predict that it is more thermally stable than the C~C bonds

The advantage in thermal stability of polyol ester compared to diester is well documented and has investigated on a number of occasions. It has been found that the absence hydrogen atoms on the beta carbon atom of the alcohol portion of an ester lead to superior thermal stability. The presence of such hydrogen atom enables a low energy decomposition mechanism to operate via a six membered cyclic intermediate producing acids and I alkenes groups . When beta hydrogen atoms are replaced by alkyl groups this mechanism cannot operate and decomposition occurs by a free radical mechanism. This types of decomposition requires more energy and can only occur at higher temperature.

Hydrolytic stability.

The hydrolytic stability of esters depends on two main features :

- Processing parameters
- Molecular geometry

If the final processing parameters of esters are not tightly controlled they can have a major effect on the hydrolytic stability of the esters. Such processing parameters include:

- Acid value
- Degree of esterification
- Catalyst used during esterification and the level remaining in the ester after processing.

Esters must have a low acid value (<0.05 mg KOH/g), a very high degree of esterification (>98%) and a low ash level before the effect of molecular geometry will begin to assert themselves.

Molecular geometry can affect hydrolytic stability in several ways. By satirically hindering the acid portion of the molecule (hindrance on the alcohol portion having relatively little effect) hydrolysis can be slowed down. To this purpose, geminal di branched acid (e.g. neoheptanoic acids) have been used. However, when using these feedstocks, there are penalties to be paid, namely very long reaction times to achieve complete esterification, and poor pour point. The length of the acid chain is also very important. Acids shorter than pentanoic tend not be used owing to their corrosively. The hydrolytic stability of neopolyol esters can generally be regarded as superior to that of dibasic esters.

Solvency. This can be divided into compatibility with additives and other lubricants, and elastomer compatibility.

(i) Compatibility with additives and other lubricants. Esters are generally fully compatible with mineral oils. This gives them three major advantages. First, there are no contamination problems therefore esters can be used in machinery that previously used mineral oil. In addition, they can be blended with mineral oil to boost their performance. Second, most additive technology is based on mineral oil and this technology is usually directly applicable to esters. Third, esters can be blended with other synthetic such polyaphaolefins (FAOs). This gives esters great flexibility, whilst blending with other oils gives unrivalled opportunities to balance the cost of a lubricant blend against its performance,

(ii) Elastomer compatibility. Elastomers brought into contact with liquid lubricant will undergo an interaction with the liquid diffusing through the polymer network. There are two possible kinds of interaction, chemical and physical. During physical interactions two different processes occur;

- Absorption of the lubricant by the elastomer, causing swelling
- Extraction of soluble components out of the elastomers, causing shrinkage.

The degree of swelling of elastomeric material can depends on:

- Size of the lubricant - the larger the lubricant the smaller the degree of swelling
- Molecular dynamics of the lubricant- liner lubricant diffuse into elastomers quicker than branched or cyclic lubricants
- Closeness of the solubility parameters of the lubricant and the elestomer. The like dissolve like' rule is obeyed
- Polarity of the lubricant. It is known that some elastomers are sensitive of polar ester lubricants. The non polarity index can be used to model eleastomeric sea swelling trends for specific ester types.

Several polar esters are well known industrial plasticisers. Non polar base stocks, such as PAOs have a tendency to shrink and harden elastomes. By carefully balancing these compounds with esters, lubricants which are neutral to elastomeric materials can be formulated.

Environmental aspects

growing environmental awareness has turned the threat to our waters into a major issue. The environment can become polluted in many ways, for example oils and oil containing effluent can have devastating *consequence* for fish stocks and other water faunna.

(i) Ecotoxicity. In Germany material are classifed according to their water endangering potential or wassergahrdungklasse (WGK). Substances are given a ranking of between 0 and 3.

WGK 0	not water endangering
WGK1	slightly water endangering
WGK2	water endangering
WGK3	highly water endandering

Esters generally have the following ranking:

Polyols, polyoleates, C36 dimer esters, diester	0
Phthalates and trimellitates	0 to 2

This shows esters to have a low impact on the environment.

(iii) Biodegradability. The general biochemistry of microbial attack on esters is well known and has been well reviewed. The main steps of ester hydrolysis beta oxidation of long chain hydrocarbons and oxygenate attack on aromatic nuclei have been extensively investigated. The main features which slow or reduce microbial breakdown are:

- Position and degree of branching (which reduce oxidation)
- Degree to which ester hydrolysis is inhibited
- Degree to saturation in the molecule
- Increase in molecular weight of the ester
- Shows the biodegradabilities of a wide range of lubricants as measured using the CEC~L~33~A~94 test.

Polyalkylene glycols

Introduction

The term 'polyalkylene glycol' covers an extensive range of polymeric molecules which, depending on chemical structure, can exhibit quite different physical properties. For example polyalkylene glycols can be solid or liquid water soluble or water insoluble, and can be produced to give almost any viscosity required. Polyalkylene glycols have the following inherent chemical and physical properties which make them suitable for a large number of engineering and lubrication applications:

- Wide viscosity range
- Excellent viscosity/ temperature characteristics
- Low pour points
- Good thermal stability
- High flash points
- Good lubricity
- Low toxicity
- Good shear stability
- Water solubility or insolubility
- Non corrosive to common metals
- Little effect on rubbers
- Parasitically non flammable in aqueous solution

Typical application area are industrial gear oils and greases, compressor lubricant, metal working fluids, aqueous quenching fluids, free resistant hydraulic fluids, textile lubricant, heat transfer fluids, etc. section offer a detailed account of these application.

Key properties

Water solubility. As previously mentioned, polyakylene glycols can be either water soluble or water insoluble. Water solubility is primarily governed by the ratio of ethylene oxide propylene oxide in the polymer with higher proportion of ethylene oxide leading to greater solubility. Molecular weight also influence water solubility, although to a much lesser extent, with lower molecular weight polymer showing greater solubility.

Homopolymers of propylene oxide are effectively water insoluble (except for very low molecular weight <900). Typical oxide ratios used for water soluble copolymer are between 1:1 and 3:1 ethylene oxide propylene oxide (by weight)

All polyalkylene glycol's exhibit inverse solubility in water solubility decrease as temperature increase. This is explained by the loss of hydrogen bonding at elevated temperature. The temperature of polymer/ water separation is usually referred to as the cloud point and is higher for copolymer with larger proportion of ethylene oxide.

Pour point. Polyalkylene glycol with high proportions of propylene oxide (>50%) exhibit very low pour point (down to *50C)* this is a result of the lateral methyl groups of the propylene oxide unit disrupting crystallistion. A typical comparison in table

Viscosity pressure behaviours. The relationship between viscosity and pressure is an important parameter for lubrication performance better viscosity pressure coefficient are obtained for polymer with a high degree of propylene oxide units.

Viscosity index. Polyalkylene glycol typically exhibit excellent viscosity/ temperature characteristics. For example. Emkarox VG 22 (ISO220) has a VI of 215 which is significantly better than that for an equivalent ISO grade mineral oil (-100). The viscosity index tends to be better for product with a low degree of chain branching.

Degradation . in contrast to mineral oils, polyalkylene glycol's either volatile or soluble degradation product upon oxidation and hence do not leave unwanted solid deposits during service. Thermal stability can be significantly improved by the addition of antioxidant additives.

Lubricant. Polyalkylene glycol's show very good directional behaviour and are inherently excellent lubricant. The high polar nature gives a strong affinity to metal, and thus lubricant films stay intact even at high surface pressures. This result in low abrasive wear.

Applications

Introduction. polyalkylene glycols (PAGs) were first developed in the mid 19th century but were not used commercially unit the late 1930s when an application as a replacement for castor oil in automotive brake fluid was found.

The compulsory use of fire resistant hydraulic fluids, triggered by the death of 250 miners in the Belgian pit disaster of 1956, resulted in a substantial increase in PAG consumption.

Table Comparison of pour point for two polyalkylene glycols with different proportions of propylene oxide

Product	Molecular weight	Ethylene oxide: propylene oxide	Pour point (°C)
PEG100	1000	1:0	+37
VG70W	1300	1:1	-46

During the 190s FAGs were used in heat treatment foundries to quench metal. A combination of inherent inverse solubility and fire resistant properties provided an alternative to mineral oil bases products.

Following strong growth during the 1970s and *1980s,* PADs are now used for many application worldwide, and constitute the largest market share within the synthetic lubricant sector.

Brake fluids. Two predominant type of brake fluid formulation DOT 3 and DOT4 based on specifications issued by the US department of transport are used in western Europe. Due to increase demands placed on brake fluids, particularly with regard to water absorption, much of the polyglycol has been replaced by borate esters. However, the lubricity limited ,rubber swell and low pour point on these esters mean that a typical DOT 4 formulation may contain up to 10% FAG.

Fire resistant fluids. A major application of PAGs involves their use in fire resistant fluids. Industrial sectors such as steel production, die casting (where leaks in the high pressure hydraulic lines can create serious fire hazards) and mining (where the consequences of fire are catastrophic) have generated a large demand for these types of hydraulic fluids, indeed many countries now legislate their use.

Fire resistant fluids have been classified by several international bodies:

- ISO-International Organisation for Standardisation
- CETOP-Commit European des Transmissions Oleohydrauliques et pneumatiques
- Luxembourg Commission- Commission of the European Communities Safety and Health Commission for the Mining and Extractive Industries.
- The following designation have been used:
- HRA Fluids containing more than *80%* water, formulated with either mineral oil, synthetic chemical solution or synthetic emulsion
- HFB water in oil emulsion, water content 40-50%
- HFC water polymer solution, minimum water content 35%
- HFD water free chemical fluid

High molecular weight PAGs(12~30K) have found to be particularly suitable for the formulation of the HFC type of fluid. PAG water (35% minimum) and glycol, together with anticorrosion, antiwear and antiforum additives are formulated to conform to the manufactures specification for a particular system. Stringent flammability requirements. Corrosion protection, low level of wear,. Foam, and other demands such as viscosity and air release must all be achieved.

Compressor lubricant. Lubrication within the pressurised area of a compressor present many problems. A lubricant must not only seal, cool, and reduce friction and wear, but must also cope with the presence of compressed gases which may be aggressive or of an oxidizing nature.

The polarity of PAG particularly the water soluble type, significantly lowers the solubility with hydrocarbon gases (e.g. methane and ethylene) compared to the equivalent mineral oil derived lubricant. Form a practical point of view this means that compressors used for hydrocarbon and other chemical gases can be operated without lowering the lubricant viscosity. For example in low density polyethylene compressor operating at 2000-3000 bar the solubility of ethylene in water soluble PAG is less than 15% of that observed with white oil. This has the added benefit of reducing lubricant contamination of the final product an important consideration for polythene when used in food packaging.

Metal cutting. This operation involves the removal of metal in the form of chip from component. Two principal types of fluid are used to cool and lubricate:

- neat mineral oil
- soluble oils

Within the soluble oil sector, there sector, there is a small demand for fully synthetic true solution particularly for light duty and grinding applications. These solutions may be formulated using water soluble PAGs as base stock. Their inverse solubility characteristic is advantageous in coating the metal surface with a film of polymer, thus proving lubricating and reducing tool wear. Biostability, low toxicity and little or no skin irritancy are additional benefits.

Gear oils and greases. The main purpose of a lubricant is to reduce friction between moving parts of hence lowering temperature and improving efficiency. Increased industrial demand for high performance products. PAGs are now extensively used to lubricate calender gears and bearing, within the plastic, rubber and paper industries, and are particularly suited for heavily loaded worm gears.

The efficiency of a worm gear is related to the friction between worm drive and gear wheel. Within the contact, there is a high degree of sliding which increase operating temperature. Consequently, a lubricant must not only provide a low coefficient of friction , but must also have a high viscosity index and possess good thermal and oxidative characteristics.

Paper and concrete mills are examples of processes where the ingress of dust and moisture can present particular problems. Gear oil base on water soluble PAGs may be used to facilitate easier cleaning and to extend service intervals.

Both water soluble and insoluble types of PAGs can be used in the formulation of synthetic greases. Thickening may be achieved either by conventional soap technology, or by the addition of solid such as modified bentonite clays or fine particle silica. The clean burn off characteristic of all PAGs makes them particularly suitable as greases bases, incorporating molybdenum disulphide or graphite. The PAGs from volatile oxidation breakdown product leaving no carbonaceous residues or sludge. A typical application is the lubrication of very high temperature chains is ovens.

Textiles. During the processing of fibres, two important criteria must be considered (I) drag from hard surface causing fibre damage; cause fibre/ fibre sippage this imparting the process. An ideal spin finish formulation will strike a balance between fibre / fibre static friction and fibre/hard surface dynamic friction. PAGs offer several advantages over mineral oils and simple esters:

- little or no carbonaceous residue is produced when the lubricant is volatilised during high temperature texturing and high speed spinning.
- Viscosity and cloud point (inverse solubility) can be readily varied according to requirements.
- Scourability is good (important when polishing the fibres)
- Water solubility at ambient temperature assist application, film coverage and removal

A typical spin finish concentrate would consist of:

Lubricant (usually blended)	75-85%
Antistant	5-10%
Additives (antioxidants)	5-10%

Formulations of textile machine lubricant based on water soluble PAGs combine gear lubricity with ease of removal from fibres during processing.

Rubber lubrication. The negligible swelling characteristics of water soluble and insoluble PAGs used to effect within the rubber industry. Actual application include antistick for uncured rubber, demoulding fluid in type production, mandrel lubricants for hoses, and lubricant for rubber packing. O' rings and seals. PAGs may be formulated with solvent and wetting agents and applied directly be use of a brush or spray.

Two stroke engine lubrication. Synthetic lubricants virtually eliminate engine problem associated with deposition and fouling commonly see with mineral oil lubricant. Although esters are predominant in this application, PAGs tends to have special uses for example, with model engines where a mixture of FAG/methanol provides a cleaner alternative to castor oil based fuels.

Phosphate esters

Introduction

Phosphate ester have been produced commercially since the 1920s and have gained important as plasticisers, lubricant additives, and synthetic based fluid for hydraulic and compressor oils. Their first use in lubricant was as antiwear additives. Later development in aircraft hydraulic control systems, particularly during the Second World War, saw the introduction of phosphate esters as less flammable hydraulic fluids. Being esters of orthophosphoric acid, they have the general formula OP(OR)3, where R represent an aryl or alkyl groups or very often, a mixture of alkyl and or aryl components. The physical and chemical properties of phosphate ester can be varied considerably depending on the choice of substituent and these are selected to give optimum performance for a given application. Phosphate esters are particularly used in application that benefit from their excellent fire resistance properties but compared to other fluids they are fairly expensive.

6

Speciality Oils

Introduction

Speciality oils are those oils which are used in applications generally not directly connected with lubrication. With the increasing special needs and complexity of modern industry, more and more of special function oriented petroleum products are assuming increasing importance. Practically all the speciality oils were being imported into India before about 1953. Demands were low and there was hardly any indigenous know-how about their manufacture in India from imported base stocks. However, since 1969 the demand for most of the speciality products is being met through indigenous manufacture from indigenous base stocks.

In the manufacture of most of the speciality oil, the main process is to react a carefully selected base stock of appropriate viscosity with either concentrated sulphuric acid or oleum depending upon the degree of refinement require and then treating the acid refined oil with clay. Since acid treating and clay treating are common to the manufacture of most of the speciality product.

Acid Treatment

The acid treatment process consist essentially of treating the base stock with concentrated sulphuric acid or oleum. The sludge formed is allowed to settle and removed. The acidic oil is then neutralized with alkali usually soda ash. The neutralized oil is either washed with water to remove sodium sulphate, oil soluble sulphonates and other impurities, or if the oil soluble sulphonates are to recovered as a by product, the oil is extracted with a solvent such as cthyl alcohol isopropyl alcohol or acetone. The solvent usually isoprpyl alcohol, removes sodium petroleum sulphonates, sodium sulphate and other impurities. Sodium salts of oil soluble sulphonates may be recover by evaporating the solvent. The solvent is condensed and reused. The washed or solvent extracted oil is then given a finishing treatment with clay.

Reaction and purpose

The reaction of concentrated sulphuric acid or oleum with petroleum constituents is an exothermic and irreversible reaction lating precipitating, oxidizing and solvent refining agent. Petroleum product are acid treated for the following reasons.

1 to remove straight chain unsaturated compounds,
2. to remove aromatic compounds,
3. To remove sulphure, nitrogen and oxygen containing compounds
4. To remove wax
5. To remove asphaltic and resinous products

The purpose of acid treatment is to remove all reactive and unsaturated hydrocarbons and impurities which would cause the oil to darken, from gummy and sticky product when exposed to air and which would adversely affect colour, odour, and taste of the product.

Acid treatment improves colour, decreases viscosity, increasing viscosity index, improves electrical properties and increase oxidative and chemical stability.

Sulphuric acid or oleum treatment always gives rise to extensive side reaction due to the exothermic nature of the reaction. These side reaction are mainly, oxidation, and are responsible for some oil soluble coloured compounds which are difficult is remove afterwards. Too much acid or oleum addition at a time chars the oil. Therefore, oleum or acid is added in successive doses to control the temperature and to avoid the side reactions.

The rate of sulphonation reaction depends on the following factors:

1. Reaction Temperature
2. Strength of the acid
3. The amount of acid or the ratio of acid to base stock.

Since excessively fast reaction lead to unwanted side reaction while slow rate of reaction would not give proper refining it is necessary to control the temperature of reaction, and the strength and the amount of acid , to optimum level.

Reaction Temperature

It has been mentioned that sulphonation is an exothermic and irreversible reaction. The rate of reaction doubles approximately for each rise of temperature by 10°C. higher temperature favours the formation of over sulhonated materials and products of side reactions and hence the quality is affected.

If maximum decolourization is desired, the lowest practical temperature should be used. It is impossible to produce good colour it the temperature exceeds approximately *60°C,* because the colouring substances which are formed by oxidation are soluble in the oil and will darken it. If on the other hand, the principle objective is the separation of unsaturated and asphaltic substance higher temperature should be used.

The viscosity and pour point will determine the minimum operating temperature. If temperature is too low the treating efficiently is reduced because of the difficulty of obtaining intimate mixing at high viscosity and because of difficulty of draining sludge, causing excessive losses due to entertainment of the oil in the sludge. Also large quality of pepper sludge will remain suspended in the oil and some sludge will float in a layer on the top of the oil. Pepper sludge is difficult to settle and will require an excess of clay for its later removal. The unsetted sludge will continue to react with the oil, some of it will dissolve back into the oil and as a result, the oil will be darkened. Once this occur, the only remedy is to blow the mass again with air which may also prove harmful. High temperature decreases the viscosity so as to assist mixing with acid. Also at higher temperature setting of sludge occurs more readily because of lower viscosity and greater diffusion. Higher temperature accelerates the reaction between the acid and the aromatic and unsaturated compounds so that if colour is not of paramount importance, higher temperature can be used.

The oil should be brought to the desired temperature before the acid is added. The temperature at the time of settling and washing is generally kept higher (20-25°C) than at the start of reaction for better settling and washing. The temperature at the time of acid treatment and settling for various viscosities are give as under :

Temperature of treatment

Viscosity of oil SUS at 100°F	Temperature of oil when acid is added °F	Temperature of oil and wash water during washing and setting °F
50	70-80	110-120
75	80-90	120-130
100	85-95	130-140
150	90-100	140-150
200	95-105	150-160
300	100-110	155-165
500	105-115	160-170
1000	110-120	165-175
1500	110-120	165-175
2000	115-125	170-180

The strength of acid depends on the degree of refinement required and the type of base stock. Higher concentration of acid or higher concentration Soa(if oleum is being use), gives better refining but the yield of oil is low because more oil is sulphonated. The acid strength may be *66* Be[1] containing 93 per cent acid, 98 per cent or any other strength, however concentration below 90 per cent are not feasible except when using recovered acid for drying the oil before the main treatment.

Normally a preliminary does of *66* Be acid is used mainly for drying the oil. In the latter dozes either concentrated 98% sulphuric acid or oleum with 20% Soa is normally used. Other concentration of sulphuric acid or oleum may be use for drastic refining. Whether concentrated sulphuric acid or oleum is use the actual reacting medium is Soa.

Though concentrated sulphuric acid (98%) is also used in acid treatment oleum gives better results. Table shows the effect of ageing on transformer oil prepared with H_2SO_4 and oleum under similar conditions.

Acid dosage

The amount of acid used for treating a given amount of oil depends upon the percentages of reactive portion in the oil. The unsulphonated residue (USR) of the base stock or oil gives per cent weight of the base stock or oil that remains unreacted after the complete sulphonation. USR is a measure of the amount of oil which does not react with the acid. The ratio of acid to oil will therefore, depend on the USR of the base stock the final USR required in the oil.

Depending upon the base stock and the quality requirement of the product, the ratio of acid to oil may very from 5 to 55 per cent. The quality of acid used is normally in large excess(6 to 10 times) of the theoretical requirements. The strength of acid used determines the amount of acid required for a given degree of refinement, increasing the strength decreases the amount of acid required.

The ratio of acid to oil in each doze with depends upon the number of dozes; if number of dozes is less more acid will have to be used in each doze, The acid is added in dozes to control the temperature and to avoid side reactions.

Increasing the ratio of acid to oil in a doze lowered the oxidation stability of the transformer oil. Hence usually acid is added in two or more dozen of 5 to 15% acid. The exact number of dozes is usually determined by the laboratory by conducting test on each grade of oil to makes sure that the desired refining is achieved. Oils that contain a high percentage of impurities may be treated with three separate additions of acid, however, generally two treatments are enough. Medicinal white oils on the other hand may require more than three additions of acid.

Generally *66* Be sulphuric acid is added in ratio 5% acid, oil for the preliminary drying treatment, if the oil does not contain asphaltic material in excess of 1%. If the proportion of asphaltic material is high in the oil, the same percentage of acid may be used in the first dump as in subsequent dumps.

The methods employed in the distillation of the base stock will determine to a large extent the quality of acid required. If the oil has been subjected to excessive heating or if insufficient steam has been used in the distillation process, destructive distillation will occur and larger quantity of acid will be required to remove the products formed by this cracking. Overhead distillate will require from 30 50 per cent less acid than residual stocks, because most of the undesirable constituent will be concentrated in the residuum. The quantity to be used must be determined by trail in the laboratory.

Base stocks, operating conditions and products

Base stock	Tempe-rature °C	Viscosity cSt*	Acid ratio wt/wt	Products
1. cable oil base stock (1600 industrial)	80-90	40	30-45	Cable oil, heavy lube
2. Heavy oil base stock (500 industrial	65-75	30	25-40	Liquid paraffin, white oil, heavy lube, cattle spray component.
3. medium oil base stock (300 SUS ind. Neutral)	60-70	20	20-30	Medium liquid paraffin, white oil, machine lubricant food processing.
4. light oil base stock (150 neutral)	50-60	15	20-30	Light liquid paraffin, white oils, food processing, pharmaceutical, petroleum jelly component.
5. Transformer oil base stock (TOBS), spindle oil	50-60	6-8	15-25	Transformer oil refrigeration oils, insecticide oils etc.

Losses and yield

Great losses occur in the manufacture of speciality oils as a result of exhaustive treatment with acid for the following reasons :

1. Polymerization of some hydrocarbons
2. Formation of sulphonic acids
3. Absorption of oil by the acid sludge.

The losses depend upon the degree of refinement and the nature of base stock. Base stock with low unsulphonated residue give high refining losses if completely refined. The losses will depend upon the USR of the base stock and final product. Generally the losses are 20-25 per cent but may be as high as 55 per cent in the manufacture of liquid paraffin with some base stock.

Typical batch acid treatment plant

The typical batch speciality oil treatment plant consists essentially of the following equipments:

1. Cylindrical vessels, lead lines with concial bottoms, called acid agitators into which the oil is pumped and where acid is added.
2. Cylindrical vessels with conical bottoms, called wash agitators into which the treated oil flows in series to be neutralized.
3. Auxiliary equipment (pumps, heating coils, air blowers, instruments) necessary for the smooth and efficient functioning of the unit.

The acid agitator is equipped with a large draw off on the bottom. A tile jacket or other form of insulation is often applied to the shell to reduce thermal loss and to protect the - content from chilling effect of cold weather. Frequently the agitator is provided with steam coil from inside, to heat the content and maintain the oil in fluid conditions. Weak acid and some water lines are often made of brass to resist corrosion.

Process of manufacturing

The oil is pumped into the acid agitator. The oil is heated to the desired temperature and then 66°Be sulfuric acid is added slowly to regulate temperature. This treatment is mainly for drying the oil before the main treatment. Often acid recovered from the sludge of a previous batch is used for the first treatment.

The acid is sprayed on the oil through a spider having approximately 1/8 opening at an angle of almost 45 with the surface and about 3 feet above the level of the oil, ensuring used for required to divided the acid into minute particles necessary to increase the active surface. The air should be moisture free as any water carried into the oil will dilute the acid and tend to increase the heat of the reaction.

However, air tends to oxidise the oil to organic acids which from soaps with alklies and these oxidation products dissolve in the oil and darken its colour and give it a bad odour. If air agitation is prolonged unnecessarily, in the presence of acid, the soaps formed by the organic acids with alkali solution in the subsequent neutralization treatment, may cause troublesome emulsions. If agitation is too violent the sludge will the disintegrated into very fine particle, making it difficult to settle out.

After the application of acid the oil is allowed to remain quiescent upon 1-3 hours or more and the acid sludge settles out and is drawn off. Since sludge dissolves and discolours the oils, it should be withdrawn before it has had time to solidify. Complete separation of the sludge is important. After this has been done the acid treated oil is cooled to about 80-100°F temperature and then neutralized with alkali and oil soluble sulphonates recovered by solvent extraction. Then the next dump of acid is added.

After the preliminary treatment with 66Be sulphuric acid and after separating the sulphonate, next dump of acid is added. The acid may be 98% sulphuric acid or oleum with 20% free SO_3. After each doze of acid the sludge is separated, acid neutralized, acid sludge may also be separated from the oil by the centrifuging process. Centrifuging is much more rapid process than the usual settling process for the separation of sludge from the oil.

The duration of treatment will depend upon

1. Method and degree of agitation.
2. Size and shape of agitator.
3. Nature and viscosity of the oil.
4. Quality of the acid.
5. Strength of the acid or oleum
6. Number of treatments

Time of contact is dependent upon the degree of dispersion of the acid or intimacy of contact. For the removal of sulphur long time of contact is required, than is required for improvement in colour.

There are three stage of contact time as follows:

1. Time of agitation to effect thorough contact.
2. Time of settling the sludge.
3. Time which elapse after the sludge is withdrawn and before the oil is neutralized. This contact time is less important because refined oil can be kept in acid state for long time provided the oil is not in contact with the sludge.

Blowing or agitation should be continued long enough to ensure complete contact between the oil and acid resulting in full utilization of the acid and clean separation of the sludge. If the period of agitation is too short there will be loss of acid as much more acid will be required to obtain the desired degree of refining. More acid will result in more amount of oil coming into the sludge and consequently the sludge will not settle well.

If the period of agitation is prolonged, the result is also detrimental to the quality of the finished product for the following reasons:

1. Tendency of oil to oxidize (with air agitation) is increased.
2. Some of the coloured substance resulting from the action of the acid on the oil, back into solution to some extent, which will darken the oil.
3. Troublesome emulsions are likely to form during neutralization with cause soda solution.

4. There is loss of some of the valuable constituents which will be drawn off as sludge.
5. Pepper sludge is formed which will resist setting and will require an excess of clay for its later removal.

More time is require to complete the treatment of a large batch of oil than a small one. When the acid is applied in two dumps, the first one is blown for a much shorter period the first dump requiring probably 5-10 minutes or longer depending upon conditions while the second dump may require more than 20-40 minutes. In the first dump more easily removable materials are involved and so require less time for blowing compared to second dump when materials resistant to the acid are involved. If the oil contains more potential sludge forming compounds the blowing time of the first dump may have to be increased.

Neutralization and washing

After the oil has been completely treated with acid a large quality of unreacted acid remains in the reactions mixture. This excess acid is neutralized with aqueous sodium carbonate (20%) in the reaction. During the acid treatment sulphonic acid are formed and the upper oil layer contains oil soluble sulphonic acids. Sodium carbonate also reacts with oil soluble petroleum sulphonic acids forming sodium petroleum sulphonates.

Sodium sulphate, sodium carbonate (which is in slight excess) and sodium sulphonates are removed from the neutralized oil by repeated washing with water or if the petroleum sulphonates are to be recovered the neutralized oil is treated with solvents.

Sludge disposal/ pollution control

The acid sludge resulting from processing is usually dumped in the open pit or into sea or burn directly thus creating a lost of pollution hazard. Such a disposal system would require prior approval of authorities.

The sludge (neutralized or blended) may also be utilized by controlled burning as a fuel in suitable heat recovery system.

The sludge may be used for the recovery of water soluble sulphonic acids is described in the next section. In that process oleum is also recovered as a by product and may be used in the acid treatment of the base stock,

Recovery of sulphonates

An important groups of compound known as sulphonic acids, is produced in the course of the sulphuric acid treatment of petroleum products. Some of these sulphonic acid known as ' mahogany acid' are soluble in mineral oil and remain in the upper oil layer while other called ' green acid' are insoluble in the mineral oil and are continued in the lower acid sludge layer. Generally the sulphonic acids formed during light acid treatment are water soluble whereas oil soluble acid are generated from ore drastic sulphonation. These petroleum sulphonic acids are recovered from oil layer and acid sludge layer in the form of their sodium salts.

The sodium salts of mahogany acid are more important commercially then the corresponding salt of the green acids because they are more effective emulsifiers., detergent dispersants and rust inhibitors. Oil soluble sulphonic acids are recovered during the refining of technical white an transformer oils.

The mahogany sulphonates are isolate from the oil layers as the crude sodium salts by treatment of the oil with aqueous solution of sodium carbonate followed by extraction with ethyl alcohol, isopropyl alcohol, acetone or other solvent. This solvent is recovered from the solution by distillation and reused.

IPA process, using isopropyl alcohol as a solvent for extraction is the most widely used process for the recovery or oil soluble sulphonic acids. The oil is neutralized with aqueous sodium carbonate solution (20% solution) and subsequently extracted with 1:1 aqueous isoprply alcohol. Isopropyl alcohol extracted some water is removed by distillation and is reused. The crude some petroleum sulphonate is dissolved in benzene or other suitable solvent and water removed by azeotropic distillation. The solvent solution is filtered to remove inorganic impurities such as sodium solution is filtered to remove inorganic impurities such as sodium carbonate and sodium sulphate,. The refined sodium petroleum sulphonate are isolated after removing the solvent by distillation.

The oil insoluble sulphonic acid are also marketed to a limited extend in the form of their sodium salt as wetting agents. For their recovery the sludge is stirred with about equal quantity or water after which the organic matter form a cake on tope of the solution. The sulphuric acid underneath is discharged. The cake is washed with cold water and then dissolved in concentrated solution in hot water, cold water after which it is neutralize with caustic soda solution to dorm the sodium salts. The neutral solution is evaporated to dryness and the dry material pulverized in a mill. The oil in soluble sulphonates may also be recovered by extraction with a solvent in the form of their sodium salts.

Clay treatment and filtration

After neutralization and washing the acid treated oil is usually treated with clay or other adsorbents. Sometimes instead or neutralizing the acid with alkali, the acidic oil is directly contacted with active clays which neutralize the acid at the same time decolourizing it.

Purpose and action

The purpose of the clay treatment is to decolurize the oil and to remove carbon coke resinous and asphaltic substance , water and suspended matter. A large portion of colouring matter is removed in the acid treatment process, but traces of oil soluble colouring matter still remains. Besides traces of inorganic materials such as sodium sulphate and sodium carbonate are also present in the oil. Clay treatment and filtration process is necessary for removing such substances.

More active materials in the oil are preferentially and selectively adsorbed on the surface of the clay. The unsaturated compounds exert greatest attractive force for clay followed in order by compounds containing oxygen or nitrogen, aromatic compounds, naphthenes and paraffins. In each series the higher molecular weight hydrocarbons are absorbed more readily. Thus resinous and asphatic materials which have high molecular weight are actively adsorbed. This clay filtration removes unstable unsaturated and aomatic compounds and colour forming nitrogen oxygen compound. At the same time it also removes suspended Impurities such as sodium carbonate and sodium sulphate from previous treatments. Water is also absorbent by the clay. Sulphur is absorbed by the clay. Sulphur is absorbed only in a limited quantity and hence all the sulphur must be removed by the acid treatment.

Absorbents

The common absorbents used for decolourizing the oils are :

1. fuller's earth
2. bentonite
3. bauxite and alumina
4. activated clays (activated with acid)
5. activated carbon.

Fuller's earth or bauxite *is* used in percolation filtration. Activated clay or bauxite it is used in contact filtration. Activated carbon may be added to activated clay from better colour removal but carbon alone is not used. Coarse clay (30-60 mesh) is used in percolation filtration because resistance to the flow of oil to excessive with finer clays. For contact filtration finer clay (15-20 mesh) is used.

The clay as received from mines contains 15-20 per cent moisture which is removed by roasting in a kiln before it is used. There is strong evidence that in many cases traces of moisture in the clay may help in initial adsorption of colour through electrostatic forces. Also, the moisture on heating evaporates and protects the clay from atmospheric oxidation by maintaining a film of steam on its surface. Rotary or multiple hearth kilns are used for the roasting and regeneration of the clays. The clays usually possess a light salmon colour when the finished in a health kiln and give better bleaching than the clay burned in a rotary kiln.

Apart from natural or acid activated adsorbents of mineral and organic origin (clays and carbons) synthetic adsorption such as silica gel, alumina gel, and ferric hydroxide gel are also used but only to limited extent because of their high cost.

Methods

There are two methods of treating the oil with clay:

1. Contact filtration method.
2. Percolation filtration method.

In the contact filtration method, very fine clay is directly agitated with oil, usually at elevated temperatures, for a definite period of time and then filtered to remove the clay. In the percolation filtration methods the oil is passed through a bed of granular adsorbent clay. Generally contact filtration is practised on acid stage oil, that is , oil that has been treated with acid but not neutralized. Percolation filtration is practised only on neutralized oils and some times even those oil which have been contacted with fine clays are given an additional percolation treatment through coarse clay.

In the contact filtration method the amount of adsorbent mixed with the oil depends upon the nature of oil the nature of absorbent and the treating temperature. Generally about 5 to 10 per cent (of the weight of oil) absorbent is added at about 95-110°C. in the percolation method the bed of absorbent is used until all the absorbent has been exhausted or inactivated.

The advantage of contact filtration are:

1. the oil can be treated with clay at elevated temperature resulting in better colour removal.
2. The oil which is still acid from a previous treatment with sulphuric acid can be neutralized and decolourized.
3. Contacting is done for a definite time resulting in better control of the process.

The two process are described below. Contact filtration process

In a large clay contacting plant, the finely powdcred clay (15-30 mesh) is carried by air lift from storage bin to a contacting vessel where it is mixed with the charge oil which has been heated to a temperature of about 5F below the flash point of the oil. Superheated steam is used to agitate the mixture. The oil clay slurry flows by gravity to a rotary vacuum filter which separates the spend clay from the treated oil. The oil is then passed successively through two vacuum steam strippers and finally to a blotter press to remove any traces of clay still present in the oil. The filler operates on a cycle of 7-9 days and must then be cleaned and started again by precoating the drum with diatomite clay. Any oil removed by the steam stripping is separated from water in a steam tank.

In another type of plant the clay is mixed with oil in a clay, mixer with the help of clay hopper, which is an automatic weighing machine for the addition of clay. The use of clay hopper permits continuous and intimate mixing through a heating furnace oil slurry is pumped from the clay mixer through a heating furnace or other suitable fuel. The oil is then cooled to a temperature which is sufficiently low below 160°C to protect the filter press a number of filter presse in series or parallel. The oil is then passed through a vacuum strippers and finally to blotter presses which may have 36 leaves or other suitable number of leaves to remove any clay particular which were not removed by the presses. The finished product from the blotter presses is delivered to the finished oil storage tank.

In a small scale plant the clay treatment is done in open bleach tanks or closed vacuum tanks. The tanks are cylindrical and have shallow cone bottoms from which the mixture of oil and clay is pumped to the filter presses. They are equipped with steam coil or jacket and fitted with mechanical agitators. Vacuum bleaching is preferred because of the danger of oxidation and darkening at elevated temperature if open tanks are used. Also vacuum helps removal of moisture the oil is dired under vacuum for a while before clay is added. It is often customary to add the clay before the oil has been heated to the top temperature (usually 95°C -110°C) heating should be as rapid as possible. The bleaching earth is often mixed in concentrated slurry with a portion of the oil in a small separate tank. After 15-20 minutes the oil with clay is pumped through filter presses which may be plate and frame type or leaf type. Before breaking vacuum and filtering the oil cooled to a sufficiently low temperature to avert oxidation by exposure to air and to avoid damage to filters but high enough for easy flow to filter press.

A considerable amount of oil is retained by the absorbent the amount depending upon the viscosity of the oil and the nature of absorbent. Therefore, after filtration is complete the filter press is blown with air or sten as much as possible of the high proportion of loose absorbed oil in the filter residue. The oil is not quality and is used for other purpose or is re-refined. Even after steam or air blowing the adsorbent many contain 20-30 per cent of oil. This oil may be recovered by washing with gasoline or naphtha or some other hydrocarbon if desired. The oil obtained after washing with naphtha etc. is used for other purpose. The clay may be regenerated in a rotary or multiple hearth kiln or disposed off as waste.

Percolation filtration process

The filter used in percolation method is simply a vertical cylinder closed at both ends and provided with suitable pipe connections at the top and bottom to permit the introduction and discharge of clay and oil. A perforated plate or wire screen, at a slight distance above the bottom, is provided over which a heavy canvas blanket is placed and clamped to hold the clay in the filter and yet allow the oil to pass through and out of the filter. The size and shape of these filters vary considerably, with clay capacities from 10 to 60 tonnes.

After the canvas filter bottom is install, the filter is charged to within approximately 2" to the top with clay (30-60mesh) transferred from the storage bin using belt conveyor. The oil is heated to a temperature that ensures fluidity and is then passed through the filer press under a pressure of approximately 0.4 kg/ cm2 gauge, until the oil appears at the bottom of the filter. The outlet of the filter is then closed and the filter is gradually filled, the entrapped air being released at frequent intervals from the vent at the tope of the filter. This is done to decrease the possibility of completed, the outlet is opened and the oil is pumped through the of 100 40,000 litres of oil per ton of clay depending on the adsorbs coloured materials and must be regenerated by burning the oil remaining in the filter is blown out with air. The filter is washed with naphtha. The clay after washing should contain not more than 1 to 1.5 per cent by weight of oil, steam is finally blown through filter to remove the naphtha.

Hydrotreating process

Hydrogen treating is the newest and rapidly growing method of decolourization. Hydrogen treating is replacing the conventional acid and clay treatment process in the developed countries. However, it has not gained acceptance in India so far because of the non availability of facilities.

Hydrogen treating is a hydrogenation process carried out in the presence of catalyst usually consisting of oxides or sulphides of cobalt, molybdenum tungsten or nickel supported on bauxite or silicon alumina. Hydrogen treatment may be of two types. In the process called hydrofinishing the operating conditions are kept mild (pressure 250-900 psi; temperature 500-760°F and consumption of hydrogen 25~100ft3/bbl.) while in the hydrocarcking process the operating conditions are more severe. Hydrofinishing improves colour, colour stability and oxidation stability; sulphur, nitrogen and oxygen compounds are removed to limited extend. Hydrofinishing removes straight chain unsaturates but does not affect aromatics.

In hydrocraking under severe conditions extensive saturation of aromatic rings and an almost complete elimination of sulphur and nitrogen compounds can be attained. In hydrocarking following reaction occurs:

1. The hydrogenation of polyaromatics into polynaphthenes.
2. The hydrodecyclization of polyaromatics and polynaphtheno aromatics into mononaphthenes.
3. The hydroisomerization of normal paraffins into isoparaffins.
4. Hydrogenolysis of sulphur, nitrogen and oxygen containing hetrocyclic compounds.

Because of the conversion of polycyclic compounds into monocyclic compounds hydrocarking greatly improves the viscosity index of oil.

Hodrofinishing is usually used as a substitute for clay treating but the hydrocarking can be used as a substitute for combined acid and clay treating process. Hydrofinishing may be used before acid treating to remove part of stable sulphur.

Reaction conditions for Hydrotreating process

Operating conditions	Hydrofinishing	Mild hydrocraking	Severe hydrocracking
Pressure	30-40 kg/cm^2	120-140 kg/cm^2	150-180 kg/cm^2
Temperature	320~350°C	350~380°C	380~420°C
Recycling	200-300 1/1	*500-600, 1/1*	800-1200,1/1
Space velocity	1-2,1/1 hr.	0.5-1.01/1 hr.	0.3-1.0 1/1 hr.

Base stocks

The base stock used for the manufacture of speciality oils vary from low viscosity transformer oil base stocks (TOBS) to high . the specialty products are numerous and specific. As each product serves a specific end use selection of base stocks becomes scientifically important if proper quality has to be maintained. In the industrially developed countries, the industry can choose a particular base stock from a wide range of base stock. In India, we have no options on base stocks because of our limited resources and we have to do with the available base stocks which can result in unfavorable economies and yields.

TOBS (Transformer oil base stock) is manufactured by two refineries in India (Lube India Ltd. and Madras Refineries Ltd.) and is lowest priced product available in the lube oil family. Though it is meant to be used for the manufacture of transformer oil it is also being used for the manufacture of white oil. Although Index 10 is little more costly then TOBS, there is a lot of demand for processing for white oil or direct blending for mineral jelly and for cutting oils. HVI spindle is used for the production of white oil and also transformer oil and is available from the two refineries (LIL and MRL). HVI heavy neutral is available from India refineries as well as from imported stock from IOC (India Oil Corporation) HVI Heavy neutral is an important raw material for the production of heavy white oil and suphonates.

The base stock produced by the MRL and LIL are given below:

Madras refineries Ltd.

1. Spindle HVI (high viscosity index)
2. Spindle MVI(Medium vicosity index)
3. Spindle LVI (low viscosity index)
4. Light Neutral HVI

5. Light Neutral MVI
6. Light neutral LVI
7. Intermediate Neutral HVI
8. Intermediate Neutral MVI
9. Intermediate Neutral LVI
10. Heavy Neutral HVI
11. Heavy Neutral MVI
12. Heavy neutral LVI
13. TOBS

Lube India Ltd.

1. 150 Neutral
2. 500 Neutral
3. 1300 Neutral
4. 100 Industrial
5. 500 Industrial
6. 1600 Industrial

7

Miscellaneous Additives and Vegetable Oils

Friction modifier

Introduction

Friction modifies or friction reduces have been established for several years. Originally the application was for gear oil, transmission fluids, slideway lubricants (for elimination of stick slip from slideways) and multi purpose tractor fluids for wet brakes, etc., in fact anywhere where controlled movement is required.

Friction and lubricating regimes

Friction is defined as the resistance a body meets with in moving over another body in respect of transmitting motion. Friction coefficient is defined as

$$\frac{\text{Friction force}}{\text{Normal force}}$$

In the lubricant surface situation the coefficient of friction will be determined by the lubrication regime. In simple terms there are two lubricant regimes, hydrodynamic regime (thick lubricant film) and boundary regime (thin lubricant film) friction modifiers act most successfully in the boundary regime. The friction coefficient of hyrodynamic lubrication is between 0.001 and 0.01.

Friction modification is function of following functions:

- Pressure
- Temperature
- Surface finish
- Surface material identity
- Chemistry of the FM

Friction modifier mechanisms

Friction modifiers dissolved oil are attracted to metal surface. The resulting adsorption forces to the metal surface are very strong, and can be as high as 13 K cal/ mole. The polar head of the FM is attracted to the metal surface and the long hydrocarbon tail is left solublished in the oil. The anchoring of the molecular to the metal surface result in the hydrocarbon tail being perpendicular to the surface. At normal concentrations the FM's hydrocarbons tails will lines up with each other and through hydrogen bonding and Debye orientation forces, their polar groups can be attracted with a force up to 15 keal mole in dimer cluster. Van der Waals forces will cause the molecules to align themselves such that they form multimolecular cluster which are parallel to each other. This orienting of the absorbed layer can also parallel to each cluster to position themselves with their respective terminal methyl groups of absorbed molecules being formed. This is similar to iron filling in a magnetic field lining up along a particular force field. Such a layer of molecules is hard to compress but very early to shear, thus it early to appreciate the slippery nature of the metal surface due to FMs.

The interactive force between methylene carbon atoms and between methyl radicals are weak but positive (estimates of <lkcal/g have been recorded). Consequently, it can be seen that, under normal stress conditions, such force will lead to simple breaking and shear. On a molecular scale it is easy to imagine that for two metal surfaces moving against each other then both surfaces would have the FM absorbed to them.

Chemical aspect of friction modifiers

Friction modifiers are generally long slender molecules. They normally have straight hydrocarbon chain consisting of at least ten carbon atom. Hydrocarbons derived from natural products are ideals for such applications. The polar head group is the dominant factor in the effectiveness of the molecular as a friction modifiers. Such polar groups consist of:

- Carboxylic acids or derivatives (including their salts)
- Phosphoric or phosphonic acids and their derivatives
- Amines, amides, imides, and their derivatives

Alcohol's and mercaptans polar groups are generally poor adsorbers in this situation.

Antagonisms between friction modifiers and other additives

Lubricant additives all exert specific characteristics relative to the static and dynamic friction coefficients of a system. The effect of difficult additives on static and dynamic friction coefficient in a specific lubricating oil base stock. An incorrect balance of additives and friction modifier can alter the mechanism of movement in modern transmission system such as slideways wet brakes, automatic transmission and limited slip axles. Incorrect combination can adversely affect the performance and operation of the mechanism. Thus a high static affect the coefficient combined with a low dynamic coefficient could cause gear movement problems together with squawk in automatic transmissions. If the static coefficient is too low then sliding and delayed gear engagement may result in loss of power. Major antagonisms can occur between friction modifiers and sulphur and phosphours based EP additives. This can result in sticks up motion in slideways.

Lubricity additives in Diesel fuel

Diesel fuel normally contains low levels of sulphur containing hydrocarbon fractions which help to lubricate the fuel pump. Recent experience with low sulhur fuels (<0.02%) has shown that the fuel pump suffers catastrophic wear. This is corrected by the addition of small amount of lubricity additive (effectively a friction modifiers). A bench test has been developed to simulate the effect using High frequency reciprocating rig (HFRR).

Pour point depressants

The pour point of an oil is determined by the ASTM D97 pour point test. The method records the temperature of the oil 3°C above the point at which the oil will not move when tipped out of the horizontal.

The fluidity of an oil in an engine is very important under all circumstance. When starting up an engine from cold it is important that the mechanical part move freely. Failur to do so will lead to excessive wear with the engine becoming inefficient to the point of being inoperable. The main cause is generally lack of sufficient lubrication.

Low temperature operations

When cooled to low temperature lubricating oil can undergo a number of changes

(i) Solidification with the formation of a precipitate of macrocrystals of paraffin, and

(ii) Solidification with the formation of microcrysals which swell giving a crystalline structure which traps the remaining oil.

The circumstance under which this occurs are dependents on the thermal history, the cooling rate, and on an opaque solid phase . they have naturally low pour points. Paraffinic oil of high normal praffins tends to produce reactively strong structures made up of large crystals. Isoparaffins give smaller crystals of weaker structure in a solidified oil. If the cooling rate is rapid then crystal growth may be rapid and the oil will not remain fluid even on agitation. If a microcrystalline wax is formed (such deposits normally take place at about IOC) then the crystals can swell, behaving like a sponge with the absorption of free oil. This result in a restriction in the flow of the oil. Rapid cooling of an oil can produce a hard gel which is easily sheared. Motor oil generally use a mixture of different oils and consequently exhibit a range of behaviours. Pour point depressants are used to improve the low temperature characteristics.

Mechanism of pour point depressants

Pour point depressants act through surface adsorption on to the wax crystals. The resulting surface layer of pour point depressant inhibits the growth of the wax crystals and their capacity to absorb oil and form gels. In the absence of long interlocking crystals or swollen particles, oil can move freely through any solid wax particles that are present.

The limitations of pour point depressants are controlled by the nature of the lubricating oil and the concentration of the point depressant. The effect of pour point depressant varies widely with respect to the oil but they are most effective with thinner oil such as SAE 10, SAE 20; and SAE 30 grades. With SAE 50 grade oil only small effect are seen. Different types of pour point depressant also have different efficiencies, with the maximum effect occurring at an optimum concentration level. Above this optimum level there is usually a visible effect on viscosity at higher temperature. Typical level of application in commercial oil are 1.0 to 1.0%.

Demulsifiers and antifoams

Introduction

During normal operation internal combustion engine subject lubricant to considerable heating and mechanical shearing. In addition to the primary function of lubrication therefore, oils must also contain with various combustion product mainly acidic gases, moisture and carbon particles which could harm the engine. For this reason dispersant and detergent additives are incorporated into the lubricant formulation. These surfactants and other additives, such as viscosity index improves,. Can have a stabilizing effect on forma and emulsion that may form under the high shear regime. Emulsion and foam can seriously impair the effect lubrication of an engine by starvation of the lubricant or blockage of oil ducts.

Emulsion stabilisation

The presence of water in the lubricant will readily give rise to the formulation of water in oil emulsion stabilished by dispersant and detergent surfactants. Dispersant typically consist of a long hydrocarbon backbone and a succinimide head group formed by reaction with a polyamine. Detergents on the other hand, consist of a $CaCo_3$ core surrounded by an alkyl aryl sulphonate or a sulphursed alkyl phenol shell. Clearly either type of produce is able to form strongly achored interfacial layer which confer a high degree of steric stabilization to the emulsions. Other polar material soot and oxidation product tend to accumulate at the interfaces. Should the water droplets come into close proximity, they are kept apart by the repulsive interaction of the long oleophillic segment of the surfactants.

The widespread introduction of positive crankcase ventilation and the recycling of blow by gases has in some instance resulted in the formation of a viscous emulsion sludge, especially on the colder part of the engine. Minimizing these cold zones through better design is an important aspect of tackling this problem.

Demulsification

Demulsification can be usefully broken down into a series of stage. In the first instance droplet must approach one another top form a loose aggregate. At his point it is important to 'sweep up' small droplets before the next stage, coalescence, progresses to far. During coalescence there is a dramatic reduction in interfacial area, resulting in the concentration of solid and other debrise at the interface,. These materials which may have contributed to the stabilization of the original emulsion, have to be dealt with by dispersal into the bulk of one or other of the liquid phases, the formation of distinct phases can then be completed and the water removed.

The ease with which emulsion can be broken depends upon the ease with which the stabilising forces can be countered. A combination of mechanical and chemical means is usually employed. Typically demulsifier formulations comprise more than one component. In order to be effective they must have limited solubility in the bulk phase, preferring to migrate to surfactants. An important feature of the demulsifiers is that they reduce the inter droplet interaction. This allow the droplets to come close together forming an aggregation of droplet separated only to thin layers of oil. The rheolofical properties of this thin layer determine the ease with which it finally ruptures.

Mechanical aids to resolution of an emulsion are important. Although no chemical assistance is required for form a hard sediment of closely packed emulsion, stubborn emulsions doe require the application of a chemical agent to bring about the final film rupture stage.

Demulsifiers

The selection of an effective product relies on a 'trial and error' approach, supplemented by the selector's knowledge of what has worked before. The test procedure requires the production of an emulsion under reproducible conditions. The rate of water coalescene is taken as measure of the effectiveness of the product.

A wide range of product, including every class an type of surfactant, .has been found to exhibit demulsification properties. The most commonly used product in lubricant formulation contain anionic surfactants (e.g. alkyl napthalene sulphonates). Also used as nonionic alkoylant alkyl phenol resin and block copolymers of ethylene oxide and propylene oxide.

Foam stability

The same surfactant that are responsible for the formation of stable emulsion almost certainly play an important role in the stabilisation of foams. Foams consist of a closely packed array of gaseous polyhedral cells separated by thin liquid films. The pressure difference across the films are similar however, at the junction of the cell curved regions of low pressure the form the causeway for the liquid drainage. Gravitational liquid drainage is the prime mechanism of film rupture. This is directly related to bulk viscosity. The liquid film can be considered to consist of a sandwich of surface molecules at the gas liquid boundary separated by a layer of the bulk fluid. Clearly a point will be reached at which the monomolecular surfactant layers come close enough to create a repulsive force which will delay film rupture.

Mechanical foam breakers and chemical methods are employed to destroy unwanted foams. The strategy is similar to that discussed above for dealing with emulsion. The stabilizing monomolecular surfactant must be sufficiently displaced to create a hole *in* the liquid layer. Antifoam are typically low solubility surfactants.

Antifoams

The most important antifoam chemical used to deal with non aqueous foam are polydimethylsiloxanes. These are available in a range of molecular weight (form low viscosity fluids of 100 cSt to several million cSt). Silicone fluids of the correct molecular weight have limited solubility in oil and surface tension of 21mNm. Lower than that of hydrocarbon oils. Flurosilicones exhibit even lower surface tension but are considerably more expensive.

A variety of other materials including alkoylated aliphatic acids, various polyethers (e.g. polyethylene glycols), branched polyvinylethers, and polyalkoxyamines, have been claimed to exhibit and anti foam properties in lubricating oils.

Foam studies

Characterisation of foams employs one of two techniques, static or dynamic. In the static method a foam is generated by sparing a gas into a liquid under controlled conditions. The foam decay is then monitored against time. The half time of the foam is termed the foam lifetime. In the dynamic method the foam is generated continuously and the equilibrium volume measured. With care a liner relationship between foam volume and gases velocity can be determined. The gradient of this liner response is the foam lifetime. Non surprisingly, form lifetime and viscosity show an identical dependence on temperature.

Traditional methods used for the study of foams of employ onc of three method generating a form, namcly single capillaries, sintered glass sparger and diffuser stones. Single capillaries give uniform bubbles buts are relatively slow. The other method generate a rapid form with considerable turbulence, which adversely affects the reproducibility of the result. A turbulent free form can be created by using a uniform mesh to generate a form of uniform bubble size.

Direct measurement of single film thickness using optical methods can yield useful information on the critical films thickness.

Corrosion inhibitors

A corrosion inhibitor is defined (ISO 8044) as 'a chemical substance' which decrease the corrosion rate when present in the corrosion system at a suitable concentration without significantly changing the concentration of any other corrosive agent. This is a useful definition as it enables us to distinguish between the function of antioxidant and overbased detergents on the one hand, and corrosion inhibitors on the other.

Antioxidant and detergents. In the course of its normal usage a lubricant is susceptible to oxidation. The process of refining strips the lubricant of its natural antioxidants (chiefly polycyclic aromatics and sulphur and nitrogen heterocyclics). Oxidation result in the formation of undesirable peroxides and acids. Antioxidants (e.g. hindered phenols and zinc dialkyldithiophosphate (ZDFAs) are added to prevent the formation of these corrosive products. In additions, moisture and acidic combustion by product invariably enter the crankcase. To protect the engine from corrosive wear by mineral acid formed in this may overbased detergent are incorporated in the lubricant.

The process of corrosion

An electochemical couple is formed between the ferrous metal and its oxide layer, invariably present. The anodic partial reaction generates electons:

$$Fe \longrightarrow Fe^{2+} + 2e\sim$$

In neutral or alkaline conditions prevalent in the lubricant environment, the corresponding cathodic partial reaction is:

$$O_2+2H_2)+4e\sim \longrightarrow 4OH\sim$$

Further oxidation result in the formation of hydrate ferric oxide or Fe hydroxide, i. e. rust. The corrosion potential (Ec) and corrosion current (Ic) for the cattodic and anodic reaction can be represented to an Evans type polarisation diagram corrosion inhibitors' interfere with the anodic or the cathodic partial reaction, or with both, resulting in a reduction in the corrosion current.

Corrosion inhibitors

In the selection of an appropriate corrosion inhibitor, an important consideration is the problem of adverse competition with other additive designed to absorb on the liquid metal interface. Extreme pressure and / or anti wear agent compete for the same sites as the corrosion inhibitor. Fatty amines are good corrosion inhibitors in the type of environment. However, their adverse effect on the performance of ZDP additives often prohibits their use.

Corrosion testing

The Ultimate evaluation of the corrosion protection afforded by a particular lubricant formulation is the Sequence IID engine test. This test simulates short trips in winter conditions. Such trips promote corrosion/ rust on the engine component due to formation of condensed water in the engine. The test least for 32 hours after which a rust rating is determined.

A variety of bench test, which attempt to evaluate the oxidative stability and or the corrosion protection of a particular formulation, exist. These invariably involve a coupon test in which a coupon of one or more metal (chiefly copper and steel) is subjected to wet conditions for a fixed period at an elevated temperature. The assessment is carried out on the basis of weight and appearance of the coupon.

Vegetable oils

Fats and oils derived from animals and vegetable sources have a long history of use in lubrication. Indeed they were the main source of lubricants before the enormous growth of mineral oil based products during the first half of this century. Modern lubricant are predominately based on mineral oil owing to price and overall performance, although there is a contusing use of vegetable oil in lubricating. In addition vegetable oils are used as feedstock for the oleochemical industry to produce a wide variety of chemical product. These chemical find use in many application, including lubricant, either as additives for the production of synthetic materials such as ester based fluids.

Chemistry and physical properties

Most vegetable oils (and animals fats and oils) have the triglyceride structure. These tri esters are derived from glycerol and carboxylic acids known as fatty acids. The fatty acid are almost always straight chains containing between 8 and 22 carbon atoms and may be saturated, mono or polyunsaturated. Vegetable oil compositions are normally described in terms of their fatty acid content, referring to the acid ester moieties, actual fatty acid present in the oil are known as free fatty acid.

Each vegetable oil is characterised by its fatty acid composition, which nevertheless may vary somewhat depending on such factor as weather, soil conditions and variety. Typical fatty acid composition of the most common vegetable oil, which together account for over 90% of world production are given in table both non systematic names and numerical notation are given for instance 18:2 refers to a fattv acid with 18 carbons and two double bonds.

Naturally occurring fatty acid components of vegetable oils virtually always contains an even number of carbons,, in nature the fatty acids in triglycerdies display positional isomerism; they are not randomly distributed among the three possible position of glycerol. For instance, plasmatic acid in both olive and soya oil is present predominately on the 1 and 3 position rather than the central position of glycerol. The double bonds are in a cis condifuration and in the case of polyunsaturated, are normally separated by a methylene groups (i.e. They are not conjugated). For instance, the structure of linoleic acid a common 18:2 acid is given in.

Difference in the physical and chemical properties of vegetable oil are largely dependent on the degree of unsaturated of the constituent fatty acids. Vegetable oil with a high proportion of saturated fatty acid are solid or semi solid at room temperature. Indeed, such oil are referred to as fats, the distinction being simply whether they are solid at room temperature.

The presence of double bonds results in a kink in the chains, which particularly owing to the cis configuration, are not able to pack together as easily. This result in a lower melting point with a consequence that unsaturated vegetable oil are liquid and free or waxy deposits at room temperature.

However, the presence of double bonds does have an effect on oxidation stability. The allylic position is labile and hence susceptible to free raidcal abstraction and subsequent formation of peroxides. In polyunsaturates the methylene groups separating double bonds is allylic and therefore particularly prone to oxidation. So called drying oils takes advantages of this process, where it ultimately lead to solid gels through the formation of a network of crosslinks Hence lubricating based on vegetable oils, in where both low temperature performance and oxidative stability are required are probably best served by using an oil high in monounsaturates. Here a compromise between low temperature performance and oxidative stability is sought, with appropriate additives being used to improve performance where required.

Since most vegetable oil are tri~ester, they are prone to hydrolysis, and this may pose problems for some application. A small degree of hydrolysis may be acceptable, or even beneficial, since free fatty acids, produced as a result of hydrolysis, are generally active as friction modifies, flash point of vegetable oils are very high, generally above 300°C but this can be affected significantly but the presence of free fatty acids.

The fairly consistent molecular weight and molecular interactions of vegetable oils result in a fluid that is viscous with a very high viscosity index for instance the VI of rapeseed oil is over 200.

Of particular importance, both historically and current is the use castor oil in lubricant. Castor oil is a triglyceride with a very high content of the fatty acid ricinoleic acid. This is an unusual fatty acid, containing one double bond and a hydroxyl group.

The free hydroxyl group is able to interact with polar groups on metal surfaces, thereby imparting superior lubricity, whilst the largely monoene nature of castor oil give it low temperature fluidity without the oxidative instability of polynsaturates. Castor oil finds use in specialist tow stroke application and can be modified for use in application such as greases.

Another oil that is of interest in lubricant is jojoba oil as a replacement of sperm whale oil, which is now banned. Jojoba oil is not triglyceride but is wax ester composed mainly of straight chain esters of C20 to C22 monounsaturated acid and alcohols. The major constituents.

Extraction and processing

In nature, vegetable oils are generally concentrated in the seeds and fruits of plants. After harvesting the vegetable produce needs to be transported and stored and these factors can have an important influence on the quality of the oil. This is because unlike mineral oil they may be affected by natural processes such as attack by insects, moulds and bacteria. Oil bearing fruits such as oil palm and olive have a high moisture contend, which favour the action of naturally occurring enzymes, and hence they must be processes soon after harvesting. Seeds, on the other have a lower moisture contend and may be stored for much longer periods.

Before extraction of the oil, the raw material is often pretreated to acid the extraction process. This may consist of some of the following.

- Cleaning
- Dehulling or decorticating
- Cooking to break down the oil cell, sterilise and coagulate the protein
- Flaking

The oil is extracted from the vegetable raw material usually by one of the following processes:

- Screw pressing
- Pre-pressing following by solvent extraction
- Solvent extraction alone

The choice of process depends very much on the type of raw material and the required plant capacity. Continuous solvent extraction is often the method of choice where high throughput is required. Direct solvent extraction is particularly used for seeds that are low in oil, such as soya.

In screw processing, the oil is expelled under pressure exerted by a revolving wormshaft. High pressures can be achieved yielding a cake with only 3-6% oil.

In pre~pressing, the pressures are about half those used in high pressure expelling and the capacities are generally must higher. Oil is obtain in the pre~pressing operation, although the main objective of pre~pressing is to obtain a cake suitable for subsequent solvent extraction.

Solvent extraction, whether direct or following pre~ pressing is performed either by a perocolation type method or by immersion, in which the pre treated seed or cake is dispersed in the solvent. Both methods employs a countercurrent technique, and the degree of extraction is controlled since relatively high levels of impurities may be extracted towards the end of the procedure. The most widely used solvent is a light paraffinic petroleum fraction, which is recovered by passing through a multistage rising film evaporator.

Finally the oil undergoes a number of refining processes to produce a purified oil. These refining processes may includes degumming in which phosphatides are removed as gums in hydration process, neutralization and washing to remove free fatty acids, trace metals and other water soluble, oxidation and deodorization to remove by product and polishing for removal of trace oil insoluble.

Uses

As noted earlier, vegetable oils have a long and continuing history of use in lubricants, even through modern lubricant are predominantly based on mineral oil owing to cost and performance consideration. However, recently there have been increased intense in extending the use of vegetable oils in lubricant driven mostly by environmental as well as health and safety issue, and also arising from changes in economic and supply factors there is a plentiful supply of vegetable oil in many parts of the world where mineral oil is expensive and in short supply. There is growing concern about polycyclic aromatics (PCAs) present in mineral oils posing a risk to human health, particularly in circumstances where, as a result of normal use, there can be considerable skin contact with the oil. Vegetable oil are free of FCA and low in potential pollutants such as sulphur containing compounds. They also have added advantage as environmental concern grow in that they are biodegradable and are a renewable resource.

Unmodified vegetables oil have a number of application in modern lubricant more often as additives but also as general base fluids. For instance, high erucic aid rape seed oil has been shown to be effective in lubricants. Jojoba oil is used in high performance automatic transmission fluids as a replacement to sperm whale oil after sperm whale was placed on the enfadered species list in 1972. Vegetable oils may also be used as base fluids for straight cutting oil. Reference has already been made to the use of castor oil in lubricant in particular in two strokes where it is used essentially as lubricity additives and is known for imparting a characteristic odour to the exhaust.

Vegetable oils are used as raw material for the oleochemical industry which supplies a vast range of material. Some of which largely retain their original trigyceride structure, whereas other are broken down and modified, perhaps with the addition of moieties from petrochemicals. In this way various alcohols and acids of vegetable origin are used in manufacture of esters for use in synthetic esters lubricants.

Most modification, initially at least are concerned with reaction involving the ester or double bonds of vegetable oils. Hydrolysis gives the free fatty acids, which are generally active as friction modifiers, transesterification result in fatty acid esters which in the case of rapeseed methyl ester, has been shown to be potential substitute for diesel oil.

Soaps of 12 hydroxystearic acid derived from castor oil have superb thickening and lubricity properties and are hence used in greases. Sulphated castor oil is used in mineral based lubricant for presizing polyester fibers and thus minimizing abrasion. Ethoxylated castor oil is a hydrophilic emulsifier which has found use in metal working fluids.

The presence for increase use of vegetable oils in lubricants, due to both environmental and health and safety consideration, is likely to continue. New genetic varieties, commercialization of existing varieties, together with new chemical modification will increase the type of material available. Economic trends are likely to make vegetable oil materials available. Economic trends are likely to make vegetable oils increasingly more attractive than in the past in many areas of the globe. All these factors will probably result in an increase use of vegetable oils in lubricant as trend that may be evidenced by the number of patent and other publication in this area. However, the predominant position of mineral oils are based fluids is likely to contain for the foreseeable future; in terms of volumes vegetable oil surpluses could only ever replace a small share of the total mineral oil based lubricant market.

8

Various Formulations of Lubricants and Grease

Textile Lubricants

		Ingredient	*Lb.*
1.		Monoamylamine/oleate	4
		Paraffin oil (28°Be')	96
		Mix the above and stir into water	100
			G
2.	(a)	Rosin	6.4
		Mineral oil	20
	(b)	Olein, light	10.5
	(c)	Spindle oil	73.4
	(d)	Alcohol	5.4
	(e)	Caustic soda (40°Be')	2.2

Melt up (a) with agitation, until clear. Add (b), (c), cool down to 45°C, add (d) and, with vigorous mixing, (e) in small portions, until the cloudiness disappears.

Some olein may also be needed if it does not work clearly.

Lubrication for Wool

Ingredient	*G*
Olive oil	87
Oleic acid	10
Trigamine	3
Water	100 cc.

The above emulsion is suggested as a wool lubricant so that the wool fibers in the carding and combing operations pass over one another with the least possible amount of frictional resistance. The oil in emulsions made with trigamine is of an extremely fine particle size and comes into contact with the fibers very rapidly, thoroughly and uniformly. Furthermore, the oil emulsion is very easily removed during scouring.

Lubricant for Worsted Yarn

Ingredient	*kg.*
Oleic acid	40
Triethanolamine	2
Water	60

Stir together at about 35°C, and transfer immediately into a homogenizer, where the emulsion is homogenized under about 150 atmosphere pressure.

Textile Lubricant for Spinning Jute, etc.

Ingredient	*kg.*
Train oil, dark	30 - 50
Spindle oil, distilled	30 - 50

Rope Lubricant (British Patent 455,652)

Ingredient	*oz.*
Mineral oil	72
Aluminium oleate	2½
Hydroquinone	1/2

Warm together and stir until disolved.

Some Important Formula

Ingredient	*Parts*
Sea-fish oil soap (50%)	31.8
Menhaden oil	5.0
Sodium hydroxide	3.0
Residuum of a Furol viscosity at 210°F of 850 sec.	49.5
Lowcoldtestoilof80-85SUSat100°F	10.7

The procedure of manufacture is as above. The menhaden oil being added to the mixture before the sodium hydroxide is introduced. This lubricant is stirred as it cools to 300°F, at which point it is filled.

U.S.Patent 2,349,058

Ingredient	*Lb.*
Tallow	28.4
Sodium mahogany soap	14.2
Dry caustic soda	7.8
Litharge	22.8
Petroleum oil	8.6

The tallow and the sodium mahogany soap are added to a mixer, together with about 5 pounds of oil. After this mixture is heated to 160 to 180°F the caustic soda is added as a 48°Be'solution and the temperature of the batch maintained at 180 to 200°F until the mixture thickens. The litharge is then added and the temperature raised slowly to about 500°F. The batch is held at this temperature until it becomes smooth, after which the remainder of the oil is added and agitation continued until the temperature drops to about 300°F at which point the product is filled into containers or further processed.

Such lubricating greases are formulated with a slight excess of litharge and alkali and will therefore have from 0.02 to 1.2% of such material in the final product. Lubricating greases prepared from these complex lead soaps are smooth, stringy, and tacky, but still fibrous enough to be pulled back to the face of the gear teeth after each revolution. These lubricating greases have good worked stability and are resistant to hot water.

Preparation of Complex Soap Lead Base Greases

Another U.S. Patent 2,292,672, gives a method for lead based complex soap greases : A very small amount of low viscosity oil is added to mixer, followed by the required amount of litharge. This mixture is stirred until a smooth paste results. The menhaden oil and an equal amount of low viscosity oil are then mixed with the paste and the entire mixture heated at 300 to 325°F for two to three hours, by which time the reaction should be complete. The remainder of the mineral oil and also blown asphalt are then added and mixed at a temperature of 200 to 250°F.

Formulas, as given in U.S. Patent 2,292,672:

	Light(%)	Medium(%)	Heavy(%)
Menhaden oil	4.49	4.49	4.49
Litharge	3.51	3.51	3:51
Blown asphalt.	30.00	40.00	51.00
80/85 at 100°F, Low cold test oil	26.00	30.00	41.00
175/185 at 210°F, Bright stock	36.00	22.00	X

Lead Base Lubricating Greases Containing Fillers

Lubricating greases containing complex lead soaps and also from 1.0 to 20.0% of carbon black are described in a US Patent 2,349,058. Its containing free litharge, is considered a filler. Another filler added is the carbon black. It increases the water resistance and improves the heat resistance of the lubricant and greases. Other fillers are asbestos, talc, and graphite.

Lead based Lubricating Greases Formula

		Heavy (%)	*Medium* (%)	*Light* (%)
(i)	Lead-sodium soap	15.0	11.3	4.2
	Sodium grlyceroxide	1.8	1.3	0.5
	Sodium mahogany soap	2.5	1.9	0.7
	Carbon black	6.0	4.5	1.7
	Litharge and free alkali	0.5	0.5	0.2
	Oil 5900 SUS at100°F	74.2	80.5	92.7 *Parts*
(ii)	Litharge			5.95
	Menhaden oil			11.80
	Sodium hydroxide			2.55
	Low cold test 80/85 SUS at100°Foil			29.40
	Residum 850 Sec. Furol at 210°F			35.30
	Heavy black oil			15.00

Application of Lead Base Lubricating Greases

Except in the case of the lead soap of 12 hydroxy stearic acid, lead soaps are not employed as thickeners for lubricating oils, because,

(1) lubricating greases in which they are present resist the scrapping and sliding action of such mechanisms as worm gears, etc., (2) and to provide a carrier for lead which may later react with another ingredients, such as chlorine and sulfur for preventing seizure and scoring of metal surfaces under heavy loads.

Types of Greases Manufactured in India (According to information received from Standard Vacuum Oil Company Ltd., Bombay):

Industrial Greases

Lime base cup greases for plain bearings.

Lime base greases for open gear lubrication.

Lime base semifluid greases for loose boss arbors, weight hooks, light duty guarded open gems, etc., in textile industry.

Lime base graphite greases for heavy duty plain bearings.

Lime base soft grease for mechanical grease lubrication systems.

Lime base grease for cold roll necks in steel mills.

Soda base grease for open type bearings in industrial machinery.

Aluminium base graphited grease.

Asphaltic base grease/Lubricants for open gears.

Automotive Greases

Lime, soda, and aluminium base greases for different parts of automobiles, and other vehicles.

Railroad Greases

Fraction gear greases.

Lime base rail and flange lubrication greases. Lime base low consistency grease for locomotive lubrication.

Soda base journal and road cup greases.

Soda base grease for general lubrication.

Specifications

Greases are graded on the basis of their worked penetration values. The 'dropping point' that is the temperature at which grease drops out of cup having an orifice at the bottom, is also employed for characterising greases. It gives an approximate idea of the maximum temperature at which the grease can be used in a bearing. Free alkalinity, and free acidity are generally specified, so also the ash content which provides a check on the soap content of the grease. The viscosity of the lubricating oil component is also spacified as this is useful to lubricating engineers in recommending greases for different purposes. The Indian Standards Institution has formulated various standards. Some of the main standards' content is given here:

Specification for Soda and Lime Greases

Nature of soap base	S.S. of loco Grease Soda	Grease 1 No.3Lime
Ash (sulphate), % max.	5.50	5.00
Evaporation Loss, max	1.00	1.50
Consistency of worked material at77°F, penetration in 0.1 mm.	200-250	230-280
Free acidity as oleic acid, % max.	0.40	1.00
Free alkalinily as $ca(OH)_2$,NaOH,%max	0.30	0.25
Drop. Pt. min	150°C	25°C
Water content, % max.	X	1.0
Viscosity of mineral oil Component, redwood No.	64-86 at 210°F	93-136 at 140°F

Strontium Based Lubricating Grease

Use: Strontium bases are particularly important because unlike other bases, they are soluble in water-cold as well as hot.

RAW MATERIALS

For forming strontium base grease the strontium compounds needed are (1) strontium hydroxide, and (2) strontium stearate. The former is primarily and mostly useful as they can be procured during manufacturing process, and comparatively economical as well. Strontium hydroxide may also contain some barium or calcium compounds.

As a soap base, tallow, lard oil, hog fat, stearic acid, oleic acid, the higher molecular weight acids resulting from the oxidation of petroleum fractions, rosin, higher molecular weight naphthenic acid, sulfonic acid, beeswax, sperm oil, and degras are needed for the manufacture of strontium base greases.

A variety of lubricant oils can be employed in strontium base lubricating greases. Oils varying from a viscosity of 55 SUS at 100°F to 200 SUS at 210°F and with a V.I. range of 20 to 105 is to be used.

Additives are the same as in other bases.

Preparation of Lubricating Grease from Normal Strontium Soap

A US Patent 2,417,430 describes the procedure as follows, two processes are cited:

In the first, 18.5 grams of dry powdered normal strontium oleate having 5 ml. of water is to be added drop-wise and stirred into wet soap thoroughly. Approx. 200 grams of naphthenic type mineral oil of a viscosity of 207 SUS at 100°F is then added and the mixture is heated to 400°F. Subsequent cooling to 250°F resulted in a partial gelation.

In the second method a normal strontium soap lubricant is prepared as follows :

50 grams of tallow fatty acids, 25.3 grams of strontium hydrate, and 200 grams of SAE 40 solvent extracted 90 V.I. oil. The tallow fatty acids were first melted with 50 grams of oil. The strontium hydrate is then added and while being stirred the mixture is heated to 450°F. After foaming had almost ceased, the remainder of the oil was added, and after a heat of 450° was reached the product was set aside to cool to room temperature. The resulting, substantially anhydrous product, containing 22.0% of normal strontium soap and having a free acid content of 0.03% (calculated as acetic acid), had a melting point of 300°F. The mixture is now semifluid in consistency and too soft for a conventional ASTM penetration determination and analysis.

Preparation of Strontium Base Lubricating Greases with Complex Soap Thickeners

According to US Patent 2,417,430, this type of grease is prepared :

A mixture of 109 grams of cottonseed oil, 16 grams of sperm oil, 60 grams of SAE 60 lubricating oil and 46.4 grams strontium hydroxide is heated to 200 to

300°F until the vigour of the reaction subsided. Then an additional 250 grams of the same oil is added, and the mixture is heated for about 12 hours at 500°F at which time no substantial amount of free alkalinity remained. Finally 466 grams of oil was mixed in and the mass is cooled at room temperature.

The lubricant obtained about 17% of soap, and 0.01 % of the strontium hydroxide. This lubricating grease is smooth, unctious, dark in colour, and exhibits no syneresis. The worked penetration of the product remains 229, dropping point over 400°F.

Additional Formulas and Processes

	Ingredient	*grams*
(1)	Tallow fatty acids	50
	Acetic acid	10.7
	Strontium hydrate	48.0
	SAE 40 grade solvent extracted 90 V.I. oil	200.0

The fatty acids are melted in a beaker and mixed with 50 grams of oil. When the temperature of this mixture reaches 180°F the acetic acid is to be added, followed by the strontium hydrate. While the material is being stirred its temperature is gradually increased, and after partial dehydration, the remaining oil is gradually added. The mixture is finally heated to 450°F before it is set aside for cooling.

	Ingredient	*kg.*
(2)	US Patent 2,595,556	
	Prime tallow	7.0
	Tallow fatty acids	21.0
	Urea	1.5
	Acetic acid (80% strength)	1.8
	Strontium hydrate	24.3
	SAE 40 grade naphthenic base oil	82.2

The tallow, tallow fatty acids, 14 kg of oil and the strontium hydrate is to be charged to a steam jacketed kettle of about 1 barrel capacity, equipped with a means of agitation. This mixture is heated to 235°F and while agitation is continued the urea and 14 kg of water is introduced. The acetic acid is next added, after which the temperature is raised to 250 to 275°F while agitation is continued for 1 hour. The remainder of the oil was mixed with the batch while cooling to 200°F, after which 0.5 kg of water is added to hydrate the lubricating grease. Dehydration is subsequently effected by raising the temperature to 285°F. The resulting strontium soap complex lubricating grease

Mixed Base Strontium Soap Lubricating Greases

A US Patent 2,540,533 cites the composition of mixed base grease ; a description of the formation of this type of grease is as follows :

20 to 50% concentrate of the strontium salt of a 450 molecular weight petroleum sulfonic acid is dissolved in an acid treated coastal oil having a viscosity of 55 SUS at 210°F, 20% aqueous solution of calcium acetate in sufficient quantity to introduce the desired amount of calcium acetate is then added and the batch is partially dehydrated ; lead acetate is then added as a 30% solution ; finally the mixture is dehydrated at 240°F and then placed in an oven at 300°F for 2 to 3 hours.

Another Formula

	0%
Strontium sulfonate	10.0
Calcum acetate	5.0
Ethane sulfonic acid	3.5
Hydratedlime	1.5
Coastal mineral oil, 55 SUS at 210°F	85.0

To manufacture this type of grease, the ethane sulfonic acid is to be dissolved in twice its weight of water and neutralized with the hydrated lime. When the reaction appeared to be complete, the solution is added to a blend of the strontium sulfonate and the mineral oil and the batch is stirred to 180 to 200°F until no solid particles are present. The calcium acetate is then added as a 20% aqueous solution and the mixture is dehydrated slowly, with stirring, until a temperature of 300°F is reached. The product is to be cooled at room temperature, without stirring.

Applications and Characteristics of Strontium Base Lubricants

(1) Resistance to the disintegrating effects of water, at ordinary or elevated temperatures; resistance to the leaching action of hydrocarbons.

(2) Reversible character over a wide temperature range, due to their anhydrous character and their freedom from gelation.

(3) Superior protective action against moisture or salt spray corrosion.

(4) Relative stability when used at high temperatures.

(5) Stability of grease structure when subjected to mechanical working.

Other Specific Applications Are

In rubber plants, bearings operating in ovens at approx. 325°F. and in an atmosphere where sulfur and solvent vapours are present, these can successively be lubricated.

Mixed Base Lubricating Greases

It is estimated that mixing two metals for a base in producing lubricating greases is more effective. It gives the structural stability in some mechanical devices. It also gives the variety, and thus effects on nature or texture of a grease. It actually softens the greases.

Only some of important greases are discussed below :

I. The addition of zinc soap together with phenyl alpha naphthylamine is found to stabilize acid reacting lubricating greases against oxidation. This is mixed with sodium, calcium, barium, aluminium, or lithium base greases.

A Suitable Working Formula is

Ingredient	%
Hydrogenated fish oil acids	13.00
54% lithium hydroxide	2.05
Aluminium stearate	0.50
Zinc naphthenate	0.50
Low pour coastal lubricating oil	41.875
Low viscosity, low pour point oil	41.875
Phenyl alpha naphthylamine	0.20

The fatty acids are dissolved in about one-quarter of the oil in fire heated kettle. The lithium hydroxide, dissolved in boiling water is added at a temperature of about 150°F, and heating and agitation are continued until the temperature reaches about 200°F. At this stage the aluminium stearate is added, after which heating and agitation are continued along with intermittent additions of lubricating oil until all but a small portion of the oil has been added. When a temperature of 370°F is reached and the mass is fluid, the phenyl alpha-naphthylamine and the zinc naphthenate, dissolved in the remainder of the oil, are added. Heating is then discontinued and the mixture is stirred until the temperature has dropped to below 100°F when the lubricating grease is drawn into containers.

Graphite Lubricating Greases

Graphite lubricating greases for general application consists of a cup grease which contains upto 5 per cent of powdered graphite as filler, Graphite is most commonly used filler in calcium base lubricating greases. Graphite lubricating greases are widely used in water pumps, ocean vessels of different types and in slides for elevators. Graphite used for lubricating greases must contain at least 95 per cent of graphite carbon and must be free from gritty materials. These types of lubricating greases are particularly effective for use in rail and flange lubricants for rail roads. Such greases reduce the wear on both the rail and the flange of the car wheels, especially on high rails on curves. Colloidal graphite, commonly as a water dispersing agent, is employed as a lubricant for drawing tungsten wire through diamond dies at a temperature of 600°C. Another advantage of graphite solid lubricant is that it is effective at higher temperature and does not oxidise upto a temperature of 650°F.

Fine grade graphite powder as a filler in aluminium base lubricating grease is most widely used as sealant or pipe-thread lubricant. It is used to seal the irregularities in pipe threads better than most lubricants. Commonly used composition is 50 per cent of lubricating grease and 50 per cent of high clay content graphite powder. Graphite is also used in antiseize compounds for general use. One of the composition is -

Ingredient	%
White lead	60
Petrolatum	10
Graphite	10
Asphalt	10
Lubricating oil	10
Total	**100**

GENERAL PRECAUTION

Addition of graphite to calcium base lubricating greases has a softening effect. For this the addition of graphite is done when the product is partially or almost completely finished. This can be achieved by having a separate mixing kettle, as it is difficult to entirely free a vessel of the filter once it has been used in equipment. Secondly an appropriate oil must be used, so that slurry can be fed to the finishing kettle without dusting, as addition of powdered graphite is accompanied by dust which settles on the sides of the mixing vessel.

II. Mixed Base Lubricating Greases having Extreme Pressure Qualities

Ingredient	%
Fatty oil	40
Caustic soda	8
Lead soap	10
Mineral oil	33
Water	9
Total	**100**

Or

Ingredient	%
Sodium-lead tallow soap	15 to 4.2
Sodium glyceroxide	1.8 to 0.5

Sodium mahogany soap	2.5 to 0.7
Carbon black	6.0 to 1.7
Litharge and free alkali	0.5 to 0.2
Petroleum oil	74.2 to 92.7

A water-resistant, high temperature, extreme pressure lubricating grease is made from 78 to 81% of sulfurized asphaltic base oil, of 50 to 100 SUS viscosity at 210°F, 9% of lithium soap, of hydrogenated fish oil acids, 9% of lead oleate, 0.5% of aluminium stearate, 0.5% of zinc naphthenate and 0% to 2% of chlorinated wax.

Ingredient	%
Magnesium soap of C_{10} to C_{12} alkenyl succinic acid	10
Lead soap of menhaden (fish oil) acids	10
Sulfurized sperm oil.	10
SAE 20 grade paraffin base lubricating oil	70
Total	**100**

III. Mixed Soap Lubricating Greases which are Reversible

The U.S. Patent 2,332,247 gives an excellent formula for a grease which is water-insoluble, transparent, temperature stable and reversible :

Ingredient	%
Animal fatty acids	6.72
Cottonseed fatty acids	6.72
Soyabean oil fatty acids	6.72
Hydrated barium oxide	12.00
Aluminium stearate	5.00
Lubricating oil, 50 SUS viscosity at 210°F	62.80

The fatty acids and one-third of the oil is heated to 150°F and the barium hydroxide added. Stirring and heating were continued until a temperature of 200°F is reached, when another third of the oil, is added. Following this, the aluminium stearate, dispersed in the remaining oil, is added and the temperature of the mixture raised to between 300 and 350°F. When the mass is fluid and clear it is poured into containers and permitted to cool. The cooled lubricating grease has a penetration of 200 and melting point of 265°F.

Thermally Reversible Lubricating Greases (US Patent 2,389,523)

Composition	I %	II %
Stearicacid	17.85	16.50
Barium hydrate	7.52	6.95
Hydratedlime	0.47	0.44
Magnesia	0.20	0.18
Solvent refined oil 350 SUS viscosity at 100°F	73.96	X
Naphthenic oil 450 SUS at 100°F	X	75.93

Characteristics

Penetration 77°F, unworked

Penetration 77°F, worked

Melting point °F

Methods of Production of Mixed Base Lubricating Greases

Mixed base lubricating greases may be produced by one of the following methods or by a combination of these processes:

(1) By **saponification,** employing a mixture of bases, all of which may be added at once or they may be added in sequence.

(2) By formation of one soap from fatty material and alkali in a portion of the lubricating fluid; followed by addition of a preformed soap.

(3) By the addition and **dispersion** of two or more preformed two soaps to lubricating fluid.

(4) By **preparation** of lubricating greases of individual bases followed by cold mixing of the finished products.

Use of Alkalies and Salts in Mixed Base Grease Production

Formulas and methods of preparation of special valve or cock lubricants are suggested by Mass, W. (**Petroleum** Z, 28, No. 38 1 -16) in which not only more than one base is used but also salts of metals, which will convert some of the soaps formed by the bases into soluble soaps. Such products are made from fatty acids in the presence of mineral oil or petrolatum.

After the fatty acids are melted in the hydrocarbon material, calcium hydroxide is added, if this is to be used. Next sodium or potassium hydroxide is introduced, after which heating is continued until the acids are neutralized. Finally, salts such as aluminium sulfate or magnesium chloride are added as solutions. If aluminium or magnesium soaps are thus formed, sodium or potassium sulfates or chlorides must remain in the mixture.

Ingredient	*Parts*
Stearic acid	13.0
Calcium oxide	1.0
Sodium hydroxide	1.5
Aluminium sulfate	3.0
Maganesium chloride	2.0

To this fillers of various kinds may be added.

Ingredient	*lbs.*
Stearic or any other fatty acid	100
Tallow or other glycerides	100
Petrolatum or oil of 150 SUS at 210°F	200
Caustic soda in aqueous solution of 35°Be'.	42
Aluminium sulfate, in 20 gallons of water	54

The method of manufacture consists of melting the acids and fit in the petrolatum or oil in a kettle provided with agitation. After these ingredients are thoroughly mixed, the caustic soda solution is introduced, while heating is continued. As soon as saponification has started, the aluminium sulfate solution is slowly added. As the aluminium sulfate is mixed in, the heat of the mass is raised to 375 to 425°F. Agitation and heat are continued until the product is dehydrated. After the batch is dehydrated, the lubricant is permitted to partially cool before it is drawn.

Formed Soaps with Preformed Soaps

In the production of mixed base lubricating greases the predominate soap is frequently formed in the lubricating oil by saponification of a fat or fatty acids, after which a preformed soap is added.

A barium-aluminium soap mixed grease is described here

Ingredient	*Parts*
Animal fatty acids	6.76
Cottonseed fatty acids	6.72
Soyabean oil fatty acids	6.72
Hydrated barium oxide	12.00
Aluminium stearate Lubricating oil of 50 SUS viscosity at 210°F	62.80

Procedure

The fatty acids are heated to 150°F in a third of the total oil. The barium hydroxide is then added and agitation and heating continues until the temperature reaches 200°F. Another third of the oil is then stirred into this mixture. The aluminium stearate is mixed with the remaining oil and then it is added to the barium soap mixture, after which the temperaure is raised to between 300 and 350°F. When the mixture becomes fluid and clear it is poured into containers to cool.

A **lithium base** lubricating grease containing both aluminium and zinc soap has the following proportions and ingredients

Ingredient	%
Hydrogenated fish oil fatty acids	13.000
Lithium hydroxide, 54% strength	2.050
Aluminium stearate	0.500
Zinc naphthenate	0.500
Low pour coastal lubricating oil	41.875
Low viscosity, low pour lubricating oil	41.875
Phenyl alpha naphthylamine	0.200

In compounding the above, the acid and about one-fourth of the oil are charged to a fire-heated kettle and, mixed and heated to about 150°F until the acids dissolved in the oil. The lithium hydroxide, dissolved in boiling water is then added. Heating and agitation are continued and the temperature is permitted to rise to 200°F. The aluminium stearate is then added and heating and stirring is being continued alongwith intermittent additions of lubricating oil until all but a small portion of the oil is added. After the mixture becomes fluid, at about 370°F, the phenyl alpha naphthylamine and zinc naphthenate, dissolved in the remainder of the oil, are added. Heating is then discontinued and lubricating grease to be stirred until the temperature drops below 100°F.

Fillers in Mixed Base Lubricating Greases

Generally, fillers are not mentioned by the industrial consultants. But a small-scale manufacturer may add, 20% of leaf lead mixed with the thickened petrolatum (temperature below 150°F).

Complex Soap Lubricating Greases

"Complex", is theoretically described as "A complex salt or absorption compound", but in manufacturing industry it is really meant "to refer to the soap modifications ; i.e. hydrated soaps, basic soaps, and soaps associated or combined with various other compounds, as complex soaps". Since many such soap combinations, and lubricating greases formed from them, has been accepted over a considerable period as normal products, they are important as well for a manufacturer like other grease products.

There are many kinds of complex soap lubricating greases, such as hydrated soaps, hydrated calcium soaps, hydrated aluminium soaps, barium soaps, lithium soaps, sodium soaps, strontium soaps, acid soaps etc. only some of the important of these complex soap lubricants will be discussed here.

Importance of Soap Salt Complexes, and their Characteristics

The particular characteristics which make soap-salt complexes valuable for the manufacture of lubricating greases are:

(1) Their solubility characeristics;

(2) Their freedom from change in aggregation state over a wide temperature range; and

(3) Their stability as regards dissociation of soap and salt.

Most soap thickeners for lubricating fluids should be soluble or dispersible in the fluid at elevated temperatures, and, as the temperature decreases, crystallize in fibrous crystallites which serve to immobilize the fluid. Still, all complex soaps formed from metal soaps and salts will not exhibit this characteristic. Some will not exhibit this characteristic. Some will be so soluble that they will fail to crystallize and consequently no plastic body will form. Other complexes may be too insoluble and either not disperse, ever, by a proper choice of the metal, of the higher fatty acids and the low molecular weight acids, suitable complex soaps can be found for the production of lubricating greases.

General claims for Soap-Salt Complexes for -Lubricating Greases

The most generalized claim for soap-salt complexes is to thicken the lubricating oils. It covers complexes at least two metals, one of which must be polyvalent. This polyvalent metal is preferably selected from the alkaline earth metals, such as : barium, calcium, magnesium, and strontium. But, aluminium, beryllium, zinc, cadmium, boron, tin. zirconium, cerium, vanadium, antimony, bismuth, arsenic, copper, molybdenum, germanium, columbium, chromium, selenium, tellurium, tungsten, manganese, iron, cobalt, nickel may be used as the polyvalent metal.

The second metal of the soap complexes must be different from the first and is preferably an alkali metal, namely: lithium, sodium, potassium, or cesium, or an alkaline earth metal, such as: barium, calcium, magnesium or strontium. The other metals listed above may also be taken as substitutes. These soap complexes are not limited to the use of two metals, as three or even more metals can by used provided at least one is polyvalent.

The saponifiable materials which contain high molecular weight fatty acids, either in a combined or a free state, include tallow, lard oil, hog fat, horse fat, stearic acid, oleic acid, higher molecular weight acids resulting from the oxidation of petroleum fractions, rosin and other related products, higher molecular weight naphthenic acids, sulfonic acids, and saponifiable waxes such as beeswax, sperm oil, degras, etc.

Suitable organic acids of low molecular weight whose salts may be employed for formation of complexes include monocarboxylic and polycarboxylic acids containing less than carbon atoms per molecule. Included in such groups are formic, acetic, propionic, valeric, oxalic, malonic, succinic, the low molecular weight alkyl and aryl sulfonic acids, and the low molecular weight carboxylic acids such as glyceric, glycollic, thioglycollic, etc., heterocyclic carboxylic acids, such as furoic, etc., and phenolic and thiophenolic compounds such as phenol, cresol, thiophenol,etc.

Some Methods for Forming Soap-Salt Complexes

There are numerous methods for manufacture of metal soap-metal salt complexes. Some of them are :

1. The one method for the formation of the complex soaps, and the resulting lubricating greases, consists of starting with a normal soap, which may be preformed or produced by reacting a saponifiabie material with a basically reacting compound. Such normal soap is dissolved in all or a portion of the mineral oil to be used, and subsequently a solution or a dispersion of the desired metal salt or salts in a polar solvent is added Agitation and heat are maintained on this mixture until all or a portion of the polar solvent is removed. Once the complex soap is formed, the production of the lubricating grease follows the usual pattern.

2. Another method for the manufacture of complex soaps and the resulting lubricating greases is to dissolve a normal metal soap in mineral oil, add to this solution a quantity of basically reacting compound, followed by sufficient low molecular weight carboxylic acid to neutralize a portion, only, of the base present. Finally,carbon dioxide is led into the mixture to neutralize the remaining base. A modification of this method is to mix mineral oil, normal metal soap, metal salt of a low molecular weight carboxylic acid, saponification reagent and water, and contact the mixture with carbon dioxide until the product is substantially neutral. The neutral product may then be dehydrated and finished in a normal manner.

3. Still another method is one in whcih a dry metal soap-metal salt complex is formed without any mineral oil being present. A suggested formula and procedure is given below

Ingredient	*lbs.*
Tallow fatty acids	50.0
Glycerol	5.0
Calcium oxide	9.5
Water	50.0

The materials are added to a steam jacketed kettle, mixed and heated to 240°F to effect saponification and partial dehydration. After cooling to room-temperature a brittle solid is obtained. This is removed from the kettle, powdered, and returned to the vessel. This powder is then heated in contact with air for 4 hours at a temperature of 300 to 350°F. Under these conditions the free calcium hydroxide content decreases to a value of 0.1% and the water content to 0.1%. Under these conditions the free calcium hydroxide content decreases to a value of 0.1% and the water content to 0.1%. Then this product is being dispersed in a mineral oil.

Complex Aluminium Soap Lubricating Greases

The complex greases are produced from a mixture of low molecular weight aromatic carboxylic acids and higher molecular weight acids, are again a combination of co-precipitating water solutions of soaps of alkali metals with an aluminium salt.

Examples of such soaps are aluminium benzoate stearate, aluminium toluate stearate, and aluminium didodecyl benzene sulfonate. These soaps are said to impart high melting points and resistance to emulsification with water to lubricating greases. For instance, 12 parts of aluminium benzoate stearate is dispersed in 108 parts of refined paraffin oil by heating to 450°F. The resulting product is a light brown, translucent lubricating grease with a dropping point of over 400°F.

An aluminium-barium complex lubricating grease can be formed thus:

Ingredient	*gms.*
Aluminium stearate	300
Urea	15
Acetic acid, 80%	19
Barium hydrate	160
SAE 30 naphthenic type oil, of 35 V.I.	600

The aluminium stearate is dissolved in about one-half of the oil, the barium hydrate, urea, and acetic acid are then added during constant agitation. The reaction mixture is heated to a temperature of 300 to 350°F for a period of two hours, after which the remainder of the lubricating oil is added while the batch cooled to about 200°F. Finally 0.05% of water is added to improve the body and smoothness of the lubricant. This product contains 3.9% of metal soap complex.

Complex Barium Soap Lubricating Greases

A US Patent 2,595,556 gives the following ingredients to form such a grease

Ingredient	*Kilos*
Prime tallow	7.00
Tallow fatty acids	21.00

Urea	1.50
Acetic acid (80% strength)	1.88
Barium hydrate	28.50
SAE 40 naphthenic type oil	82.20

The tallow, tallow fatty acids, 14 kg. of oil, and the barium hydrate are charged to a steam jacketed grease kettle and heated to about 235°F with agitation. The urea and an additional 14.0 kg. of oil are then added and the mixture is heated to 300°F while agitation continues. After 1¼ hours at this temperature, the batch is cooled to 200°F and 0.5 kg. of water is added. The acetic acid is then added to the kettle and the temperature increased to 250 to 275°F while mixing is continued for 1 hour. The remainder of the lubricating oil is then added while cooling the charge to 200°F, after which 0.5 kg. of water is added. Dehydration is then accomplished by heating to 285°F. The finished lubricating grease is slightly fibrous and had an unworked penetration of 272.

For barium-sodium complex greases the following formula is found suitable:

Ingredient	%
Stearic acid	14.0
Candelillawax	4.0
Glacial acetic acid	4.0
Glycerol	6.5
Barium octahydrate	19.0
Lubricating oil	52.5
Total	**100.0**

Complex Calcium Soap Lubricant

Ingredient	%
Hydrogenated fatty acids	5.5
Cottonseed fatty acids	5.5
Refined or crude montan wax	4.0
Acetic acid	4.0
Lime flour	4.6
100 second paraffin oil	76.4
Total	**100.0**

The method of production is the usual compounding procedure followed by dehydration to the extent of giving the finished product increased temperature stability.

A calcium soap-calcium chloride complex formula is

Ingredient	%
Hydrogenated fish oil	20.0
Hydrated lime	2.9
$CaCl_2.H_2O$	0.3
Ethylene glycol mono-butylether	2.0
Lubricating oil	74.8
Total	**100.0**

The hydrogenated fish oil, calcium hydroxide, calcium chloride and a trace of water are stirred and slowly heated to 450°F. With the calcium chloride present, it is said to be necessary to heat the mixture to 450°F in order to form a calcium soap. After all the water is removed at 450°F the mineral oil is mixed in at such a rate that the temperature is maintained at 400 to 450°F. Following the oil, the ethylene glycol monobutyl ether is added and the batch is permitted to cool, without any agitation, to room temperature after which it is stirred until smooth. The melting point of the product is 375°F.

There is a considerable choice of either mineral oils or soap stocks for the manufacture of these calcium soap-calcium chloride lubricating greases. The points which are emphasized about the manufacture of such lubricating greases are that the soap be prepared before mineral oil is added and the reaction carried out at 400 to 500°F.

A reversible high-temperature lubricating grease can be prepared by the following procedure:

A steam jacketed kettle is charged with 3000 grams of a 30% concentrate of calcium sulfonate of approx. 900 molecular weight, and 3000 grams of naphthenic oil of 65 viscosity SUS at 210°F. This mixture is agitated and heated to 180 to 200°F, after which 180 grams of calcium acetate as an 18.4% aqueous solution is added. Five drops of an organic silicon polymer are added to control foaming and the temperature of the charge is readily increased to 250°F. Cold water is then poured into the kettle jacket and agitation continues until the charge reaches a temperature of 100°F, at which point the lubricating grease is packaged. The finished product has a melting point above 400°F, and unworked penetration of 242 and a worked penetration of 278.

The recommended ingredients for producing a **calcium sulfonate complex for thickening lubricating oils** is as follows:

Ingredient	%
Calcium sulfonate as 40% concentrate in oil	41.0

Technical calcium acetate		18.0
Calcium stearate		1.5
Naphthenic type mineral oil		39.5
	Total	**100.0**

The procedure for compounding is to dissolve the calcium sulfonate concentrate in half the lubricating oil to be used and add the calcium stearate while agitating. When a paste is obtained with the above mixture, the calcium acetate is added as a 15% aqueous solution. This addition is gradual and when the mixture acquires the appearance of a homogeneous, milky emulsion, heating is started. When the charge is substantially dehydrated, at about 280°F, heating is discontinued and the remainder of the oil is added. Agitation is continued until the temperature drops about 280°F, heating is discontinued and the remainder oil is added. Agitation is continued until the temperature drops to about 150°F when the lubricating grease can be drawn. The lubricating grease thus formed is a stable, having worked penetration of 285, and dropping point of 425 to 450°F.

Another Example is:

Ingredient	*grams*
Prime tallow	450.0
Urea	24.3
Acetic acid (80%)	34.0
Calcium oxide	51.5
Sodium hydroxide	42.0
SAE 30 naphthenic type oil, 35 V.I.	1200.0

The tallow is mixed with 225 g. of the oil and the slaked calcium oxide is added. The batch is heated and mixed to effect saponification, after which the mass is cooled and another 225 g. portion of oil is added. The sodium hydroxide (as a solution) and the urea are then added to the mixture, which is re-heated to 300 to 350°F for a period of 45 minutes. After cooling to 200°F the acetic acid is added to neutralize the remaining sodium hydroxide. A substantial neutral lubricating grease resulted with a melting point of 275°F.

Complex Lithium Soap-Salt Lubricating Greases

A preparation of lithium soap complex lubricating grease is described in an US Patent 2,417,428, in which 980 grams of stearic acid, 3940 grams of sperm oil, and 5000 grams of waxy gas oil are mixed in a steam jacketed kettle before a slurry of 1130 grams of lithium monohydrate in 1060 grams of gas oil is added. While the temperature is increased to 300°F the remaining gas oil, consisting of 10,000 grams, are added. The batch is then cooled to room temperature and worked through a 200 mesh screen.

The finished lubricating grease is smooth, buttery, and translucent. This product has an unusual character i.e. it bodied up when heated to 200 to 300°F and yet when it is cooled to room temperature the lubricant grease returns to a soft consistency.

A lubricating grease containing both the lithium soap of a fatty acid and lithium acetate has the following ingredients :

Ingredient	*grams*
Hydrogenated fish oil fatty acids (54 liter)	150
Palm oil	25
Naphthenic acid	25
Acetic acid	40
Coastal pale oil, 100 viscosity at 100°F	700
Lithium hydroxide (added as a water solution)	80
Coastal red oil, 2000 viscosity at 100°F	800

Complex Strontium Soap Lubricating Greases

One method of the preparation of lubricating grease from a strontium soap complex is as follows : 109 grams of cottonseed oil (approx. 0.38 equivalent), 16 grams of sperm oil (0.04 equivalent), 60 grams of a naphthenic type SAE 60 grade lubricating oil, and 102 grams of strontium hydrate (equal to 46.4 grams of strontium hydroxide or 0.76 equivalent), are heated at 200 to 300°F until the vigour of the reaction subsided. Then an addition 250 grams of the some oil added, the mixture is heated for about 12 hours at about 500°F at which time no substantial amount of free alkalinity remains. Finally 466 grams of the oil is stirred in, and the mass is cooled to room temperature.

An Extreme Pressure Lubricating Grease in which the preferred thickening agents for lubricating oil are strontium sulfonate, calcium acetate, and the calcium salt of ethane sulfonic acid

Ingredient	%
Strontium sulfonate	10.0
Calcium acetate, anhydrous	5.0
Ethane sulfonic acid	3.5
Hydratedlime	1.5
Acid extracted coastal oil of 55 SUS at 210°F	85.0

The ethane sulfonic acid is dissolved in twice its weight of water and neutralized with the hydrated lime. When the reaction appears to be complete, the neutralized solution is added to a blend of the strontium sulfonate and the oil. The batch is stirred at 180 to 200°F until no soild particles remained. Then the calcium acetate is added as a 20% aqueous solution and the mixture is dehydrated slowly, with stirring, until a temperature of 300°F is reached. The product is cooled to room temperature without stirring.

9

Asphalt Technology

SOURCE OF ASPHALT (BITUMEN)

Asphalt is obtained as the ultimate bottom product of a vacuum distillation column. The residuums may still contain some oil, but further distillation serves no use at all.These residuums are rich in asphalts and form the starting materials for air blown bitumen. Asphalts are also obtained in large scale, from deasphalting units. Reduced crudes, waxy distillates, lube oils and long residuums are usually deasphalted for getting quality lube oil base stocks. Naphthenic crudes leave more asphaltic bodies in high boiling fractions, hence deasphalting operations are necessary for producing bright stocks and quality lube oils.

Cat. cracker feed stocks are also necessarily subjected to deasphalting operations.

Chemical Structure of Asphalt

Asphalts do not have general representative formula and are very complex in nature exhibiting inconsistent properties. Asphalts are colloidal in nature and contain asphaltenes in oil which are stabilised by resins to maintain the colloidal form. A sample of asphalt contains:

Oil	—	35 to 50%
Rosins	—	5 to 20%
Asphaltenes	—	20 to 30%
Acids etc.	—	upto 10%

Asphalts obtained from vacuum distillation units shall have less pour point (usually between 30 to 60°C) where as asphalts from deasphalting operations show a high pour point (45 to 90°C). Asphaltic materials are usually responsible for some of the physical properties of crude oils. High sulfurous crudes give more asphaltic materials.

Asphaltic materials are black in colour and display agglutinating properties and hydrophobic tendencies. These are the properties which are industrially explored for road making and water proof works.

Structure of asphaltic materials has been the subject for numerous investigations. These investigations have revealed the significant details of the structure.

Most of the asphaltenes contain carbon to an extent of 82 ± 3% and hydrogen to 8.1 ± 0.7%. It can be seen that the carbon hydrogen ratio is greater than 9 but surprisingly the ratio for various asphalts remains same. Nitrogen, oxygen and sulfur are the usual hetero elements present in asphalts in varying amounts. With increasing aromaticity and hetero elements, the molecular weight of the material also increases. Oxygen content vary from 0.3 to 4.9 and sulfur content reach upto 10%, while variation in nitrogen content is not appreciable-goes upto 3% only.

The structure of asphalts has been open to question for some time. The present NMR studies show that they are condensed aromatic structures of sixteen carbon atoms or more. The idea of such big molecule may be difficult to conceive. X-ray analysis has furnished the valuable information regarding the dimensions of interlamellar distance, layer diameter and height of unit cell.

Indeed, the solubility of asphalt in different solvents varies. This advantage has been capitalised in precipitating different grades of asphalts by the use of solvents.

Sulfuric acid[2] is quite destructive to asphaltenes. Some salts like aluminium chloride can successfully remove the last traces of asphaltenes. The facile interactions of metal chlorides with asphaltenes may prove as a possible means of petroleum deasphalting in future.

The molecular weight of asphalts vary considerably from 900 to 2000 or even more, but no structural investigations have emphasised the nature and location of the inorganic materials in these asphalts.

Action of Heat on Asphalt

Thermal cracking of asphalts result in more or less the same products as contemplated in heavy oil cracking. Thermal decomposition of asphaltenes is a good method for identifying and estimating the hetero atoms. A spectrum of compounds like saturates, unsaturates, and oxidation products are obtained during thermal decomposition of asphalts. Some of the decomposition products of asphalt are:

H_2, CO, CO_2, H_2S, SO_2, H_2O.

C_2H_4, C_2H_2; RNH_2, CH_2, C_4H_6, C_3H_6

C_4H_{10} ' C_5H_{12} ' C_6H_{14}

Dealkylation of aromatic rings at low temperatures; and formation of benzene and naphthalene structures at high temperatures are quite contrary but pronounced.

However, the oxidation of asphaltenes by common oxidising agents like acetic acid, peroxides etc. is exceedingly slow. Phenolic and carboxyl groups are formed during oxidation. There is some up-take of oxygen by the molecule which effectively results in decreasing the solubility of asphalt in heptane. During oxidation dehydrogenation also takes place, with the result, unsaturates and aromatics tend to increase. Blowing air through asphalts brings about orientation in molecular structure, usually decreasing the molecular weight but producing necessary functional groups to give more agglutinating properties. Moschopedis *et al.* have shown that during oxidation of asphaltenes oxygen to carbon ratio increases with increase of time, further the colour and consistency are progressively increased.

Types of Asphalts

Asphalt is categorised into three distinct species, depending upon the source. The primary source is the residuums of vacuum distillation unit, second source is from deasphalting operations.Third is a mixed source comprising all the above two and solvent extracts. The necessary qualities like ductility, penetration index and API gravity are not available with these raw stocks; hence are to be imbeded. Some qualities are enhanced by air blowing of asphalt, the product of which is commercially known as air blown bitumen.

AIR BLOWING OF BITUMEN

Air blowing is done mostly in batch units although continuous air blowing of bitumen is also in existence. In this operation, asphalts from various sources

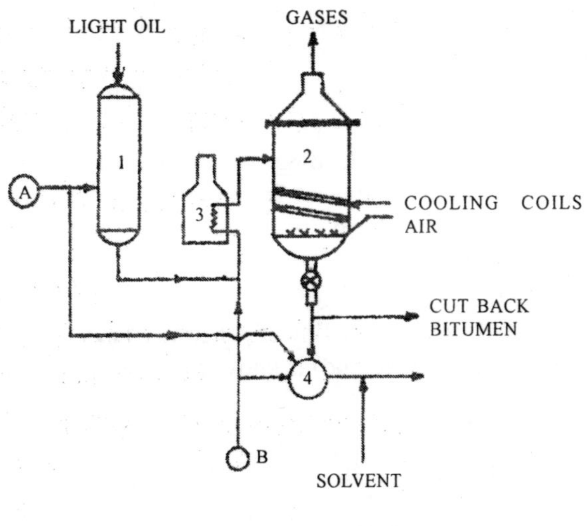

(1) FLASH COLUMN (4) BENDER

(2) REACTOR (A) ASPHALT FROM DEASPNALTING UNIT

(3) HEATHER (B) VACUUM RESIDUUMS.

are mixed and heated to a temperature of 200 to 210°C and sent into the reactor. Fig. 6.1 shows the outlines of the operation. The reactor may be horizontal or vertical type, usually made of mild steel, of a capacity to hold 1000 tons of charge stock. These reactors are fitted with air distributors at the bottom and also cooling and heating coils. During oxidation the temperature may increase rapidly, hence as a precautionary measure provision for cooling is made available.

The reactor should be maintained at a temperature of 200 to 320°C, and air rate of 0.5 to 1.5 m^3 at a pressure of 1.1 to 1.2 Kgs/ cm^2 per hour, per ton of charge stock is necessary.

Blowing time lasts for 10 to 14 hours depending upon the required consistency of bitumen. Heat of reaction is dependent upon the consistency of bitumen as shown below:

Initial softening point °C	Final softening point°C	Heat of reaction kJ/Kg.
41.4		16.9
21.7	120	170.75

Gases are allowed to escape into refinery flare up or/combustion system after being stripped with water.

The product, air-blown bitumen is obtained from the bottom of the reactor.

With sulfur also oxidation is possible and the product is found to have the comparable qualities as with air blown bitumen; but the cost of such process is exorbitant.

The time of air blowing can be considerably reduced by adding certain chemicals like ferric chloride, phosphorous pentoxide etc. A concentration of 0.3% ferric chloride is found to reduce the air blowing period by half.

Cut back bitumens are not really manufactured ones, but blended ones. These are obtained by blending various asphalts with a suitable solvent; in fact these are liquid bitumens. Their action prevails after the solvent is dried off.These are mostly cheap grade bitumens. Simple blending of asphalts also may serve common needs.

Penetration index, the most important property of bitumen judges the quality of bitumen. Arbitrary estimation of penetration index is possible if the softening point (Ball and Ring method) is known; by the following correlation:

$$\frac{20\text{-P.I.}}{10+\text{P.I.}} \times \frac{1}{50} = \frac{\log 800 - \log \text{P.I. at } T\,^{\circ}C}{\text{Softening point } at\ T\,^{\circ}C}$$

This equation is based upon the assumption, that penetration index of all asphalts at softening point is approximately 800.

UPGRADATION OF HEAVY CRUDES

Heavy crudes are different from light crudes in many ways. They possess high gravity, high viscosity, high asphalt and metal contents.

Table 9.1 Results in Different Upgradation Processes.

Property	Heavy crude oil	Visbreaking	Visbreaking after deas-phalting	Deasphalting after visbr-eaking	Visbroken-Hydrocrack-ing	Hydrocracking after deasphalt-ing
API	17.5	21.5	30.6	27.1	32	33
Viscosity (CPs)	740	50	18.0	30.0	10	10
Pour point (°C)	8.5	-1.5	-5.5	-6.0	-12	-15
Distillation %						
IBP-110°C	2	6.7	13.0	7.5	7.3	7.0
110-200°C	3.2	17.0	15.0	17.0	13.0	13.0
200-250°C	4.4	15.-9	16.5	17.5	29.6	30.6
250-300°C	6.8	18.5	16.0	19.5	18.6	21.6
300-350°C	4.6	6.1	8.0	5.0	5.3	8.6
+350°C	79.0	31.5	33.5	26.2	26.2	19.14

The distillation characteristics usually show a very small amount of recovery of light and middle distillates. These properties are definitely different from the crudes of normal category; hence they cannot be processed by the conventional refineries. To feed these crudes into normal refineries a sort of pretreatment is required which goes by the name upgradation.

Thermal cracking, hydrocracking and deasphalting in combinations are suitable for the upgradation of heavy crudes. Visbreaking and separation of lights and then deasphalting the remaining portion, then feeding into light hydrogenation and cracking reactors may be worthy. If the asphalt rich crude can be deasphalted and fed into the hydrocracker, thermal cracking may be eliminated but processing may become uneconomical. It is better to reduce the load on hydrocracker. Hence visbreaking, distillation, deasphalting of heavy fractions and then feeding to the hydrocracker may result in an artificially excellent crude.

The processing of heavy crudes in future is a must not only for our country but for others too, in view of the huge deposits available as heavy crudes and shale oils. Table 9.1 shows some results on upgradation of heavy crude available from north Gujarat zones.

10

Speciality Products

A. INDUSTRIAL GREASE

The consumption of grease bears a direct relation with industrialisation, however in our country it is far from the truth as the importance of application of grease ignored. Hence causes disruption in service of the equipment or machinery. Commercial advantage of the lubrication must be thoroughly explained to users. Though different types of lubricants are employed for the purpose, it is not followed as per specification. Grease application is still not received adequate importance. In fact grease is nothing but soap dispersed in oil. Calcium grease is the most versatile grease and is largely consumed in the industry.

Manufacture of Calcium Grease

Grease is manufactured by two processes (a) Continuous (b) Batch. Batch process description is given below:

Batch process can be followed by two operational adoptions, namely, either open kettle or closed kettle. The process begins with the saponification of oil and hydroxide. Usually non edible oils are employed for this purpose and cheap hydroxide like calcium hydroxide. However the quality of lime is important. It is first hydrated with 2 to 3 times of water and allowed to pass through screens of 60 to 100 mesh size grizlies.The line is now reacted with equivalent vegetable oil (fat) and the temperature is slowly raised to 100 + 20°C. The addition of fat continues till the neutrality is viscible. Saponification lasts for four hours. During saponification water separates out which is evaporated. Now addition of palc oil equal to the weight of the fat is done. The whole mixture is vigorously agitated keeping the temperature around 100°C. Anti oxidants colours can be added at this stage. The whole mixture is now drained for kneading operation.

During kneading which lasts about an hour some more pale oil can be added. Any additives, fillers can be added, after the temperature is brought down to 56°C and the mixture transferred into small drums. Calcium grease is suitable for most of the industrial non specialised type of application. Silicone grease is useful for vacuum and moderate temperature ambients. Molybdenum and Tungsten greases are also available for pressure applications and high temperature operations. It is essential to see the greases are non corrosive i.e.

essential neutral, Greases are tested for load bearing capacity water washability, penetration melting point and oil separation etc. If the grease is water soluble it can be used in water or steam atmospheres. Similar considerations are given priority for selection of grease application.

B. LIQUID PARAFFIN

Depending upon the boiling point range the paraffins can be classified as light or heavy. Most usually light paraffins are used for medicinal purposes such catharacting hair oils, body oils, ointments, sprays etc. Heavy oils are more suitable for industrial applications like paints, solvents, ointments, chemical preparations etc. These are also known as white oils.

Production of Paraffins

The boiling point range for light liquid paraffins is 200 to 250°C, free from wax. The fraction is first isolated and tailored if required depending upon the density and viscosity. The fraction must be free from fluorescence otherwise it has to be eliminated. The stock is to be completely free from aromatics. If the aromatics are more than 5% it is better to remove them by physical extraction like phenol extraction or furfural extraction. If the material is having pugnacious materials like high sulphur and nitrogen components it is even better to go for hydrotreating operation. The cost factor only has to be judged. After removing the solvent from the feed it is treated with concentrated (above 98.4%) strength sulphuric acid till the coloration disappears. Finally it may be given oleum treatment may be upto 2%. Sulfuric acid requirement may vary from 100 to 200%. The treated stock is now extracted with propanol-alcohol mixture. This extract forms good detergent and can be employed for house-hold phenyl making or for cheap detergency actions.

The extracted feed is now thoroughly washed with water and dried by passing air or adding molecular sieves or silica gel. After drying the feed is allowed to pass through a column of bauxite, fuller earth or silica gel of 60 mesh. The finished product will be colorless transparent, odourless and tasteless and does not react with con. sulfuric acid; usually a flash point of 100°C. It should be nongreasy oil with a viscosity not more than 30 cst. at 100°F. Pour point should be as low as possible, perhaps 5°C is sufficient. However it should satisfy U.V. reading not more than 0.1 at 240-280 rim. for a 2% solution in iso octane. The stock being free from aromatics and resins its refractive index will be in the paraffin range, i.e. less than 1.44. For medicinal applications U.V. reading of the sample has to be passed.

C. PETROLEUM JELLYS

Jellys are fine dispersions of wax in oils. These are like greases though there is no saponification. Quality oil i.e. paraffinic oil is preferred as the viscosity variation with temperature is less. Microcrystalline wax is dispersed and to maintain the viscosity and viscosity index it is mixed with polymers like poly butene, poly ethylene liquids. Usually about 5 to 6% polymer is needed. In addition to the polymer an anti oxidant is added. These jellys are thixotropic and non melting. Phase changes do not take place appreciably over temperature variations. These are meant for cable filling operations and act as highly water repelents.

Usually the density of these gels is between 0.9 to 0.83. Cone penetration at 23°C for 3 days is 270 to 310 mm at -10°C, 250 to 270 mm. Oil separation is less not more than 6%. Flash point of these gels is above 250°C. Vaselens are also a sort of jellys but pure paraffinic dispersions sometimes with moisturisers, colorants and perfumes. These can also form as the bases for ointments.

11

Treatment of Lubes

By providing a thin film of oil between sliding surfaces, lubrication increases mechanical advantage, efficiency, and the life of machine. Another function unnoticed by many, is the disposal of heat developed in frictional movements. A carefully chosen lubricant must maintain fluidity and viscosity at the conditions of operation like temperature, load, shocks etc. Truly a single oil cannot contain all the requirements for different conditions and operations thus necessitating several formulations for specific functions. The basic nature

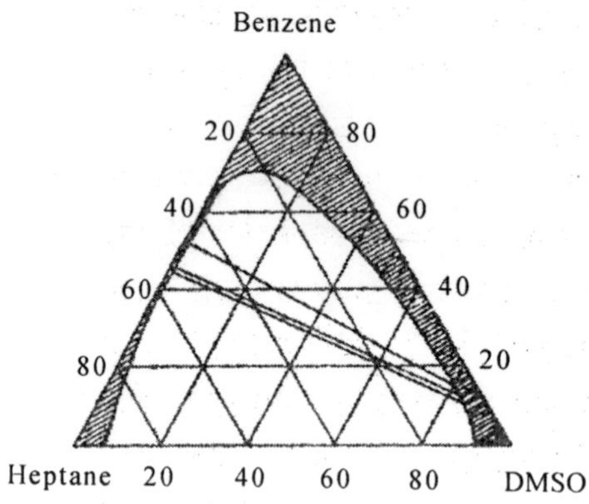

Fig. 11-1a Mutual Solubility Envelope showing Tie-lines for Extract and Raffinate when using Undiluted DMSO

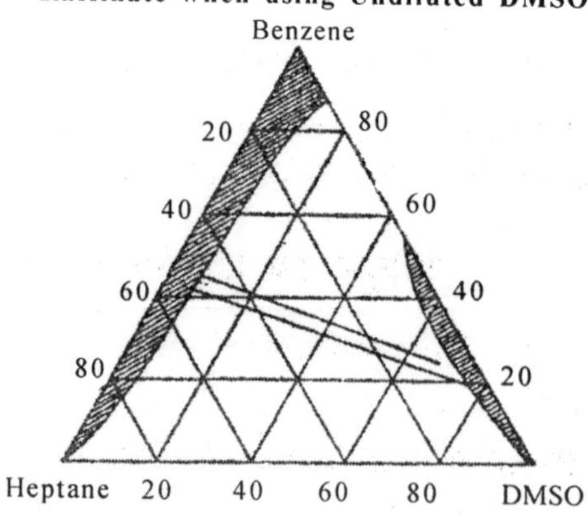

Fig. -11-1b The Mutual Solubility Envelope has Greater Area when DMSO is Diluted with 10 wt.% Water Phase Diagrams for the System DMSO and Heptane, Benzene

of the oil rests upon the source of oil (base of crude); some properties of allegiance are incorporated by blending with other oils or additives. A raw lube oil having a boiling point of above 350°C is composed of the following genera! groups, (except purely synthetic ones).

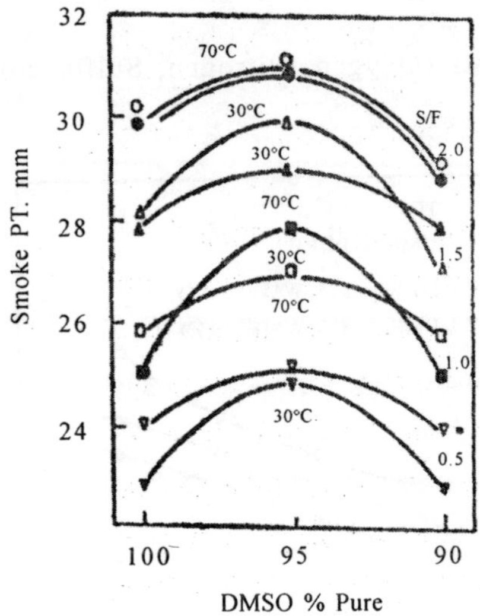

Fig.11-1c Dimethyl Sulforide as Solvent for Improvement of Smoke Point (Effect of Temperature (30°C AND 70°C) S/F Ration and Dilution)

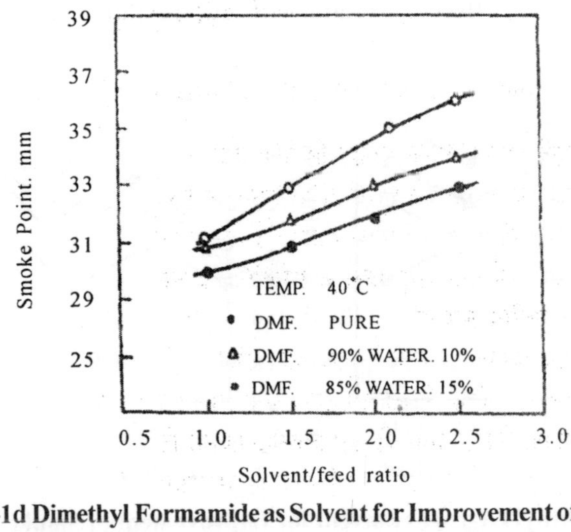

Fig. 11-1d Dimethyl Formamide as Solvent for Improvement of Smoke Point (at 40°C) (Effect of S/F ratio, with and without dilution)

Paraffins

Naphthenes

Aromatics (Poly, Condensed, Branched chains)

Waxes

Asphalts and resins

Inorganic constituents (Oxygen, Nitrogen, Sulfur compounds and contaminants like metals)

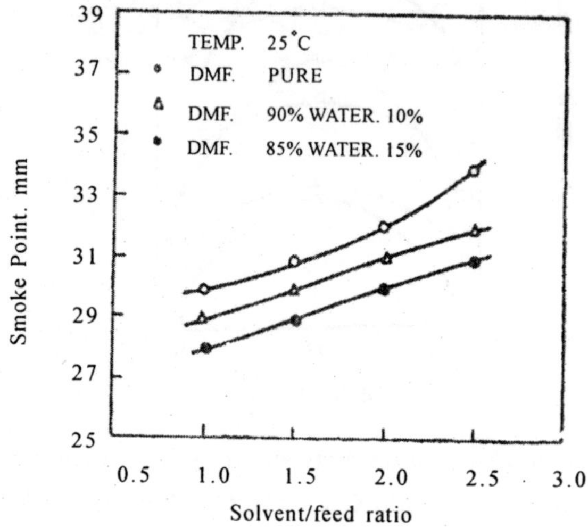

Fig. 11-1e Dimethyl Formamide as Solvent for Improvement of Smoke Point at 25°C (Effect of S/f Ratio with and without Dilution)

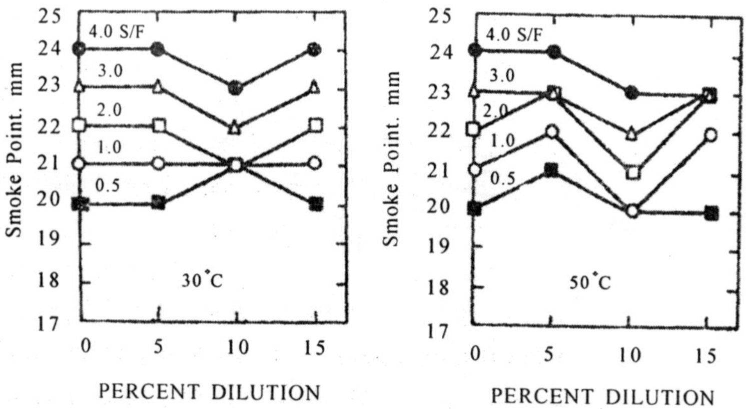

Fig. 11-1f Dimethyl Glycol as Solvent for Improvement of Smoke Point. (Effect of S/S Ratio at 30°c and 50°C)

Table 11.1 Properties of Solvents used for Smoke Point Improvement.

Solvent	Mol.wt.	MP°C	BP°C	Sp.gr. at 20°C	Sp.heat J/gm°C	Latent heat J/gm	Viscosity Cst at 20°C	Surface tension dynes 25°C	R.I. at 25°C	Solubility in water wt. %
1. Sulfur dioxide	64	-93	-10	1.45 at-14°C	1.338	387.76 at17°C	-	-	-	19 at0°C
2. Dimethyl formamide	73.1	-61	152.8	0.9489	2.09	575	0.83 at25°C	35.2	1.4629	fair
3. Dimethyl sulfoxide	78.3	18.49	188	1.101	2.05	-	19 at25°C	-	1.4770 at20°C	fair
4. Ethylene glycol	-	-14	197	1.116	2.41	450.0	19.0	53	1.43	fair
5. Diethylene glycol	106.11	-	245	1.118	2.09	627.0	30.2	48.5	1447 at 20°C	fair
6. N-formyl-morpholine	115	+20	244	1.1528	1.588 at25°C	435.0	8.13	-	1.4869 at20°C	fair

All these kindred groups offer their own properties to oil without any reservation. Paraffins are credited for high viscosity index, while aromatics for low viscosity index. Comparatively, aromatics are generally more viscous than paraffins. Paraffins in higher ranges are more branched and invariably increase the pour point of oil. So evidently starting fluidity, viscosity and maintenance of viscosity at different temperatures cannot be satisfied by any single species. Naphthenes being intermediate in properties, can naturally form a bridging gap of these extremities. A high viscosity index oil, thus can be produced from paraffinic-naphthenic base or paraffinic base crudes only. Wax is an undesirable constituent in any oil due to its high pour point, although its viscosity index is very high.

There are four established processes for improvement in quality of lubes as given below:

(a) Sulfuric acid treatment
(b) Clay treatment
(c) Solvent refining
(d) Hydrotreatment

Sulfuric Acid Treatment

Acid treatment for lighter fractions was already discussed. This method is now reluctantly adopted although its disappearance is not yet complete, as some refineries practice it today also (like Assam Oil Company etc.). The main disadvantage of this process is inherent loss of material; further there is no improvement in viscosity index. However it is good for stocks containing more inorganics. Sludge disposal, material loss and tedious procedure are all the repugnant reasons for its systematic disappearance.

Industrially, acid treatment is done with 93% of sulfuric acid at a temperature of 60°C. 2 Kgs to 50 Kgs of acid are required per barrel of stock treated, covering light to drastic treatments.Treatment is done in cylindrical lead lined tanks with conical bottoms. Air is used for agitation. Required temperature is ensured by steam coils placed in the agitators. After the reaction is over the sludge is carefully removed and the oil is subjected to severe washing with water till the P_H is in neutral region. Caustic neutralisation is inevitable for naphthenic stocks. Naphthenic acids are prone to form sulfonates and these sulfonates offer considerable resistance during sludge settling. In this treatment, improvement in colour is significant as asphaltenes, resins and unsaturates are gradually depleted in the treated product. This treatment is most convincing for speciality oils like transformer oils, medicinal and white oils, where the material loss is of no significance (some times the loss goes upto 50%). Acid treatment is followed by clay treatment to avoid any emulsification difficulties during caustic or water wash.

Clay Treatment

This treatment is listed as one of the oldest methods and even now-a-days also it is followed in a limited scale. Various mineral clays and synthetic adsorbents are the listed materials for this treatment. Asphalts and resins are adsorbed on these clays. Resins being the colour contributors to oil, removal of these reflects in improving colour of the oil (unsaturates are preferably adsorbed over saturates). Further, clays have the tendency to adsorb some sulfur compounds and metallic bodies. Material loss is very much because of wetting the whole quantity of clay and retention of some in pores.The material adsorbed is governed by Freundlich equation and this is useful only for decolorising operations and the equation is given as:

$$\log \frac{X}{M} = \log a + \frac{1}{n} \log c$$

where X = units of impurities adsorbed

M = quantity of adsorbent

c = concentration of impurities in equilibrium at surface

a & n = constants

Clay treating was once a technique for decolourising and stabilising cracked gasolines and also for desulfurising virgin gasolines and kerosenes. In the treatment of light fractions the clays acts as catalyst; for heavy oils it is an adsorbent purifier.

Gasolines are also clay treated to eliminate materials inclined to , give colour or form gums. The tendency of natural clays like fuller's earth or bauxite to polymerise unsaturates cannot be set aside during this treatment. For this reason, the clay treated gasolines may have to be further processed (distilled) to remove the resultant polymeric groups. The Gray, the Stretford and the Osterstrom processes are enlisted for such kind of treatment. Clay being catalyst in this case, the treatment is frequently conducted in fixed beds containing 40 to 60 mesh size particles. The charge may be in vapor or liquid state. Slurry type reactors are the new comers in this field and are condigned for cracked stocks.

Most of the clay treatment operations are conducively carried at a temperature of 125 to 250°C, desirably at a high pressure, almost in the vicinity of 20 atmospheres. These operating conditions are quite typified in Gray and Stretford operations. In other processes the pressure is still higher. In contrast, when desulfurisation of virgin gasolines is attempted, a temperature of 400°C is opted, and this helps in venting sulfides and mercaptans in the form of hydrogen sulfide. Clay treatment for cracked stocks, enriched with thiophenes is not sound as these are refractory. Due to fine deposition of coke on the clay, the activity of clay diminishes. Some refiners try to regenerate the clay by burning off the coke under controlled conditions, others discard. A ton of bauxite can usually handle 10,000 bbls of virgin gasoline, 1200 bbls of cracked gasoline or 5,000 bbls of kerosene. A comprehensive information regarding removal of sulfur compounds from naphtha cuts using different adsorbents and sulfuric acid treatment was presented by Kalichevsky and Kobe and is furnished in Table 11.2. Evidently sulfuric acid is superior in removing sulfur compounds especially like thiophenes.

In case of lube oils of naphthenic origin, clay treatment seems to be effective, and succeeds acid treatment. Acid treated stocks in such cases pose problems for caustic washing due to emulsification tendency. For materials having high surface area, such as Attapulgus, bauxite can adsorb acidic, resinous and asphaltic materials from heavy oils.

Table 11.2 Comparison of Adsorbents and Sulfuric Acid Adsorbent used about 13.6 Kgs. per Barrel of Stock Acid used 24.5 kgs per Barrel of Stock % Sulfur Compounds Removed.

	Silicagel	Fuller's earth	Al_2O_3	Sulfuric acid 93%	Sulfuric acid Fuming
Free sulfur	8	4	4	0	0
H_2S	12	12	12	12	12
1-amylmercaptan	69	3	17	24	100
Dimethyl sulfate	100	100	25	100	100
Methyl-p-toluene solufonate	80	67	0	77	100
CS_2	0	0	0	0	0
n-butyl sulfide	57	3	0	93	100
n-propyl sulfide	37	11	5	58	100
Thiophene	11	11	0	89	100
Diphenyl sulfoxide	100	100	0	90	100
n-butyl sulfone	100	100	12	100	100

Clay treatment is conducted in two ways, namely contact filtration and percolation technique. After treatment the clays are regenerated by burning (controlled oxidation) carbon deposits; although it is not possible to completely remove these deposits without suffering the efficiency of adsorbent. Properties of different adsorbents are presented in Table 11.4.

Residues upto 6% are left behind even at temperatures (500-600°C) of regeneration. A close look at the percolation data given in Table 11.3 by Kalichevskey and Kobe reveals, that by increasing the ratio of oil to fuller's earth (adsorbent), the sulfur compounds increase in treated oils after an initial depletion; hence a proper oil to adsorbent ratio has to be found out and utilised.

Table 11.3 Percolation Data.

	API	Sulfur %	C. Residue wt. %	Viscosity SUS (at10°C)
Unfiltered stock	41.6	0.134	2.25	156
4.5 Kgs	48.3	0.02	0.027	87
34 "	43.2	0.08	0.546	125
68 "	41.9	0.13	1.49	140
225 "	41.8	0.13	1.61	140

A survey of different adsorbents was made available by Felix Heinemann and Henz Heinemann and is presented by Table 11.4.

Continuous contact filtration is shown in Fig. 11.2. It is based on the principle, that finely divided clay (-100 mesh size) is thoroughly mixed with the stock and allowed to stay in a tower to complete the reaction (adsorption). Then the slurry is filtered in suitable filter. Heavy oils are viscous and try to settle, this will bring unlimited snags by choking the lines and filtration equipment. Suitable measures, like addition of diluent or elevation in temperature of operation are necessary. Addition of sulfuric acid is desirable to keep the activity of clay.

In contact filtration or percolation the size of the adsorbent plays a significant role. Adsorption is favoured by smaller sizes, on the contrary filtration

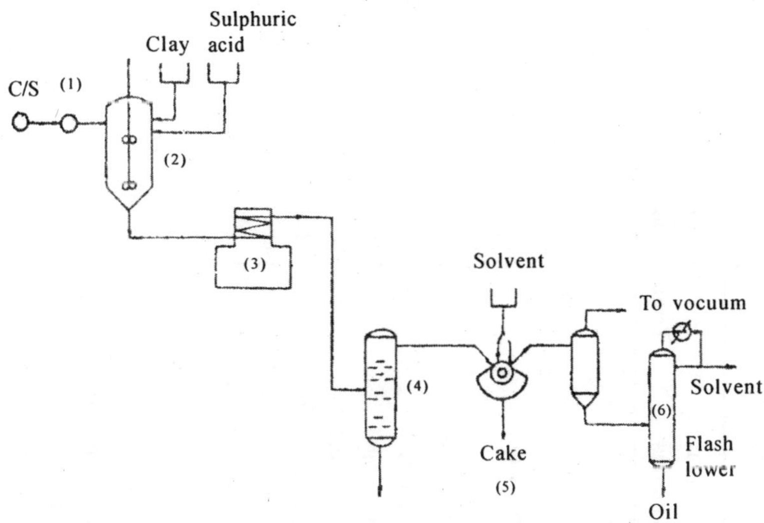

Fig. 11.2 Contact Treatment.

Table 11.4 Adsorbents and Properties.

Activated alumina	Activation Temp. (appox)°C	Bulk density	% voids	Surface area M^2/gm	Pore dia A	Heat of wetting kJ/gm
Grade F-1	194			200		58.980
		0.88	44		72	
H-151	194			300-350		
Bauxite	233	1.33	44	27	76	79.477
	200	0.94	42	151	43	87.843
Silica gel	194	0.82	41	602	10	121.725
Synthetic						
Silica gel	194	0.82	41	374	15	
Fluid catalyst						
Pelleted Cat. A	194	0.64	34	372	33	
Cat. B	194	1.00	36	280	16	
Head catalyst	194	0.79	30	420	22	
Fuller's earth	194	0.56	44	126	95	99.137
Attapulgite	600	0.56	42	119	109	
Bentonite	372	0.68	41	236	43	
Diatomaceous						
earth	194	0.32	49	4	5500	
Activated carbon		0.42	44	1397	112	39.738

may not be easy with small sizes. The process begins with heating the charge stock by exchanging with out-going hot oil in exchanger (1). Oil and clay are now mixed in required proportion, and thoroughly agitated in mixer (2). The slurry is then routed through a convection of a heater (3) to reach a temperature of 200 to 225°C.The hot slurry is pumped into a contact tower (4). Usually an empty tower, fitted with steaming arrangement will suffice.The residence time in the tower is approximately one hour, and by that time the decolonisation operation comes to end. The slurry is now transported to filtration equipment (5). Filtration is sometimes difficult with highly viscous stocks, hence calls for fresh additions of diluent. Neutral high cylinder stocks, oils for reclamation are processed in this way. Filtrate containing diluent is distilled or flashed in a stripper (6); diluent is collected as top product which is cooled and kept ready for recycle. Treated oil from the stripper is also cooled and stored.

Though, spent clay recovery is disliked in most of the cases, it can be practised. Firstly, the cake is extracted with diluent to remove the adhering oil. Mixture of this oil and diluent is flashed to recover the diluent.The extracted cake may be regenerated by burning the carbon in a suitable kiln.

Percolation Technique

The beauty of commercial percolation technique is its simplicity; it consists of only one step i.e. the oil is allowed to flow through a bed of clay. Treatment of viscous oils is also possible by diluting with naphthas and then percolating. The treated product can be used directly without other operations.

The controlled oxidation of carbonaceous material on clay is not a simple one as sometimes the temperature goes off uncontrollably, spoiling the very nature of adsorbent. However, the difficulty has been overcome by using Thermofor Kilns.

Thermofor Kilns are the best available Kilns for activating these spent clays. Here the spent clays do not directly come in contact with flame, but are heated by means of molten salts under circulation in tubes at 500 to 600°C. The spent catalyst from the top of the Kiln travels downward through baffles. In this process, the clay comes in contact with hot tubes. This ensures burning of coke particles without fusing surface pores. With the introduction of this type of kiln, clay treatment has regained its lost importance and continued to be used in industry on a moderate scale.

Solvent Treatment

Solvent treatment, in refinery operations enjoys a unique position due to its multifunctional designs. Viscosity index improvement, deasphalting and dewaxing etc. are some of the major applications. A number of solvents for each of such operations are in service and more are being introduced. Each of these operations are discussed below.

Viscosity Index Improvement

A strong temptation to produce high viscosity index lubes has led to a prolific growth of solvent extraction. Solvents widely used for this affair are furfural, phenol, mixtures of cresols and propane. May other solvents like aniline, sulfur dioxide are enlisted; but without much use. A solvent credited with many irrevocable properties also is not free from controversies, as it cannot be hundred per cent foolproof. General characteristics responsive towards good extraction tendencies for any solvent are

(a) High electronegativity of the hetero atom.

(b) High dipole moment.

(c) Presence of atoms of O, N, S with activity to form hydrogen bonds.

(d) Increased selectivity by substitution in *ß* (5-ring) or *m* (6-ring) positions.

(e) Free rotatability of the molecule, no screening by further substituents.

(f) Accumulation of selectively acting groups.

Invariably, some of the functional groups are sacrificed and the final selection of a solvent is based on other factors as indicated below:

1. Solubility relationship
2. Adoptability to various feeds
3. Ease of recovery
4. High density (high molecular weight)
5. Less corrosiveness and good stability in presence of moisture
6. Low viscosity, less cost, less toxicity
7. Low interfacial tension
8. Low freezing point and less latent heat.

Even though high selectivity and solvency power govern extraction process, sometimes highly selective solvents are disregarded in favour of other solvents having less assuming properties. As an example, even though DMF, DMSO are good solvents for extraction of aromatics but are not considered favourably, because of accruing difficulties in recovery.

Phenol and furfural are very competitive solvents in field. Both these solvents accomplish the task satisfactorily; a survey on the performance of these two solvents is presented below:

1. Furfural extraction may require a higher temperature of extraction and more number of stages.
2. Yield of raffinate is more with phenol.
3. Phenol treated lubes have better oxidation stability.

4. VI. improvement may be same in both cases, however solvent dosage may be slightly more for furfural on comparative basis. •
5. Phenol is more adoptable to different stocks and is unavoidable when naphthenic acids are more.
6. The selectivity of phenol increases with water (upto 10%). This is deemed to be a great advantage over furfural.
7. Furfural is unstable, hence requires nitrogen seal, during storage and recovery.
8. Losses can be negligible with phenol.
9. Residual solvent in treated stocks is not harmful; provided the solvent is phenol.

After extraction, the pour point of the stock increases, sometimes as high as 12-15°C. Despite this, refineries, without any doubt keep the extraction units before dewaxing units, and the result is, extraction units are destined to carry more loads. The following dewaxing operation naturally tailors the lubes to required pour point. Even with many of the above points in favour of phenol, furfural is able to sustain its position (in fact trying to replace) in view of pollution and toxic nature of phenol. Properties of solvents used for lube treatment are shown in Table 11.5.

Phenol Extraction of Lubes

Plate or packed bed extractors are generally employed in phenol extraction. Phenol extraction cannot be carried out at a temperature less than 50°C, because of the high melting point of phenol (40°C). Addition of water upto 10% is approved in all operations, although anhydrous phenol can do the extraction. Common operating temperatures range from 60 to 100°C. In practice a thermal gradient of 10 to 20°C from top to bottom is imposed on the column; this enhances the internal turbulence due to mixing of hot solvent and relatively cold feed. Solvent to feed ratio of 1.5 to 2.5 for processing paraffinic and naphthenic stocks is conducive. An increase of V.I. by 25 to 50 Units is confirmed. Some authors had utilised the viscosity gravity constant as parameter instead of viscosity index.

Raffinate yields vary from 50 to 90% depending upon the solvent to feed ratio. Higher solvent ratios give better quality of raffinate but with less yields. Some of the operating data on phenol extraction is presented in Fig. 11.3, *a, b* and *c*. Phenol treated oils possess good oxidation stability with less sludge forming and carbon depositing tendencies. Number of stages required for phenol treatment is less than four with most units operating at three. In India, Barauni Refinery and Bharat Refinery (Bombay) are practicing this process. Description of the Process: (Fig. 11.3a).

Solvent to feed ratio is one of the closely guarded parameters in extraction operation and for phenol extraction it lies in the range of 1.5 to 2.5 in going

Table 11.5 Solvents & Properties (Lube Treatment).

	B.P. °C	M.R °C	Sp. gravity at20°C	Sp. heat Joules/gm°K	Latent heat J/gm	Solubility °C in water at 38°C
1. Furfural	161.6	-36.6	1.162	1.757	419.137	9.0
2. Phenol	182	41.5	1.07	2.342	445.480	15
3. Sulfur dioxide	-10	-74	1.45	1.338	387.764 at—17°C	19 at°C
4. Chlorex	177.8	-51.8	1.22	1.548	260.183	1.02
5. DuoSol	180-205	—	1.045	2.217	418.3	3.1
6. Propane	-42	-190	0.51	2.509 (liquid) 1.966 (vapour) 1.422	422.483	—
7. Nitrobenzene	211	5.4	1.207		296.575	0.1at20°C
8. Aniline	184.4	-6.2	1.027		433.777	

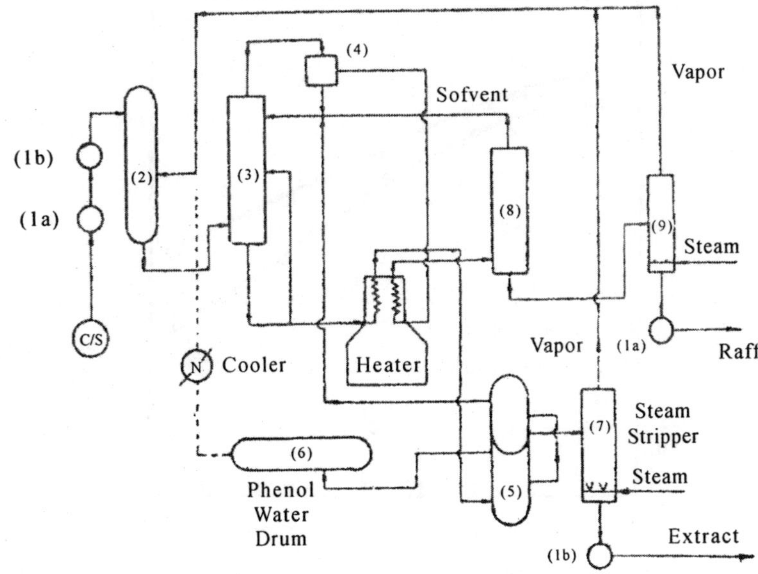

Fig. 11.3a Phenol Extraction.

from paraffinic to naphthenic oils. In an extraction process number of stages play a vital role in determining the size of extractor, in phenol extraction the stages are about 4, and in general 3 stages are satisfactory. Solvent power and selectivity of phenol at lower temperatures matches with chlorex and at high temperature it is near to furfural. Hence the dual nature of the solvent at all temperatures is quite convincing.

Charge stock heated to 80-100°C by exchanging heat with raffinate and extract in exchangers (1 a and 1 *b)* is first allowed to absorb the phenol vapors in absorber (2); these vapors are delivered from the strippers. The stock then goes to extraction unit (3).This consists of a counter current extractor (packed bed or sieve plate column, or centrifugal extractors) where a continuous down flow of solvent takes place from top of the tower. Feed being lighter is admitted at the bottom of the tower. Extract and raffinate are separated as distinct layers Raffinate from the top is led into a separator (4) to settle solvent drops, if any.The collected solvent is mingled with the solvent stream that goes into extractor. Bottom product is extract, and always a part of this is circulated back to extractor as a reflux and the rest is processed for recovering solvent.

Raffinate phase contains less solvent; hence it is easily stripped off in fractionator (8) under vacuum. The stripped raffinate is again blown with steam to separate the remaining solvent from oil phase (9). If amount of solvent is small then it may be directly steam stripped.

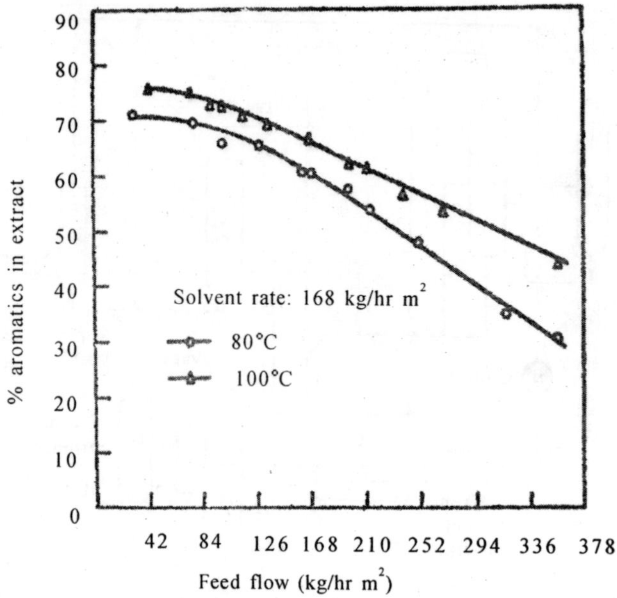

Fig. 11.3b Effect of Feed Rate and Temp. Operating Data on Phenol Extraction.

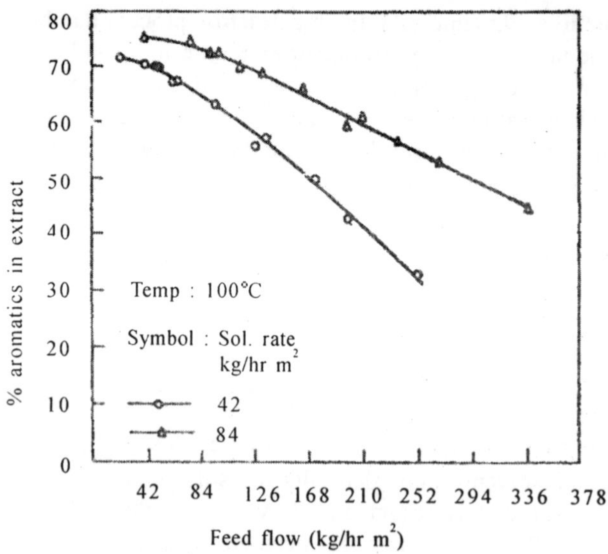

Fig. 11.3c Operating Data on Phenol Extraction (Effect of Feed and Solvent Rate).

On the contrary, difficulty may be experienced while separating solvent from extract. It is done usually in two stages i.e. carry the distillation under pressure (in lower section) and under pressure and vacuum.

Fractionator (5) is fitted with such kind of arrangement to vacuum (upper section). The recovered solvent is fed back to extractor. Steam stripping of extract is done in a separate unit (7).

The steam blown vapors from extract and raffinate are absorbed by the fresh feed and extraction continues as shown in Fig. 11.3a. It is general practice to introduce one liquid in continuous phase, and other in dispersed phase. Solvent being in large quantities forms continuous phase. Some of the operating data on phenol extraction is presented in Figs. 11.3b, *c*.

Furfural Extraction

Naphthenic stock treatment of may not yield convincing results with this solvent, yet modern refineries are decisively inclined to use this solvent due to enraptured services rendered by rotating disc contactor. In India, Haldia, Cochin, Madras refineries are using this process and planned refinery (Mathura) is also to follow the predecessors. A temperature range of 75 to 125°C under a gradient of 20 to 30°C makes the operation a success. Demands of furfural are slightly more, and number of stages in furfural extraction are also more in contrast with phenol for the same elevation of VI. Furfural extraction is practised not only for lubes but also for gas oils, catalytic cycle oils and for special applications like butadiene extraction and removal of low cetane index components from diesels.

In raffinates of furfural treated stocks, very much less quality of solvent is present, and hence vacuum distillation unit may be skipped and opt for direct steam stripping operation.

Furfural has tendency to react with atmospheric oxygen gradually resulting in polymers of furfural; as a consequence to this change, the solvent power is lost. To arrest such unwanted contacts, a nitrogen or an inert gas seal over the extractor and storage tanks is necessary, as also feed stock should be necessarily deaerated before extraction. Fig. 11.4 describes furfural extraction.

Charge stock is heated by passing through heat exchangers HE and HE_2 through which raffinate phase and finished extract pass before reaching storage tanks.This may raise the temperature of feed to 70 to 80°C. Feed then enters the extractor RDC(1) at two or three points and solvent is admitted into the upper portion. Raffinate phase being lighter leaves from the top of the contactor. It is heated in a heater (H_1) and flashed in evaporator (2) working at a low pressure.

This ensures the removal of solvent contaminated with water vapor if any, the heavy stream goes into the bottom portion of the evaporator. Steam stripping

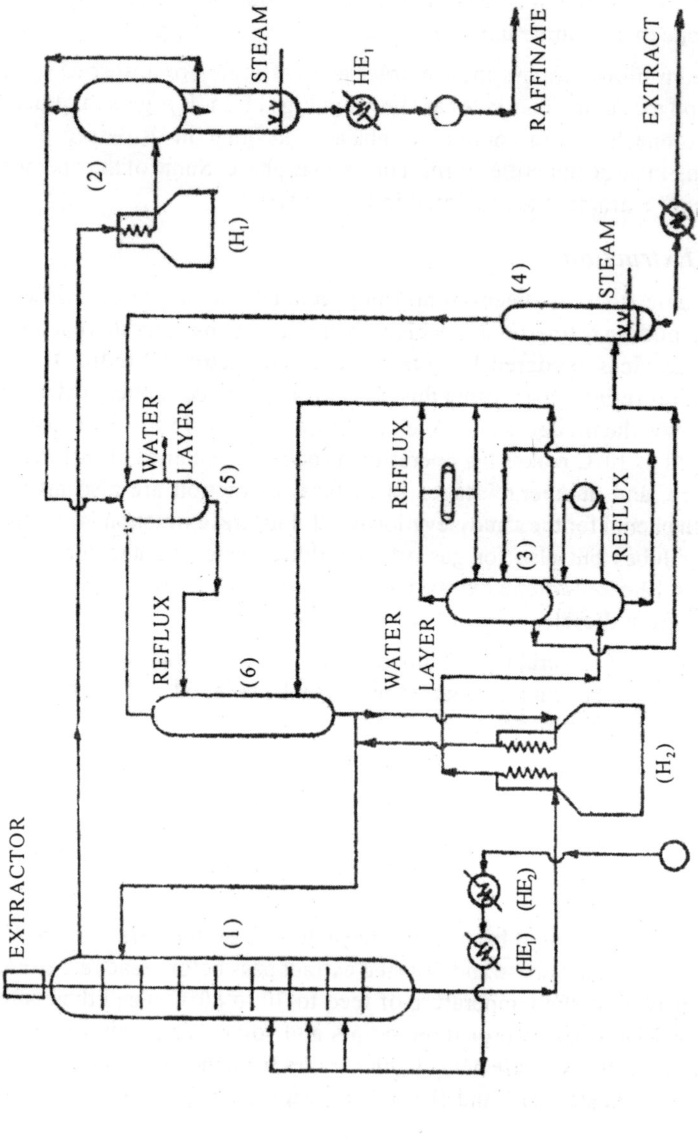

Fig. 11.4 Furfural Extraction.

in the evaporator facilitates the removal of last traces of solvent as solvent vapor-steam mixture. The mixture is cooled in a settler drum (5).

From the bottom of the evaporator, concentrated raffinate (free of solvent) is obtained as the finished product and sent for storage through heat exchanger (HE_1). Relatively solvent stripping from extract water mixture is tedious but has to be done.

Extract from the bottom of the column is heated in a heater (H_2) and then admitted into high pressure zone of a flash tower (3). Solvent with accompanying water is flashed here and later sent for rectification into furfural column (6). Heavier portion of extract, is flashed in the low pressure zone of flash tower to remove the solvent. An efficient reflux in the tower aids flawless separation. Rich extract is now transferred to steam stripper (4), to remove the last traces of solvent.

Extract is obtained as a finished product from the bottom. Vapors from the strippers (of extract and raffinate) are condensed in solvent drum to separate furfural and water layers. Furfural water mixture forms azeotrope (b.p. 97.7°) in which 34% of furfural is present by weight. After cooling to room temperature, the furfural rich layer contains 96% furfural, whereas water layer contains 8% only. Furfural rich layer is admitted as a reflux into furfural column (6).

Duo-sol (Selecto)

Hitherto only single solvent extraction has been dealt with. Duo-sol, as its name indicates two solvents are simultaneously employed, as is the case with unisol extraction for selective removal of groups. Solvents are used in this process are propane and selecto or cresylic acids (+ phenols), propane, extensively dissolves paraffinic groups, while the other solvents are good for naphthenic groups. Both the solvents are fed simultaneously to the extractor at both the ends, while the feed enters at an intermediate point. Extract and raffinate are permitted to leave from either ends. The extractor in this case differs from the conventional types, being horizontal with separate mixing and settling zones. These different zones cause a perfect counter current extraction. In one end, the outgoing cresylic phase is stripped off paraffinic material by incoming propane, and exactly the opposite thing happens at the other end.

Selecto (mixture of phenol 35% and cresol 65%) requirements are 200% to 400% with equal amount of propane, though naphthenic oils require more propane and paraffinic oils require more cresols.

Figure 11.5 illustrates the operation. Extractor (1) is charged with phenols (cresols) at one end, while liquid propane is fed at the other end. Propane being lighter, leaves from the top, while heavy naphthenic layer leaves from the bottom. Propane from naphthenic layer is first freed by evaporating in an evaporator (2). Propane from this evaporator, joins the propane vapors of raffinate evaporator (5) to begin the cycle.

Naphthenic layer is heated and sent to selecto evaporator (3), where steam stripped vapors of selecto from extract steam stripper (4) circulates as a reflux. From the bottom of the steam stripper, extract layer finally leaves to storage. Selecto vapors from selecto evaporators [both raffinate (6) and extract (3)] mix and enter the distillation unit (8), where selecto is obtained. From the steam stripper (7) finished raffinate is obtained. It is seen from this operation that both the phases have to be systematically separated from the solvents. Propane is separated from the phases by evaporation at high pressure while selecto is recovered at ordinary pressures. In general practice raffinate layer requires 3 stages,

Table 11.6 Duo-sol Extraction — Effects of Paraffinic and Naphthenic Stocks.

	Stock 1 (naphthenic)	Stock 2 (paraffinic)
API gravity	15.2	26.2
Viscosity SSU (99°C)	76.0	47.4
VGC	0.876	0.839
Raffinate yield %	44	73
Dewaxed raffinate API	26.5	29.9
Dewaxed raffinate viscosity (SSUat99°C)	143	48.0
Carbon residue	0.4	0.002
Dewaxed raffinateVI.	95	95

while extract phase requires 5 stages during contact. Main advantage of this process is, its ability for removal of asphalt. The operation is supposed to be in the regions of above melting point of phenol and below vaporisation temperature of propane at that pressure.

Results of extraction work carried out by Martyn Noel are presented in Table 11.6.

About Extraction

Extraction is a physical operation and thrives on good contact between feed and solvent; and separation of the solvent from resulting phases. All extraction operations are governed by distribution law which states that the ratio of concentrations of a compound distributed into two phases at equilibrium is a constant.

i.e. $\frac{C_1}{C_2} = K$; where C_1 and C_2 are the concentrations of solute in phases 1 & 2 respectively

K = distribution coefficient.

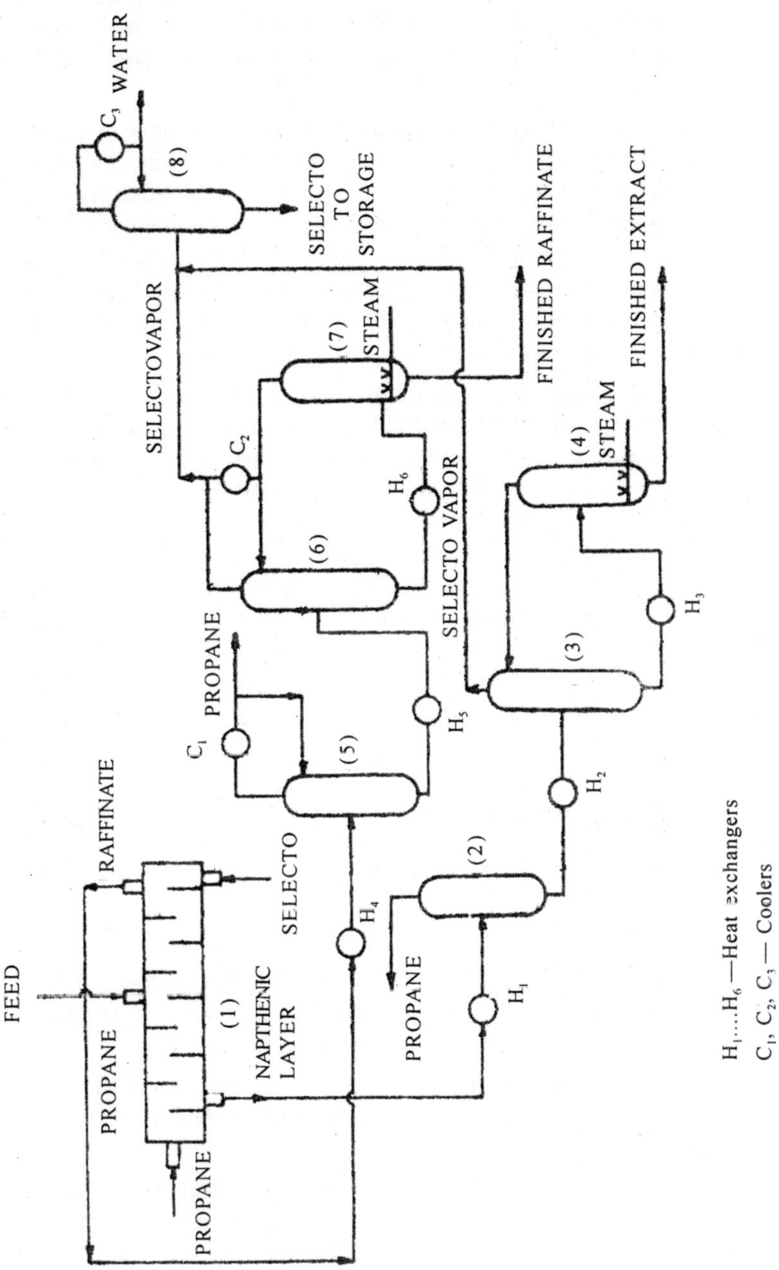

Fig. 11.5 Duosol Extraction Process.

Selectivity term is more often used in extraction work, it is expected that selectivity away from unity will lead to better extraction with less difficulty. Solvent power is the capacity of a solvent to dissolve a substance at a given temperature. A good solvent should possess high solvent power and good selectivity.

Conventional procedure of representing ternary system is done in triangular plots. Equilateral triangles serve the purpose most, as the apex to opposite side perpendicular distance remains same. Each apex is assigned with 100% purity of a component. The concentration at any point inside the triangle can be found by drawing perpendiculars to opposite sides from that point. Percentage concentration can be found by measuring the height. Binodal curve demarks the miscible region with immiscible; thus acts as a boundary of the heterogenous area and bears the tie line points too.

With higher heterogeneous region better extraction is possible, due to the flexibility in handling feeds of quite variable concentrations. As the temperature of extraction increases, the area shrinks impairing extraction very much. Though higher temperature increases solubility and selectivity the operational region shrinks very much, hence the flexibility choosing very high concentrations of feed diminishes. A method to increase such area is by adding and antisolvent (some times water) which can open the closed hionodal curve to give liberal access to extraction. For example in DMSO, Benzene, Heptane system (Fig. 11.1 a and *b,* heptane is in fact a better solvent for removing benzene from DMSO, but DMSO is used to remove benzene from heptane-benzene mixtures, because the selectivity is away from unity.

Tie Lines

The equilibrium compositions of extract and raffinate lie on binodal curve; line that joins these two points is known as tie line. The slopes of the tie lines vary even for the same system and distinction disappears between extract and raffinate at one point, which is known as plait point.

Slope of a tie line furnishes valuable information regarding the capacity of solvent; if the slope of the tie line is away from the solvent apex, then, the solvent is considered to be very good, otherwise not. In most of the cases the solvent may not be satisfying the needs theoretically.

Tie line concentration can be plotted on *x-y* diagram, as in the case of McCabe Thiele equilibrium diagrams which simplifies the evaluation of number of stages involved in operations.

Minimum solvent required in the operation can be obtained by extending the tie lines, the larger the distance between meeting point of highest tie line and lowest tie line from solvent apex, the higher the solvent required.

When extraction is conducted in conventional packed bed extractors the column diameter and packing size are important. Packing size to column size should be as large as possible (Minimum 8) to avoid channelling. The minimum size of packing required for a system is given by critical packing size (d_{FC}) defined as

Critical packing size {d_{FC}) = 2.42 (γ/Ap)^{05}

where γ : Surface tension of the system at boundary

$\Delta\rho$: difference in densities of phases.

Problem 4.1

In a phenol extraction operation conducted over a packed bed at 80°C the following data is obtained. Judge the necessary size of packing and column diameter.

Data :	Surface tension of	
	Phenol at 80°C	= 37.3 dynes/cm
	Lube oil at 80°C	=26.8 "
	Extract	=35.88 "
	Raffinate	=29.14 "
Density of Phenol at 80°C		= 0.9692 gms/cc
	Lube oil at 80°C	=0.8161 "
	Extract	=0.8873 "
	Raffinate	=0.8043 "

d_{FC} determined on the basis of properties of solvent and Lube oil.

$$d_{FC} = 2.42\left(\frac{37.3 - 26.8}{(0.9692 - 0.8161)\,980}\right)^{0.5} = 0.6402$$

On the basis of Extract and raffinate

$$= 2.42\left(\frac{35.88\text{-}29.14}{0.8873\text{-}0.8043 \times 980}\right)^{0.5} = 0.6966$$

The higher size of packing is chosen. To avoid channelling a minimum diameter of column required is eight times critical packing size.

Problem 4.2

Phenol extraction operation conducted at 100°C to extract aromatics from pressable waxy distillate; given the following data, find out the number of stages used in extractor:

Feed gms/min	160
Solvent gms/min	100

Extract gms/min		110
Solvent free extract	—	40.28 gms/min
Aromatics (As) in feed	—	21%
Aromatics (As) in extract	—	21.85%

Equilibrium data:

As in extract Solvent free extract	As in raffinate Solvent free raffinate
40.00	12.14
63.69	27.08
50.90	14.79
44.12	14.08
10.05	3.8

Solution: Total aromatics in feed: $\frac{160 \times 21}{100} = 33.6$

Aromatics in raffinate = 33.6-21.85=11.75

$$(E_1) = \frac{AS}{SFE} = \frac{21.85}{40.28} = 0.5426 \times 10^2$$

(% As in solvent free extract)

$$(E_1) = \frac{AS}{SFR} = \frac{11.75}{120} = 0.098 \times 10^2$$

(% As in solvent free extract)

Solvent free raffinate (SFR) = Feed-solvent free extract.

Plot the equilibrium (x- y) diagram as shown in Fig. 11.6. In

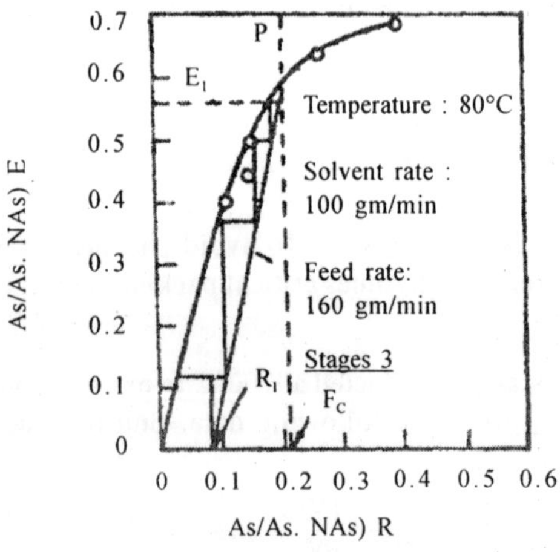

Fig. 11.6 Determination of Number of Stages in Extraction.

phenol extraction the feed is introduced at the bottom of the column, so the extract and feed are in contact (equilibrium) with each other i.e. the feed concentration (F_c = 0.21) and extract concentration are in equilibrium. So F_c and E_1 shall be fixing the point P. R, lies on x axis, as initial concentration of aromatics in solvent is zero. These two points are joined by a straight line, which forms the operating line. Steps are drawn from top to bottom, joining the operating line and equilibrium line.

Another method is by fixing raffinate composition and drawing a straight line with slope equal to feed to solvent ratio until it touches the concentration of extract.

12

The Formulation of Automotive Lubricant

Introduction

Producing a lubricant can be simple process. Refineries produce lubricating basestocks of an appropriate viscosity. Additives companies produce chemical components and 'additive packages' which contain a specially developed blend of these components. Chemical companies product polymer which help to maintain the viscosity of the oil at elevated temperatures. Sometimes two or threes of the above are produced by the same company. The information on which basestocks, additives and polymer can be used together can be obtained from the additives companies who attempt to pay a co-ordination role in the lubricating and industry, supplying additives packages and recommending the basestocks and polymer required for the formulation. Contacting an additive company can be the first step in the formulation of a lubricant. Following, this the necessary contracts can be decided, arrangements made for the additives package, basestocks and decided, arrangement made for the additive package, basestock and polymer to be supplied,. Blended and packaged, a quality control system developed, and the result is a lubricant that can be sold and used, this produce would be generic lubricant suitable for some but not all applications. However, this is unlikely to be what the lubricant supplier, the distributor to the consumer, or the consumer actually wants.

Why there are so many type of lubricant

Originally a lubricant was simply the non volatile or vacuum distilled base stock that came out of the oil refineries. There were several viscosities that were used according to the season of the year. The unstablised lubricant had to be changed frequently and this was normally covered by lubricant changes between seasons a light oil was used in winter and a heavy oil used in summer. The same oil were suitable for virtually all applications. As automotive technology developed, speeds, loads and temperature increased and there were problems in different parts of different vehicles at different times. These problems could of course, be overcome by redesigning the vehicle hardware but that did not help the vehicles that were produced before the problems were identified. The most cost effective solution was to modify and strengthen the lubricant enabling it to be used for a specific application in both new and existing vehicles. In this way engine oil were developed which had better resistance to oxidation, better wear protection, better engine cleanliness which had improved ware protection axle oil were developed for highly loaded sliding contact in. This method of lubricant development has been referred to as the 'basketful of broken parts' methods because lubricant were only change when there was a hardware problem in the field. It is easy to criticise this method as being reactive rather than pro active and as no being in line with todays view of quality; however with hundreds of vehicle manufacture each making a small number of vehicles it was not possible to foresee every condition to which a vehicles might be subjected and mistakes were bound to occur. In addition, reliability expectation were much lower than they are today.

The result of this has been the need for different lubricant for different application and even different lubricant for the vehicles of different manufacturers. This makes the development of new lubricants extremely expensive particularly if the new lubricant is radically different from current established technology. As well as developing the new lubricant it is necessary to prove its performance through a wide range of hardware test as specified by the hardware manufacturer, by the industry bodies and by the end user. Field trial demonstrations may also be required.

Before any formulation work is begun it is necessary to carry out a detailed commercial review of the performance that is or is not required. Several commercial options are likely to be generated. The technical options on feasibilities of producing such lubricant can be fed back into the commercial options and through an iterative process it should be possible to identify a performance profile for the oil that has a chance of being achievable at certain development and formulation cost and within a certain timescale. This procedure is extremely complex as it continually generates new ideas but the time well spent in identifying the performance require of a new lubricant is time well spent. It is not uncommon for this phase to take as long and to use up as much human resource as the formulation programme itself.

Multifunctional lubricants

To a vehicle operator the ideal lubricant may well be one that can be used with confidence in all major application in all vehicles. Special lubricant have been developed for some applications, for example universal plant oils for the construction industry super tractor universal oil (STUOs or STOUSs) for agriculture use and heavy duty diesel engine oil with moderate transmission and clutch performance for off highway application. In each case the one oil can be used in almost every area of the vehicle and there is a simplified inventory with virtually no opportunity for misapplication (Misapplication can be a major concern where on site maintenance is carried out on complex equipment by personnel who have no qualification in vehicle maintenance) however the price paid for such multifuntionality is the compromise between different aspect of performance because such lubricant are unlikely to meet the latest requirements in all aspects of performance. Passenger car engine requirement are the fastest chaning and are the most likely to be compromised. However if a lubricant claims to be multifunctional or universal then it is likely to be applied in any vehicle. Consumer studies have shown that most motorists believe that all engine oil are suitable for all cars and they do not read their owner manuals or check to see if the oils is of the correct quality. In the above example there is a fairly closed environment which limits where the lubricant will actually be used, the plant contractor, farmer or engineer may use the oil in his Jaguar, Mercedes or Range Rove, for which it is not designed and there is good chance that the vehicle will be none the worst for it. It would, however, be irresponsible to introduce such as oil to the open market place as misapplication would be commonplace and field problems at a level of only 5-10% are totally unacceptable. The lubricant industry has a responsibility to protect the vehicle operator from anticipated misapplications and therefore must produce oil with a wide margin of safety in all possible areas of application. The lubricant industry does not only sell lubricant, in effect it sells protection, safety and insurance against equipment failure. This only rarely appears in the lubricant description but suitability for use is implicit in the acti of supplying the lubricant. Lubricant technology is complex and responsibility for its cannot be developed to the end uses as many of them would not have expertise to handle it.

Although there are constraints on how universal a lubricant can be it is clear that it must have a relevant degree of universality for its area of application. Heavy duty truck engine lubrication provides an interesting example for this. Historical factors have led to engines being designed differently in North America compared to Europe. Two stroke diesel engine built by Detroit Diesel and used particularly extensively in buses, have proven to be an attractive powerplant with a high power to weight ratio, low maintenance, and low initial cost. These engines prefer low ash oil since high ash oils can lead to exhaust port blocking in two stoke engines. The North American lubricant industry adopted the strategy of marketing universal oil for both four and two stroke engines and these were low in ash compared to their European equivalents. The designers of successive generation of North American four stroke engines used the lubricant available in the market for their development and therefore their engines are designed around low ash oils. In Europe there has been no such constraint and the ash level of the oil has been allowed to increase in order to provide certain benefits with the result that European engines are now designed around high ash oils. Trucks and engines are exported around the world in this international business and there are truck fleets that use both types of engine. In such a fleet there is a need to satisfy both types of engine and the oil must therefore be universal. In other fleets, however, one type of engine for example a high ash European oil may allow the operator to extend the engine oil drain interval in a European fleet, or a low ash North American lubricant may extend the engine life of North American fleet.

The art of developing and formulating a new lubricant lies in identifying and building in all the desired performance benefits for the end user while marking it tolerant to anticipated misapplication.

13

Industrial Lubricants

Introduction

General aspects of industrial lubricants

Industrial lubricants comprise a wide variety of products which, depending on their application, differ widely in their chemicals and physical properties. With respect to the properties, one can say that industrial lubricants involve all classes of lubricants applied in practice. They include gases (mostly air), various kinds of liquid product (mineral oil, animals and vegetable oil, synthetic oils, water based fluids, etc) grease (simple soap greases, complex soaps greases, greases with pigment, minerals, polymer and other materials) and solid lubricants. The latter comprise

(i) inorganic compounds, e.g. molybdenum disulphide, boron nitride, tungsten disulphide and many other chemicals and materials

(ii) solid organic, compounds and materials, e.g. phthalocyanine and tetrafluroethylene,

(iii) chemical conversion coatings, and

(iv) soft metals.

Furthermore, industrial lubricant make use of many additives which comprise practically all the known additives classes used in other type of lubricant and additionally, numerous additives that have been developed specifically for industrial lubricants, particularly for water based fluids. Thus the importance of additives in the formulation of industrial lubricant is difficult to overestimate.

High speed and lightly loaded plain bearings needs a low viscosity plain mineral oil. The viscosity of the oil is essential for ensuring hydrodynamic lubrication. Higher loading and lower speeds require higher viscosity oils. From the point of view of the chemistry of lubricants, these oils are the simplest, being composed of crude oil components. They mostly include isopraffinic, naphthenic, naphthenic aromatic and to some extent, aromatic hydrocarbons. All the rings structure are substituted by alkyl chains. The viscosities of these hydrocarbons depend on their molecular weights.

Apart from this simple lubrication of plan bearing, the lubrication of tribological elements being rubbed under mixed and / or boundary friction requires lubricants in the form of very complex mixtures of appropriate mineral base oils and a number of possible additives.

The selection of additives to formulate industrial lubricants involves consideration of the requirement of the equipment to be lubricated or the metal/ process type for a metal working operation. Although hundreds of product have been used as industrial lubricants, and some other lubricant (e.g. engine oil) may be applied in lubricating some industrial equipment, equipment and lubricant manufactures usually recommend lubricant for particular applications.

In terms of quantities, industrial lubricants represent the largest group (over *50%)* among the lubricants. Lubricating oils are the most important type of industrial lubricant.

Classification of industrial lubricants

Industrial lubricant includes a very large number of specialised products form all the lubricant classes. Therefore, with the exception of some lubricant groups, such as hydraulic fluids, it is rather difficult to classify them as clearly as say engine oil.

The majority of industrial oils for which viscosity is a significant criterion, for example fluid bearing lubricants, are classified according to ISO 3448 viscosity grades this classification consist of eighteen viscosity grade in the range 1.98 mm^2 to 1.650mm^2/s. Each grade is represent by the whole number of which is obtained by rounding off the mid point viscosity at 40°C, expressed in mm^2/s. this classification does not imply any quality evaluation.

So- called general machinery oils classified according to ISO viscosity grades encompass mineral oil products from light oil for spindle lubrication, to heavy black oils for lubrication of wire ropes. This category includes products that cover the full range of speeds and loads used in industrial machinery. Usually these products contain mineral oil raffinates of suitable thermochemical stability, providing long-lasting lubrication of the machinery, especially bearings. Sometimes these oils are included in a group of machine lubricants oils together with slideway oils, multipurpose oils, and lubricating oils precision instruments and watches.

Viscosity grades for industrial lubricants according to ISO standard 3448

ISO viscosity grade (ISO VG)	Kinematic viscosity a 40 °C, mm^2/s		
	Minimum viscosity	Maximum viscosity	Mid-Point viscosity
2	1.98	2.42	2.20
3	2.88	3.52	3.20
5	4.14	5.06	4.60
7	6.12	7.48	6.80

10	9.00	11.00	10.00
15	13.50	16.50	15.00
22	19.80	24.20	22.00
32	28.80	35.20	32.00
46	41.40	50.60	46.00
68	61.20	74.80	68.00
100	90.00	110.00	100.00
150	135.00	165.00	150.00
220	198.00	242.00	220.00
320	288.00	352.00	320.00
460	414.00	506.00	460.00
680	612.00	748.00	680.00
1000	900.00	1100.00	1000.00
1500	1350.00	1650.00	1500.00

Another category consists of metal working lubricant which, in many cases, are treated separately in conjunction with their tribology. These lubricants are not classified under the viscosity grade system since properties other than viscosity (e.g. cooling and lubricating properties) are much more important, and a viscosity grade is not required as part of the identifying mark.

A further classification approach might include the following categories; production engineering lubricant) e.g machine tool and metal working lubricant), lubricant for engineering components (refrigerator, heat transfer and transformer oils) and plant maintenance lubricants (compressor, hydraulic, turbine and gear lubricants).

To simplify the problem of industrial lubricant classification the names of the lubricants, gear lubricants, compressor lubricants, hydraulic lubricants, gear lubricants, metal working lubricants etc., are derived form their application. Such classification is consistent with other lubricant categories, i.e. lubricant for internal combustion engines, aviation lubricants, and marine lubricants.

14

Lubricating Greases

Introduction

A grease a solid or semi solid lubricant consisting of a gelling of thickening agent in a liquid lubricant. Other ingredient such as fillers and additives mat also be incorporated to form mineral lubricating oils with soaps as gelling agent but now synthetic lubricating fluids and non soap gelling agents are also finding increasing use.

Grease Vs oil

Oil lubrication is more versatile than grease lubricating however, there are number of applications, where grease lubrication offer advantages over oil lubrication. Such applications vary from light loaded ball bearing on small electric motors and fans to heavy duty plain and anti friction bearing on the largest of steel mill rolling equipment. Because of their many advantages over oil greases are now the first choice for the lubrication of ball and roller bearing in electric motors, household appliances, aircraft accessories, automotive wheel bearing, machine tools, railroad, apparatus etc. they are also used for the lubrication of small gear drives and for many slow speed sliding applications.

Advantage

The advantage of grease lubrication over oil lubricant are as follows:

1. Greases are handier lubricant than oils.
2. Greases lubricant gives better protection under extreme operating conditions such as extreme pressure, low speeds, shock load and bearing operating intermittently or reversing.
3. Grease lubrication provides more effective sealing against contaminants such as water and dirt.
4. Oil Lubrication requires complicated design of housing and bearing enclosures. Grease lubrication permits simplified design of housing and enclosures because grease clings to metal surface more easily and more firmly.
5. Grease reduce possible damage to the process or product from leakage. In oil lubrication there is danger of damage from oil spilling or leakage.

6. Grease lasts longer than oil and therefore, requires less frequent maintenance or replacement then oil lubricant.

Disadvantage

However, greases lubricant has many disadvantages also:

1. Grease is not suitable for high speed applications. In general it is not employed for speed factors above *2,00,00* although higher speed have been successfuly employed with specially designed ball bearing and selected greases.
2. Grease though more effective in sealing, cannot flush away contaminants such as dirt and dust accumulated in the system.
3. Grease is not good heat transfer or cooling agent compared to oil. Therefore, in heavily loaded or high heat duty applications where cooling effect is important grease is not suitable.
4. Grease cannot be circulated while in case oil lubrication centralized systems can be used.
5. Less labour is involved with oil than with grease when the lubricant is to be changed.

Thus grease lubrication is preferred over oil lubrication in high pressure, low speed of shock load applications; in dusty and dirty locations such as cement plant, coal mining, saw mill, mining and quarying etc, in inaccessible locations where the lubricant cannot be easily replaced frequently; for the lubrication of exposed bearings, gears wire ropes, chains etc, and on textile or food machinery to avoid dripping or splashing which may causes contamination or staining of the food or textile articlcs. It should, however, not be applied in high speed, low torque or high heat duty applications and in bearing with complication layouts.

The constituents of grease

Greases are mainly composcd of petroleum oils, or synthetic oil together with thickening agents additives and fillers. The important constituents of greases are discussed below.

Petroleum oils

Petroleum oil are used most of the greases. Essentially petroleum oil of same viscosity and other characteristics is employed in compounding a grease as would have been normally selected for oil lubrication itself. Petroleum oil of viscosity 200-500 SUS at 100F are used for moderate temperature general purpose grease.

Generally solvent refined oils are preferred for making greases for use in roller bearing or other critical applications. However, sodium and calcium based greases are difficult to make with these refined oil conventionally refined oil are used in making these greases. Since conventionally refined oil have poor oxidation resistance and are also not so responsive to antioxidant additions, sodium and calcium bases grease are used for general purpose non critical applications. Greases intended for high temperature serve in particular are made with solvent refined oils and generally have a lithium soap or clay base as thickener since these thickeners readily accept solvent refined oils.

Thickeners

Thickeners or gelling agents are compounds which thicken or solidify the liquid phase of the grease. Their main function is to help keep the grease close to bearing surfaces. Gelling agents can be divided in two broad classes (a) soap gelling agent (b) non soap gelling agents.

Soap gelling agents

Soap gelling agent are the most commonly used thickeners in greases. Common soap gelling agents are fatty acid soaps or sodium, calcium, lithium, barium and aluminum. Lead soap are incorporated in certain types of greases, generally as waterproofing or extreme pressure agent rather than as gelling agent. The fatty acid employed are usually oleic, palmitic, stearic and other carboxylic acids derived from, tallow, hydrogenated tallow, hydrogenated fish oil, hydrogenated sperm oil, hydrogenated cottonseed oil and less often wool grease and rosin. Fatty materials derived from animals origin are preferred to these derived from vegetable origin. Special properties are obtained by using more than one type of acid at the same time and forming complex soaps.

Non soaps gelling agents

Non soaps gelling agents are either inorganic or organic. Organopilic clays, carbon black and silica are the common inorganic gelling agents. Finely divided clay particles of the bentonite and hectorite types have come into common use after being given a surface coating with organic materials such as quaternary ammonium compounds. Carbon black is used as a thickener in some high temperature petroleum and synthetic greases. Also coming in broader use are organic powders and pigments such as aryl substituted areas, phthalocyanines, indanthrene, sodium octadecyl terphthalamate and ureides. These new gelling agents are specially helpful in making synthetic fluid base greases.

Synthetic fluids

All the synthetic fluids which have been used in the formulation of oil lubricant have also been used in the formulation of greases. Dibasis ester, polyalkylene glycols, silicones, fluroractons and polypheny ethers are the common synthetic fluids used in the formulation of greases. Generally petroleum oil base greases are satisfactory for most of the operating conditions found in practice and it is only when special properties are desired in the grease that synthetic fluids are used. Synthetic fluids are generally used when the grease is to be used at very high or very low temperature particularly in aircraft, military equipment and refrigeration machinery.

Additives

As in case of lubricating oils, chemical additives are also required in greases to improve oxidation resistance, rust protection in lubricating oil.

Oxidation inhibitors of amine, phenolic or silphur types are commonly used at about 0.1 -1.0% concentration while selenium compounds are used in the range of about 2.0-5.0% to impart high temperature stability. In many greases 0.01-0.05% of a metal deactivator, such asmercaptobenzothiazole is also added to avoid staining of copper and to minimize any catalytic effect of the copper *on* oxidation of grease.

Greases offer better protection against rusting of coated surfaces than the oils because of their better adherence to the surface. However corrosion and rust inhibitor are still often added to provide added resistance to water and salt spray corrosion. The additives are often added in the concentration range of *0-2-3.0%* or even upto *6.0%.* a dispersion of sodium nitrate has been especially effective in some multipurpose greases.

Extreme pressure additives are generally not required in greases but these are necessary in greases for use in steel rolling mill, in many gear applications and in conditions involving boundary lubrication. Lead soaps, and various sulphur chlorine and phosphorous EP additive are used for this purpose. Solid powders, such as graphite, molyblenum disulphide asbestors talc and zinc oxide are also added in greases for extreme conditions of boundary lubrication.

Structure modifiers such as glycerol propylene glycol, propylene, glycol, glycerolmono oleate, propanol and higher alcohol, fatty acid in soap oil system in the concentration range of 0-1.0%. glycerol often remain after the formation of metallic soap thicker when natural fats are employed as raw materials instead of fatty acids. When with some soaps produced from fatty acid, structure modifiers may be added for stabilizing the sop structure when used in combination with small amount of water. These modifiers change the solubility characteristics of the thickeners. Other additives such as foam inhibitors colour stabilizer and dyes may also be added to the grease.

Fillers

Fillers are added in some greases to impart special properties such as bulk, density, mechanical properties or extreme pressure properties. Among the various filler that are employed are mica soap stone, graphite, asbestos, molybdenum disulphide, zinc oxide lists the various additives, the proportions in which they are used and their applications. It is to be noted that greases containing fillers are not generally recommended for use in antifriction bearing.

Fillers used in lubricating greases

Filler	Proportion normally used %	Most common soap base	Purpose for which the grease is recommended
Graphite			
(a) Colloidal	0.01-1.0	Any	General application
(b) Flake	2-10	Calcium	do
(c) Powdered	2-10	Calcium	do
Lead powder	1-20	Aluminum	Chasis lubrication
	1 -20	Calcium	Thread lubrication
Red lead (lead oxide)	10-20	Calcium	Thread lubrication
Molybdenum disulphide	0.5-18	Any	General application
Zinc dust	10-40	Calcium	Thread lubrication
Lead powder	30.2-30.8	Aluminum	API high pressure thread lubricant
Graphite	17.7-18.3	do	do
Zinc dust	12.0-12.6	do	do
Copper flake	3.1-3.5	do	do

Filler are also used in plug and value lubricants in the proportion of 5 to 10 per cent with calcium, sodium or zinc soap thickness. Sodium or calcium based brick greases contain from 25 to 60 per cent of fillers.

Classification of greases

Lubricating greases can be classified on the base of the type of gelling agent of fluid component used and on the base of application. The modern tendency is to classify greases on the basis of use pattern rather than on composition. However, such a classification though useful would be quite complicated because of the many applications of greases. A simple classification based on composition is given on. The soap bases greases may be further divided into calcium soap grease, sodium soap grease, etc., depending upon the soap different alkali metal compound . Similarly non soap greases may also be divided according to different organic compounds and pigment used as gelling agents. All these grease will be described below in brief. Since synthetic grease are a class apart from petroleum greases they will be described below separately although there may be some overlap in the description.

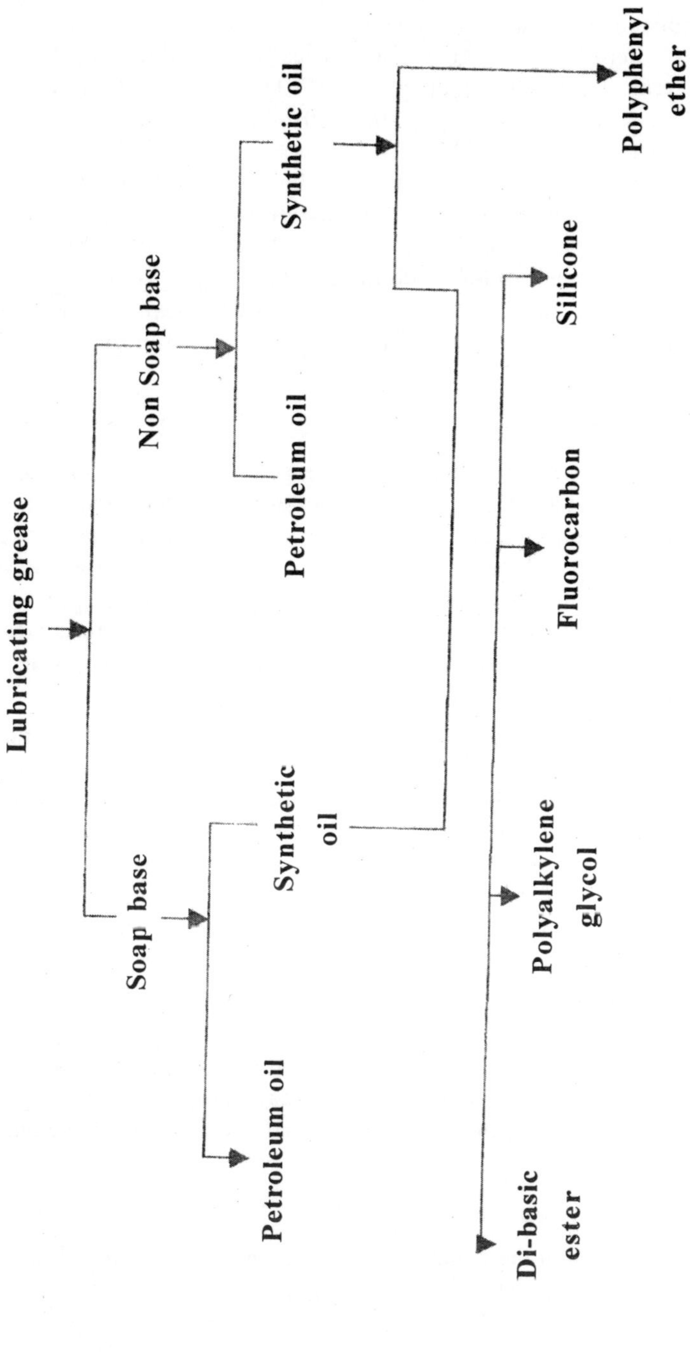
Lubricating grease
Soap base
Non Soap base
Petroleum oil
Synthetic oil
Petroleum oil
Synthetic oil
Di-basic ester
Polyalkylene glycol
Fluorocarbon
Silicone
Polyphenyl ether

Sodium soap greases

Petroleum oil greases thickened with sodium soaps are currently used extensively in rolling element bearing because of their suitability over a broad range of temperature from ~ *30C* to 120C . Greases of this types have short fibrous structure and are, therefore suitable only for very low speed applications. The nature of fibrous structure depends on the nature of fatty materials high unsaturation yielding very fibrous structure. To aid in obtaining a less fibrous structure a small percentage of calcium soap is usually added with sodium soap. This class of greases generally have excellent rust preventive properties but because of the solubility or emulsifiability of the soap in water the greases is into water resistant and may be washed away by water. Sodium soap greases have high as 200c. They are therefore useful for relatively high temperature service.

Calcium Soap Grease

These greases are also called cup greases. These grease have a smooth buttery texture and are water resistant. They are water stabilized , that is water is present in the soap crystals as water of cystallization. The optimum amount of water varies considerably with the type of formulation, fatty material and mineral oil, used, but is usually within the range of 0.4-1.0 per cent. At high temperature the water is gradually lost and the soap structure is weakened, consequently calcium soap grease are restricted to use at fairly low maximum temperature about *60°C.*

Calcium based greases stabilized with water turn liquid after exposure to high temperature (above *60°C* and may separate into oil and water phase. Only those greases which contain other stabilizers besides water will regain structure on cooling. Now a days the availability of other stabilizers or structure modifiers such as glycerol, glycol mono oleate, propylene glycol, wool greases etc. has made the presence of water in calcium greases less important. Calcium greases stabilized with these new stabilizers can be used at higher temperatures because these stabilizers are lost at much more higher temperature than water, special calcium greases such as calcium hydroxystearate greases can beused upto 120°C.

The use of calcium soap grease is limited to moderate speeds because of its somewhat poor mechanical stability. Oxidation stability of these greases is poor since oxidation inhibitors are rarely used, these are also deficient in rust prevention.

Lithium soap greases

Depending upon the composition lithium greases are smooth or slightly grainy in appearance. They have the highest drop point (about 90°C) of the conventional greases and the highest service temperature. They can be used from ~30°C to 150°C. they are water resistant, mechanically stable and can be made with a greater variety of oil, then other greases. Their versatile and wide operational scope, specially in high speed services, has led to wide their use as multipurpose grease top the displacement of earlier types of more specialized greases. Lithium soap greases used to be made from lithium stearate greases, made by saponification in situ from hydrogenated castor oil, predominate. Synthetic greases are generally based on lithium soaps.

Aluminum soap greases

These have an attractive, transparent, smooth and polished appearance. The drop point are low about °C the mechanical stability is poor and the grease tend to become rubbery at high temperature. They are almost invariably made from high viscosity oil and often incorporate polymer. These grease are water resistant, stringy and adhesive and find application as chassis and gear lubricant. They are not recommended for rolling bearings. They should not generally be used above *80°C*

Other greases

Barium soap greases are water resistant and their texture varies from fibrous to smooth. Barium soap greases are similar to lithium soap greases in mechanical stability and can be used upto 175°C. Lead base greases withstand extreme pressure and do not emulsify or dissolve in water these are generally used as thread lubricant. Zinc base greases are water repellent. They are usually employed for lubricating plungers of hydraulic elevators and piston rods of water pumps and as slushing compounds to prevent rusting of wire cables under water. Potassium, strontium, and magnesium base greases have also been produced for some specialized purpose. In fact greases can be produced from any of the heavy metal soaps.

Mixed soap grease

Mixture of a variety of soaps can be used to product mixed soap grease, the most common being a mixture of sodium and calcium soaps. The grease are generally prepared by sponifying the fatty materials with mixed alkalis derived from different metals. One of the soaps usually predominates and determines the general characteristics of the grease while the other modifies the structure in some way. This result for example, in change in texture and improved mechanical stability.

Silica Based Greases

Silica is an abrasive substance and it seems most unlikely components of lubricants yet it can be used as a gelling agent if the particles are of colloidal dimensions. Silica particles of upto 50 microns are non abrasive. It has been proved that silica greases cause not greater wear than conventional soaps greases.

Finely divided silica (50 micron macron Max) will disperse easily in a suitable liquid lubricant to *give* a grease but such a product may be very unstable owing to the hydroscopic nature of silica. Treatment with a water proofing surface nature of the silica. Treatment with a water proofing surface active agent e.g. butyl alcohol, is necessary unless silicones which are themselves highly water repellent from the liquid phase.

It is possble to make silica based grease merely by dispersion of the powder in the liquid, with addition of the water proofing compounds if required. Another process being with sodium silicate, which is acidified, washed and treated with an alkyl ethoxysiloxane, the ethoxy groups reacting with the silica to provide water proofing.

Silica based greases have good water resistance and can be used at high temperature upto 120°C. they have relatively poor mechanical stability unless special cares Is taken in formulation and manufacture. They have good resistance to both high temperature and oxidation if combined with synthetic fluids. However these greases are costly and commercially they are restricted to special applications. A water repellent grease for electrical apparatus, where the liquid phase is silicone, is one important application. Another is radiation resistant grease containing special aromatic petroleum oils for use in the inert gas atmosphere.

Clay based greases

Finely divided clay particles of the bentonite and hectorite types have come in common use. Montmonillonite clays, particularly bentonite, has been used for sometime in the petroleum industry as thickeners for drilling muds before they were investigated as gelling agents for greases. Clay based greases also require a water proofing coating as in case of silica base greases and are coated with organic materials such as quaternary ammonium compounds of fatty acid amides.

Montmonillonite clays are composed of primarily hydrated magnesium aluminum silicate with micaceous structure. Of those bentonite and hectorite are used commercially for greases making, the former generally as a proprietary pre water proofed powder under the trade mark "Bentone" or "baragel" and the latter is made by a patented shell process.

After the natural clay has been refined in an aqueous dispersion to remove impurities. It *is* water proofed and either dired to fine powder or processes immediately into a greases.

Clay thickened greases are readily manufactured by simple mixing without the high temperature cooking at carefully controlled temperature which is necessary with soap thickeners. The comparative simplicity of processing, economic formulation and valuable properties of these greases, have led to their rapid industrial exploitation and they probably account for the major part of non soap greases product in India as well as the world.

Clay based greases have been produced with high melting point, excellent water resistance and long time for multipurpose application in industrial and automotive equipment. In general, however, they seem still unable to match the lithium and sodium greases for high speed application in ball and roller bearings. In texture these are smooth and polished and polished and are normally transparent.

The organophillic clay greases are of specials interest for high temperature applications. These grease do not pass through transitions and so do not normally show a drop point by the standard test. They, however, show a drop point by the standard test. They however, tare sensitive to metal soap greases and care should be taken in practice to avoid such mixture. The traditional extreme pressure additives also exert a de gelling effect on clay greases and other EF additives such as metal sulphides are being explored for use in heavy duty application as in rolling mills. Anticorrosion additives are also incorporated to protect the bearings, the level of protection, however, is not normally as high as that obtainable with appropriately constituted metal soap greases.

Carbon Black greases

Though not common, greases made with carbon black may have advantages in certain situation e.g n high temperature environments where other gelling agent might produce objectionable deposit. Both petroleum and synthetic greases can be max with carbon black as gelling agent. Acetylene black is normally used for the purpose. Carbon black based greases can be used upto 200°C

Phthalocyanines Based greases

Copper phthalocyanines were the first organic pigments to have their grease making properties studied. These greases are of interest because of the high resistance of the phthalocynanine pigment to oxidation and heat. This can be seen from the fact that these pigment subline in vacuum at *5OO°C* without decomposition. It has been found that only-such phthalocyanines as did not grow large crystals in liquid are suitable for greases making. Silicone fluids are better suited to these thickeners because silicones are less critical in producing crystal growth.

The disadvantages of these thickeners is that the amount of thickener required for a given consistency is about two or three, time as much as in lithium or clay based greases. This result *in* higher cost of these greases. However, their properties are of great interest for service at very high temperature. It has been found by experiments that, but for the limitations imposed by the liquid phase, the phthalocyanine greases could be used above *300°C.*

As the greases tend to stiffen with rise in temperature softer greases than are normally necessary for critical application may be acceptable. This would result in saving of gelling agent thus reducing the cost of the greases.

Indanthrene bases greases

Indanthrene blue greases are used at extreme temperature for rolling bearing and other high temperature applications. In addition to their high temperature properties, they grease also have good water resistance and good mechanical stability. A greases made with indanthrene blue RS and a silicone fluid is reported to given more then twice the life normally obtained from greases based on other gelling agents. These greases also have good antioxidant properties because these greases absorb oxygen less readily. For example it was found that a grease based on diester fluid and 5% indanthrene blue absorbed the same amount of oxygen in about twice the time than the time taken by diester alone.

The amount of gelling agent required by these greases to obtain a given consistency is large and greases are very costly. These grease, therefore have limited commercial application, mostly in aircraft and military application.

Sodium octadecyl terephthalamate bases greases

Greases based on sodium octadecyl terephthalamate as gelling agent are commercially available. They are claimed to have very good high temperature properties, not softening sufficiently to allow a drop point determination by the manufacture for temperature upto and even above 150°C with petroleum oil as the liquid phase, and 200°C with silicones as the liquid phase. Synthetic esters and other synthetic lubricating oils can also be used with this gelling agent to make greases for services at abnormally low or high temperatures.

Unlike conventional sodium soap based greases, these greases are highly water resistant. Mechancial stability is good and they are not so sensitive as clay based greases to admixture with other gelling agents. The usually antioxidant and corrosion inhibitors may be incorporated in these greases where required. These grease have a good future if they can be made at competitive prices.

Sodium octadecyl terephthalamate may be made separately or more conveniently generated in the grease making process. In either case it is prepared by the reaction of sodium hydroxide on the methyl ester of N octaecyl terephthalam acid, which itself is synthesised from dimethyl terepthalmate an amines derived from hydrogenated tallow. The amount of gelling agent required for a given consistency is of the same order as in lithium greases.

Aryl substituted urea based greases

Aryl substituted urea (ASU) bases greases are claimed to offer good high temperature performance, particularly in association with silicone. In a standard test no drop point was obtained when the grease were heated upto 315°C and one ASU/ silicone grease was found to give *$00* d performance in bearing tests at a temperature of 232°C. good water resistance and mechanical stability are also claimed for these greases.

Unfortunately, in the manufacture o these greases two to three times as much gelling agent is required for a given consistency than in lithium or clay based greases. This makes the grease very costly though if silicones are used as liquid phase the amount of ASU required for thickening may be less.

The ASU can be dispersed in the oil as a pre made compound or generated in greases making process. Suitable ASU can be made by the reaction of amines and isocyanates.

Diamidodicarbonyl based greases

diamidodicarbonyl (DAC) based grease are closely related to ASU based greases and are made in a similar way by reaction of an amine with an isocynate but in such way that a diamidocarbonyl linkage is created. A low percentage of gelling agent for a given consistency is claimed compared with the typical ASU greases and even lithium soap grease. A drop point of only about 250°C is indicated in the literature and their high temperature performance in bearing is of a lower order than that claimed for some ASU grease described earlier . the DAC grease could be proceeded more cheaply as less gelling agent is required. So far however, they have little commercial impact.

Synthetic greases

Synthetic greases are rapidly gaining acceptance even though at present they share only about 1% of the total grease market. Diester greases are the most widely used of all the synthetic greases, about *-55* to 120. Polyester fluids are also finding increasing application because of their lower evaporation losses.

Silicone greases can be used over an even wider temperature range than the organic ester. The silicon fluids have very low evaporation losses even at very high temperature upto 150. These fluids are commonly thickened in commercial greases with lithium soap as are most of the other synthetics. Conventional silicone grease thickened with soap gelling agents can be used at temperature upto 170°C. silicone grease thickened with non soap gelling agent can be used at even higher temperature upto 230°C.

However, the lubricity of the high temperature silicone, grease is relatively poor for gear and other sliding devices. Therefore diesters have been blended with silicone oil in some wide temperature range greases for improved lubrication of sliding parts. The diester oil provides better solubility for the lithium soap during grease manufacture and some of the silicone diester greases offer low torque at temperatures well below ~75°C.

Folyalkylene glycols and flurocarbons greases are also being produced for specialized purpose. A variety of high temperature radiation resistant greases have been formulated with alkyl biphenyl and polyphenyl ether oil in combination with high melting non soap thickeners.

Phosphate esters, silicate esters and chlorinated compounds have also been used as the fluid in lubricating greases. The chapter on synthetic fluid should also be consulted for detailed information on synthetic fluids and the observation made there are also applicable in case of synthetic greases,

Classification according to use

Grease have also been classified in trade according to commercial uses. Some of the important commercial grades are cup greases fiber, and sponge greases (sodium base), ball and roller bearing greases, chasis greases and universal joint grease. Table 14.2 shows the different type of greases according to service, their desirable qualities and product normally used.

Structure of greases

Lubricating grease are essentially thickened petroleum or synthetic oils in which solid particles of gelling agents are finely dispersed. The dispersed particles from a collodial structure with the oil. Lubricating grease may exhibit a wide variety of structure depending on the nature of gelling agent and the size, shape and degree of dispersion of the solid particle

Classification according to Use

Designation	Desirable qualities	Product normally used
Axle greases	Cheap satisfactory for rough, slow moving machinery	Calcium rosin oil soap based
Cup grease	Water resistant, low torque	Calcium with low visco sity oil.
Ball or roller bearing greases	Long service life, stable.	Lithium, sodium, sodium calcium, Calcium complex Arylureas or polyureas
Chasis greases	Quite hard or stiff with a high m.p so that consumption is low	Most often sodium or sodium calcium
Chasis grease and form greases	Adhesive, resistant to washing effect of water, oil viscosity preferably 700 SUS at 50°C or above	Any thickener base except water soluble ones

Brick grease	Quite hard or stiff with a high m.p so that consumption is low.	Most often sodium or sodium calcium products
Graphite or molybdenum disulphide greases	Clings to metal well	Cup or chasis grease containing graphite or molybdenum disulphide.
EP grease and steel mill grease	Resist heavy pressure or shock load, water resistant	Calcium or lithium product plus EP additives
Pipe value lubricant and gasoline resistant grease	Resistant to solvent action of gasoline etc. high m.p in most cases	Special product which may be high in proportion of both soaps and filler. Different product for steam, solvent chemicals etc.
Steering gear greases	Resistant to wiping action of worm gears	Soft greases with EP additives or lead soaps included.
Tool joint greases	Project thread and permit case of uncoupling	Similar to pipe thread lubricant
Universal joint greases	Adhesive, high m.p	Sodium base product with high viscosity oils.
Water pump greases	MP above 100°C water resistant, stiff	Cup grease NLGI no.4 grade
Wheel bearing greases	High m.p. work stable	Complex calcium, lithium or sodium base NIGI no. 2 or 3 grade
Trace roller greases	Adhesive stringly, water resistant and soft enough to feed readily,	Aluminum, calcium, lithium base product with high viscosity oils.
Textiles greases	Low torque	Calcium or sodium base semifluid grease with low viscosity light coloured oils.

Soap gelling agent

In most soap based grease the gelling agent is dispersed in the grease in the form of continuous network of fibers or ribbons varying in size from 1 to

100 microns in length, with length to diameter ratio of 10-100. The gelling action of soap is due to the ability of the fibers to form tangle or interlacing structure in the interstices of which the oil is held wither by simple physical entrapment or by a combination of capillary force and contact forces (adsorption on the gel forming molecules). The relative important of each of these mechanism of gelling would depend on the type and degree of dispersion of the thickener, the type and solvency of the oil and the influence of any stabilizing agent and additives.

The body characteristics or appearance of the lubricating greases are intimately related to the crystal or gel structure of the soap phase. Farrington el at have proposed a classification of greases based upon the average length of the soap fibres, after conducting a thorough microscopic study of various greases. The classification is as follows:

Type	Length microns	Characteristics
Long fiber grease	100 or more	Fibrous, ropy
Medium fiber grease	10-100	Clinging slightly rough
Short fiber greases	1 -100	Slight rough , short
Microfiber grease	Less than 1	Smooth unctuous.

The suitability of a grease for a specific use can be correlated with fiber length. Long fiber greases is particularly suitable for use in gear boxes since long fibers are readily worked between the moving pat by the action of the gears and take upto sack in the worm gear an reduce noise in the operation. However, long fibers are not good for ball and roller bearing as they do not cling well to ball and rollers. Short fiber greases are most suitable for locomotive journals and open type roller bearing cup greases are usually microfibrous in nature.

Long, short and medium fiber greases are made with sodium soap. The fiber length becomes greater as the fat in the soap becomes higher in iodine number, or in other words, more unsaturated. Water glycerin or polar compounds also favour the formation of long fibers.

Calcium, lithium and aluminum grease are usually classified as microfiber greases although actually the soap may exist largely in the form of a liquid crystallite phase and in some cases at least the crystals or crystallites may be absent altogether. The most finely dispersed form of gelling agent is found in aluminum soap greases and the gelling agent in these grease may be present in the form of large micelle aggregate rather then well defined fibers.

Properties of greases

The properties of a grease depend upon the composition of the grease and the nature of its constituents. The gelling agents determine to a large extent the texture and mechanical stability or the system. The liquid phase on the other hand influence flow properties particularly at very low and high temperature. However, liquid phase has it greatest significance in its effect on life at high temperature. The life of the grease at high temperature is determined largely by the loss from evaporation or oxidation of liquid phase. The important properties of the greases are discussed below.

Viscosity of the oil

In selecting the viscosity of the oil in a grease for a particular application, the temperature range of application of the grease and the torque available in the equipment are to be taken into account.

The grease should be such that the machinery can be started easily without excessive torque. This is particularly important at low temperature. The low temperature starting torque and also the pumpability of the grease at low temperature are affected by the viscosity and viscosity index of the oil in the greases. As the temperature decrease the viscosity of the oil increase resulting in increase in resistance to flow. The viscosity should be such that resistance to flow at low temperature is within the torque available in the machine so that the machine can be easily stared. Lowering the viscosity and increasing the viscosity index tend to permit earlier dispensing and starting.

The maximum oil viscosity in grease for staring medium torque equipment is about *100,00* centi stokes, thus the viscosity of the oil should not be above this level and this set a low temperature limit for oils for use in greases. This means that in a median torque equipment, a particular greases can be used only upto as low temperature at which the viscosity or the oil in the grease is below about 100,000 cSt, similarly if a greases is to be used in a medium torque equipment at a particular low temperature the viscosity, of the oil from which the greases is to be formulated should be below *100,000* cSt at the temperature. For a low or high torque equipment the viscosity limit will be correspondingly lower or higher than 1*00,00* cSt.

At high temperature the oil in the grease should be viscous enough to give adequate lubrication. If the grease is to used at high temperature it should be made from highly viscous oil because at high temperature the viscosity oil decreases. High viscosity in higher temperature greases is also desirable from another point of view. Generally petroleum oils of high viscosity are also less volatile and low volatility is important at high temperature as it increases the life of the grease.

As mentioned earlier, generally oils of 200-500SUS viscosity at 50°C are used for the manufacture of grease but oil with higher viscosities upto 3000 SUS or lower viscosities below 100 SUS at 50°C may also be used for respectively very high and low temperature. Synthetic fluids normally have been viscosity indexes, that is, they show less change in viscosity with temperature and therefore are better suited for low and high temperature applications.

Loss on evaporation

Loss on evaporation of oil at high temperature is very important property of the grease and depends mainly on the nature of liquid phase. If the grease losses significant amount of oil on evaporation, its lubricant properties would be seriously affected an the life of the grease curtailed. Synthetic fluids normally give less loss on evaporation then petroleum oil; the loss on evaporation increasing in the order silicon, polyakylene glycols, silicon diesters, high temperature petroleum oils and diesters.

Oxidation stability

oxidation stability of greases is depended on the oxidation stability of the oil. Oxidation of oil lead to acidity development, increase in viscosity, blackening caused by like bodies, and ultimately to the formation of bituminous mass. The same pattern is followed when oil is a component of grease and at some stage in the oxidation process the grease ceases to be a safe lubricant. If oil is heated to its thermal decomposition temperature t form a had carbonaceous mass which further complicates the matters.

Incorporation of antioxidant and or synthetic fluids with high resistance for oxidation e.g silicones or flurocarbons can give greases of longer life than petroleum oil alone. However, oxidation cannot be checked completely by any means and ultimately the greases losses it effectiveness. Increase in temperature increase the rate of oxidation rapidly and there is a temperature limit beyond which a greases cannot be used except for a very short time.

Heat stability

The oil is held in the grease by means of the gelling effect of the thickener. Different gelling agents have different abilities to hold the oil in the greases and this ability decrease with increase in temperature. Some gelling agents are effective beyond its melting point temperature. However, no gelling agent is effective beyond its melting point or transition temperature as the case may be. The melting point of the grease is measured in terms of standard drop point test. The drop point is the temperature at which the grease is sufficiently fluid to drip from the bottom of a small standard cup. So drop point is the upper limit of temperature beyond which the grease is not stable.

In practice, however, drop point does not always indicate the maximum unable temperature. The oil may start separating out of the greases even before the drop point is reached and greases can be used for extended period only much below the drop point.

Heat stability is the ability of the grease to hold the oil at elevated temperature (below the drop point) for extended period. This is measured in terms of the oil separated from greases in a standard test at a fixed temperature (usually 100°C) after a fixed period (usually *30* hours). The grease which gives less loss due to separation is more stable.

Temperature limits of operation

The low temperature limit of operation of a grease depends on the viscosity of the oil the torque available in the machine. At low temperature the viscosity of the oil in the grease should be sufficiently low so that the machine can be started easily. The low temperature limit for a grease is generally determined by a torque test at 100 g~cm torque in a bearing of standard size.

The high temperature limit of operation of grease is mainly determined by the heat stability of the grease and by the loss from evaporation or oxidation of liquid phase. Of course, if the high temperature gelling agent are used, the greases will be retained in the bearing housing at temperature within the scope of gelling agent but they will be effective as lubricant only for so long as the liquid phase does not deteriorate excessively by oxidation or loose significant amount by evaporation. It is evident that for a short period of time a grease can be used at any temperature within the scope of the gelling agent in the grease but the grease ca be used for extended period of time at only the temperature at which the loss by evaporation and detonation due to oxidation are within acceptable limits. The high temperature limits of a greases usually determined by standard test in which the grease is tested at various temperature for 1000 hours.

The low temperature and high temperature limit of grease made with various liquid phases are shown in table the high temperature limit of the petroleum grease will be influenced to some extent with the type of thickener used and many vary from *60~80°C* with aluminum of calcium soap thickeners to about 150°C with lithium or organic non soaps thickeners.

Table

Temperature limits for different greases

Grease type	Max. temp.for 1000hr. life,°C	Lowest temp, for 1000g~cm torque in 204 bearing °C
Petroleum	120	-29.0
Polyglycol	120	-34.5
Diester	132	-56.5
Silicone-diester	138	Less than-73.5
Polyester	150	-41.5
Conventional silicone	171	- 34.5
Special silicone (with non soap additives)	232	-73.5
Fluorocarbons	176	-18.0

Mechanical properties

Grease vary in consistency from soap thickened oil which is fluid at room temperature to brick type of greases which are so hard that they must be cut with a knife. The most common method for measuring consistency employs a penetrometer penetration is usually measured both on the unworked greases and also after working sixty or more strokes with a perforated disk plunger. The national lubricating grease institute (NLGL) of America has developed a consistency classification based on worked penetration. The NLGL classification is shown in table.

Table also shows the approximate yield values for a grease in each of the penetration range. A yield of value of 981 dyn/cm2 indicated that a grease layer (with a density of Ig/cm2) 1 com high will just be able to support its own weight without slumping against the force of gravity. Yield value thus provides a measure of mechanical strength of the grease and can help in selecting greases for various sizes of bearing and housings.

NLGL Classification of greases

NLGI number	ASTM worked penetration	Approx. yield value dyn/cm2	Nature of grease	Typical type of greases
0	355-385	1,3000	Semi-fluid	Sodium or calcium
1	310-340	18,00	Very soft	Sodium, calcium, aluminum
2	265-295	3,000	Soft	Sod., cal., alum., or sod~cal (mix).
4	175-205	13,000	Medium cup greases	Do
5	130-160		Heavy cup greases	Sodium or calcium
6	85-115		Block grease	Sodium

The worked penetration measures the ability of the grease to withstand the churing action rotating shaft in the bearing which would break down the soap fibers. Number 2 grade greases are the most commonly used *in* a wide variety of application as they combine sufficient mechanical stability with adequate softness and oiliness to supply the lubrication need of most bearing. Softer greases are used where greater feeding of the greases is necessary as is the case with multiple row roller beating for railroad axle journal bearing needle bearing and various gear mechanism. The brick or block grease re applied as block which are inserted directly in the sleeve bearing box in such as application as a paper mill. No 3 and no4 grades are widely used in doubl4e seated and double shielded perpetrated ball bearing.

Flow resistance of grease is dependent on shear stress or shear rate. The apparent viscosity of a grease at low shear rates, below about 10 reciprocal seconds, is approximately equal to the yield stress divided by the rate of shear. The apparent viscosity then drops off rapidly in a nearly straight line manner upto about 1000 reciprocal second. After this the drop in viscosity decreases and the viscosity of the grease asymptotically approaches the viscosity of the mineral oil used in the manufacture of the grease. Thus under the high shear rates prevalent in most rolling bearings, even those grease which are stiff at low shear rates provide the same viscosity as the oil in the greases.

The mechanical strength of the greases depend upon the structure of the gelling agent. The structure of the gelling agent in destroyed by mechanically agitation, heat and other factors. A part of the reduction in flow resistance is reversible on decreasing the rate of shear but a part of the resistance is permanently lose due to the destruction of the fibers of gelling agent. The ability of the fibers composition of grease and the care exercised in preparing the greases.

Abnormally high power loss, high temperature and noisy operation are indicative of the deterioration in mechanical strength of the grease. During use, periodical checks on colour, oil content and acidity will provide a useful indication of the degree of deterioration occurring in a grease.

Operating life

A satisfactory lubricating grease is one which will resist, excessive oil separation, be reasonable stable to working and not change its nature to any extent over the temperature range in which it is used.

Thc life of a grease depends on many factors including the types of liquid phase, the type of thickener, the temperature and speed of operation and the environment. Oil separation from grease and evaporation and oxidation of liquid phase are the main reasons for the deterioration in the lubricating properties of the greases.

Synthetic fluids in general are less volatile and more oxidant resistant, and therefore, have greater life. Oil separation from greasc depends on the nature of the thickcning agent. However, for a given fluid and a given thickening agent, the life of a greases depends on the temperature and speed of operation. Oil separation rate of evaporation and rare of oxidation all increase with increase in temperature factor in determining the useful life of grease. Speed of bearing is also an important factor as the lubricating properties of a grease deteriorate more rapidly at higher speeds because of higher rate of shear.

15

Manufacture of Lubricating Greases

Introduction

The manufacture of lubricating grease essentially involves incorporation of gelling agent into oil in such a manner that a stable product is obtained. There are a wide variety of lubricating greases having different liquid phase and gelling agent and therefore.., it is obvious that non single method of manufacture can be applied to all type of greases, the process of manufacture will depends upon the formulation and the properties requirement in the finished product. In general however, the manufacture of greases may be studies in terms of the type of gelling agent and on this basis the manufacture of greases may be divided into two broad classes.

1. manufacture of soap base greases
2. manufacture of non soap base greases.

Soap base greases

Soap base lubricating greases are prepared by heating a mixture of lubricating oil and soap to a high temperature to form a homogeneous solution and then cooling the mass either with continued agitation or in a static condition depending upon the type of gelling agent employed. Soap separates out upon cooling in the form of fibers or other crystalline forms and being intimately dispersed in the oil, form a plastic solid with oil.

The soap used in making the grease may be either a pre made soap or the soap may be prepared in situ by saponification of the fat (or fatty oil) or fatty acid while in solution in all or part of the lubricating fluid. When the soap is produced from fat glycerol is formed as a by product and this glycerol remains in the grease if the soap is formed in situ. The glycerol in the greases greatly influences the physical structure of the product. In small amount the glycerol may also come from pre made soap$_7$ made by saponification of fats.

The characteristics of the finished greases depend upon the mineral oil or synthetic fluid used, the relative proportion of soap and oil the fatty material and the metal used to make the soap the water content of the compound and the method of solidifying and working the greases. In addition certain minor filers may greatly influence that physical structure of the product. Lubricating and physical chemical properties of greases are also modified by the addition of chemical additive such as oxidation inhibitor rust preventive and EP additives

For a specific greases employing a particular lubricating fluid and particular soap, the properties of the grease depend on the growth of soap fibers or crystallites and the manufacturing process should be conducted under condition leading to the formation of stable soap fibers or crystallites. The growth of soap fibers depends upon the heat treatment (heating and *cooling)* process followed during the manufacture of the greases. Although it is now known that the growth of soap fibers is quite similar to the growth of other types of common crystals, at the present stage of knowledge it is not possible to predict, from the properties of the soap and oil in a particular system, what the optimum conditions for fiber growth would be in the given system.

Consistency, stability and other physical properties of grease depend to a very large degree upon details of the heating, cooling and working operations of manufacturing process and these details must be established for each type of grease before commencing their production. Preliminary investigation are necessary to find out the optimum condition for fiber growth and to establish proper method of working for the manufacture of a particular greases. Generally applicable manufacture conditions can not be laid down, since these will depend to a great extend on formulation and the properties required in the final product.

The manufacturing process for soap base greases may be divided into following step. Not all the step are required in the manufacture of a particular greases and some step may be eliminated in some cases.

1. Measuring of material wither by weighing, metering or gauging.
2. Saponification, which involves mixing and heating of fat and oil with an alkali. This step is eliminated if pre formed soap is used, saponification may be carried out in open fire kettle open steam kettle or in an autoclave. Saponification under pressure reduce the time required for saponification.
3. Dispersion of the soap formed in the lubricating oil. The dispersion may be carried out in the saponification vessel or in a separate mixing kettle.
4. Dehydration which may take place during saponification or at any other point in the processing. In the some process the final removal of water occurs by vacuum treatment of the finished or semi finished product. In some case specially calcium base cup grease complete dehydration is not desired and rehydration of the grease may be necessary.
5. Cooling of the soap dispersion. This may be done with agitation or in a static state.
6. Milling or homogenizing is done to smooth the appearance of a fibrous grease.
7. Removal of entrained air or volatile materials.
8. Packaging.
9. Storage.

Lubricating greases are generally manufactured by batch process specially in small scale sector because batch process requires less capital investment and because batch process can handle many greases in the same equipment. However, continuous processes have also been developed for the manufacture of greases. Because of closer control over the variables of production , these continuous processes are claimed to yield products of better and more uniform quality than the older batch process.

As has mentioned earlier no single method of manufacture is applicable to all types of greases. However, in general, methods of manufacturing soap base greases can be grouped under three main headings.

1. Conventional method
2. Manufacture of aluminum, lithium and similar greases.
3. Manufacture of cold sett greases.

Conventional method

In the conventional method of production of soap greases, fats or fatty acids and a portion of lubricating oils are mixed with an alkali in an open kettle or closed vessel under pressure (autoclave) and heated until the formation of soap is complete. The reminder of the lubricating oil along with necessary amount of water acid or alkali and any other additive is then mixed with the soap solution in the same kettle or if the separated mixing kettle where the remainder of an other ingredient are added. The whole mass is stirred until homogeneous and then cooled with continual stirring. The product is finally filled into packages.

During saponification water is formed if fatty acid are used in forming the soap and this water has to be evaporated during processing. Glycerol is formed in the reaction if fats are used instead of fatly acids. In case of calcium or sodium greases it is preferred to have most of the fatty mineral consist of glyerides rather than free fatty acid as the presence of glycerol liberated. In some greases particularly in calcium soap greases considerable fat as well as substantial amount of alkali may remain unreacted. Minor amount of fatty acid are often added in the latter stage of the process to adjust the alkalinity of the solution.

The metal hydroxides used in the saponification are. where possible used in aqueous solution. However, lime and other hydroxides which are only partially soluble in water are used as dry oil slurries after dispersing the metal hydroxide in a part of the lubricating oil.

Saponification in open vessel was the general practice in early years of commercial greases making but now saponification under pressure is preferred as the time required for saponification is greatly reduced if the saponification is carried out under pressure especially if fats are to be saponified.

In a grease plant the machines and kettles are so placed that the oil or greases flows from one process to another by gravity. Generally a multistoreyed building is used, fat and oil storage, tank together with measuring vessels are on the top floor, autoclaves *on* the next, measuring kettles on the floor below and filling arrangement and storage on the ground floor.

Calcium soap greases

About any fat fatty acid will serve will serve to form calcium soaps. Fats from cattles, horses, swine and fishes are best suite for the manufactures of these greases. Palm oil, cottonseed oil, castor oil rapeseed oil, soyabean oil etc., can also be used for the purpose, although the dropping point of calcium soap greases made from such oils is slightly lower than the grease made from animals fats. Large amount of degree or wool grease fatty acids are also used for the manufacture of calcium soap greases.

A few formulae and methods of manufacturing calcium soap greases are given below:

Manufacture in a open steam kettle

Lard oil Extra No. 1	205
Inedible tallow	3001b.
Hydrated lime	198 1b.
Lubricating oil	900 Ib.
Water	75 gal.
Oil mirbane (perfume)	6Ib.

The lubricating oil should be a mineral oil of viscosity 180 SUS at 50°C. the lard should not contain more than 7% free fatty acid calculated as oleic acid and should be red or brown in colour. The tallow should be clear, fresh and free from dirt. The m.p. of the tallow should not be less than and free acid nor more than 5%. The hurate lime should be finely powdered containing about 27% to 28% water and *66.6%* available CaO. The process of manufacture is a follows:

Charge in an open steam jacketed kettle 50 gallons of oil or tailing from previous batch, lard oil and tallow in the order mentioned. In a separate vessel mix 198 IB of hydrated lime$_7$ 30 gallons of mineral oil and 75 gallons water, and this mixture to the kettle and agitate.

Turn *on* steam in jacket and bring temperature of contents of kettle to 1*50°C* in from 2 to 4 hours. Allow lime soap formed to stand in kettle over night with steam on but without agitating.

Test soap to find if saponification is complete and estimate water content. Soft pasty consistency indicates incomplete saponification or too much water, stringy morc or less transparent soap denotes excessive water evaporation. Soap should be firm and break evenly but should not crumble too readily.

Corrections should be made by adding from 1 to 5 gallons. NaOH (20Be') or in case of excess lime an appropriate amount of tallow.

Now run in mineral oil till total oil in the kettle is 400 gallons. Heat to 212° F. run in additional oil to 750 gallons. Scrape form sides of kettle and add slowly 4 to gallons water, temperature should be 180° *to* 185°F. stir for 10 minutes and add oil of mirbane. Now add remainder of oil (150 gallons) stir for 15 to 20 minutes and fill at 160°F to 170°F.

Grease produced is of medium constancy known as No3. It's melting point is 190°F to 195°F and consistency at 77°F is about 180.

Manufacture of anhydrous grease

Conventional cup greases are made with a small amount of water (0.5-1.5%) left the finished grease. The water forms hydrates with the soap and stabilizers the soap structure and gives characteristics smooth buttery cup greases structure. However it is possible to make these grease in completely anhydrous from by boiling off all the water, in manufacture anhydrous greases, it is necessary to cool the grease rapidly in order to secure the desired structure. This can be done by the use of cooling coils, or chilled rolls, or by the pouring the hot greases out in layers of, preferably, not over about one inch in thickness. The result is a crystal clear greases which like those containing water will not separate at high temperature. These anhydrous greases have some marked advantages but do not have the conventionally desirable structure and properties of hydrous greases.

Anhydrous greases are stabilized by hydroxylic compounds of lower volatility then water such as n~ propanol, n~butanol, n-amyl alcohol, cetyl alcohol and other higher fatty alchols. Greases made with these stabilizing greases because of the low volatility of the agents. Since greases made with water have desirable structure and properties not possible without water, both water and a fatty alcohol stabilizing agent may be used in the same grease so that advantages of both stabilizing agent may be combined.

U.S Paten 2, 108, 643 describes a method of the manufacture of calcium soap greases based on these fatty alcohol stabilizing agents. The grease made in accordance with the patent will normally have the following weight composition.

Lubricating oil	54-96%
Soap	3-35%
Stabilizing agent	1 -8%
Water	0-3%

According to this patent these greases may be made by mixing the necessary lime with a small amount of water and an amount of mineral oil about equal to the fatty acid to be used in a streamjacked greases mixing kettle. The fatty acid to be used in the manufacture of the soap is then added and heat is applied.

After an interval of abut 40 to 60 minutes, when the temperature has reached 240~260°F, saponification is complete and the soap is ready for mixing. About 2% to 3% water is added and when the batch foam up the form is driven down by the addition of cold oil. Due to the addition of cold oil and evaporation of water the temperature drops of about 230°F oil is added until the batch contains about 25% soap and during the interval at the temperature drop 205-210°F if the soap percentage is reduced to 15% then the temperature would drop to about 180~190°F.

After the addition of the final amount of oil, but prior to final cooling the desired amount of stabilizers agent is added and stirred in. the greases is then cooled and packed in the normal manner.

The process is about the same when fats are used instead of fatty acids except that is requires. 12 to 20 hours at 240-260F to effect the saponification of the fats. It is preferable to use hydrogenated fats (such as hydrogenated castor oil, hydrogenated tallow and hydrogenated fish oil) or fatty acid derived from hydrogenated fats but animal other fats acids derived from them may also be used.

Manufacture of pressure cooking

Extra No. 1 lard	150gal.
Water	14 gal.
Lubricating mineral oil (180SUS at 100F)	900gal.
Powdered hydrated lime	198 Lb.
No.l Inedibel tallow	300 Lb.
Oil mirbane	6 Lb.

Charge in closed pressure kettle of 12 barrel, capacity 30 to *50* gallons of oil or tailing from previous batch. Then added 1*50* gallons of lard and 3001b of melted tallow. In a separate vessel mix *30* gallons of mineral oil, 198 lb of hydrated line and 10 gallons of water and add the solution to the kettle.

Chose and fasten manhol or opening. Test for leaks by admitting compressed air till pressure of 151b is reached. Release pressure close relief valve.

Turn on steam in jacket. Heat till the pressure in the kettle is about 100 psi. agitate and maintain the pressure kettle at temperature not less than 50°C and 50-80 psi pressure for 20 minutes.

In a second open steam jacked mixing kettle of 30 barrels capacity, add 50 gallons of shop grease from previous batch to temperature to 112 to 135°C open valve on pressure kettle and blow the soap in the mixing kettle.

Start the agitators and begin adding lubricating oil till the volume of oil is 400 gallons. Bring the temperature to 105°C. add mineral oil to *75* gallons. Add 4 gallons of water, keep temperature balance of mineral oil. Stir for 10 minutes. Add mirbane and the balance of mineral oil. Stir for 15 to 20 minutes and fill at 80°C to *85°C.*

Calcium soap greases may also be made by incorporating small amount of soaps of other metal such as sodium. Admixing of certain low molecular weight metal salt such as acetates and benzoate's to calcium soap greases (and also to other alkaline and alkali metal soap greases) result in remarkable increase in maximum operating temperature for many applications. These grease are called complex soap greases. Inert material such as powdered metal flake graphite, mica, asbestos, fibers etc may also be in cooperated into calcium soap grease for special purpose.

Sodium greases

Sodium soap greases can be prepared in open fire kettle, in open stream jacketed kettle or in pressure kettle with a open mixing kettle. The open fire method is know and the size of batch which can be manufactured in a open fire kettle is considerably smaller than in case of the other two methods. There is better control of temperature when steam is used as heating medium than when direct fire is used, direct fire is used when high temperature are required for cooking the greases. Dowtherm and similar oils mat be used for obtaining high temperature in jacketed kettles.

The sodium hydroxide required for saponification is used as a water solution of 20-40 Be strength. The addition of soda solution to at and mineral oil is done after heating the mixture of fat and oil at about 50~100°C. the soda solution should be added slowly. In open vessels, great care must be taken with addicting the soda solution as too much addition will cause frothing due to boiling of water in the solution. The best method is to add about 300 *500* cc at a time and heat between application toll cracking of the batch has ceased which indicates complete evaporation of moisture. The temperature of the oil is slowly raised upto 140C during addition of caustic soda. After the addition of soda the temperature may be raised to *240-Z60C.*

The time required to finish a batch of sodium greases is more than that for a batch of calcium greases because all the water in the soap must be boiled off the batch before cooling the greases. The moisture content in a sodium greases must be kept as low as possible otherwise the finished grease will have a pasty, soft texture with lowered melting point.

The sodium soap grease is fibrous in nature. These are two ways to cool the batch and aid in the formation of proper fibrous appearance. The batch can be agitated until the temperature fall sufficiently to draw or it can be run into large shallow pans and raked manually or mechanically until cooled sufficiently for packaging.

The rate of cooling and amount of agitation greatly affect the length of grease fiber formed. Quick cooling and agitation at the lowered temperature will produce long fibers and give the grease a fibrous appearance similar to universal joint greases, while if no agitation is used the grease will form into very short or fine grain fiber and have the appearance of what is known as block of brick greases.

If it is desired to smooth the appearance of fibrous grease it can be donbye milling. There are various type of mills such as ball mill, roller mill or stone mill. These mills are identical to those used in paint manufacture. Sodium soap grease are milled to smooth or reduce any lumps that may have been formed during manufacture and to work the rough grease structure into a more homogeneous mass thereby reducing the internal friction in ball or roller type bearing.

A few formulate and methods of manufacturing sodium soap greases are given below.

Lubricating grease for driving gears

Castor oil	30 kg.
Tallow	20 kg.
Rosin	20 kg.
Sodium hydroxide, solid	14 kg.
Cylinder oil	
(100 SUS viscosity at 100 °C)	1916 kg.

Add the castor oil, tallow, rosin and 66 kg. Of the cylinder oil in a open steam heated kettle with a stirring gear capable of giving at 90 °C make a 40 Be aqueous solution of the sodium hydrox idle and add it slowly into the kettle with continuous stirring.

Heatup slowly to 140 °C until., after about 2 hour the water is boiled away. Now add slowly the remaining cylinder oil. The rate addition should be such that about 400 kg. Should enter the kettle during 1 hour. Keep at 1-0 °C. test as soon as all the oil is added, if enough water has boiled away.

If the batch is ready, cool as quick as possible to secure a good consistency. Keep stirring until 35 °C is reached. Stirring should be such that too much air should not be stirring into the greases. Fill the grease into packages at 35 °C.

Another formula is :

Tallow	60 kg.
Stearic acid	10 kg.
Sodium hydroxide solid	12 kg.

Cylinder oil	
(50-75 SUS viscosity at 100 °C)	1916 kg.

Add the tallow, stearin and 200 kg.of the cylinder oil into the kettle, stir and heat to 60°C.add a 30 Be' caustic soda solution add 200 kg oil. Let stand overnight keeping warm., but without mixing.

Stir up the mass next morning and add *800* kg. Cylinder oil, mix through and add slowly the remaining 718kg. of oil.

Mix through again, the shut off the steam; cool until the consistency is correct. If necessary, more cylinder oil has to be added. Fill at about *60 °C.*

Mixed soap greases

Soaps of more than one metal are often used in the manufacture of greases to obtain properties not obtainable with one type of soap alone. Generally the proportion of one type of soap alone. Generally the proportions of one type of soap is higher and the other type of soap is used to modify the structure of the greases to give special properties.

Sodium and calcium soaps are often combined to produce mixed soap greases for use in ball and roller bearings. US patent 2,05,236 describes the manufacture of a lubricating greases for high speed ball and roller bearing. The greases consists essentially of a mixed soda lime soap of stearic acid (15 10 35%) and a light lubricating oil (*65-85%).* The ratio of calcium soap to sodium soap in the grease is around 1:5. The grease is substantially anhydrous and free from glycerin and characterized by having short fiber texture.

Calcium of sodium soaps may also be mixed with barium or other metal soaps. Examples of mixes soaps of barium with calcium and sodium are given below.

High temperature cup greases

Barium soap	15 kg.
Calcium soap	5 kg.
Diglycol sterate	3 kg.
Mineral oil	77 kg.

The grease can be made by mixing the hydrate lime and hydrated barium hydroxide stoichiometrically equipment to the desired amount of soap with the stoichiometrically equivalent of fatty acid and an amount of minerals oil equal to the amount of fatty acid. This mixture is then heated as rapidly as possible to 150°C. rapid heating avoids excessive formatting of the soap. When the foaming has subsided the batch or fatty acid, whichever is required. The diglycol stearate is then added and the remaining oil added.

The resulting greases should be cooled rather rapidly, for instance in layers one half to five eighths inch thick. However rapid cooling does not seem to be as assential as it is in some other types of greases.

One of the factors which make the mixed calcium and barium soap greases highly desirable is the fact that each soap lends a high consistency within a particular temperature range the calcium soap at medium temperature and the barium soap at high temperature.

Sodium Barium soap greases

British Patent 507,980 describes the manufacture of mixed soap greases consisting of a mineral oil and 10 to 40 per cent of a mixture of sodium and barium soaps. The ratio of sodium soap to barium soap in the mixture may vary from 1:1 to 10:1. The soap are preferably soaps of saturated fatty acid such as stearates.

As a example 425 parts of weight of stearic acid and 500 parts of weight of mineral lubricating oil of viscosity *200* SUS at 50 °C when the acid is completely melted and dissolved 25, part of weight of barium hydroxide in approximately saturated aqueous solution are stirred in the temperature is then raised to about 180 °C while 62 parts by weight of sodium hydroxide (30 per cent aqueous solution) are stirred in when saponification is complete and water nearly completely eliminated the product is cooled to about 93°C and is worked at that temperature for two or three hours.

The grease has the following composition 2.75 per cent of barium stearates 21.25 per cent of sodium stearate and 76 per cent of mineral oil.

Manufacture of aluminum and lithium base greases

The conventional method of manufacture greases is applicable to sodium, calcium and similar types of greases but there are certain kinds of greases which cannot be manufacture in this way. The essentail feature of conventional method are that the soap is usually formed in situ i.e. directly in the mineral oil and the cooling of grease is always done under continual stirring. In the manufacture of aluminum and lithium base grease the cooling must be done in the more of less static condition and the grease are usually made from per made soaps usually of stearic or other saturated fatty acids.

Aluminum and lithium soap greases have a transition temperature and the greases must be held at this temperature for the optimum growth of the soap crystallites. Hence the conventional method in which cooling is done with stirring is not suitable for these greases and special method of cooling have to be employed.

To prepare the grease, the pre made soap are dissolved in the mineral oil at elevated temperature. Cooling was formerly usually done by pouring the molten mass into shallow pans or trays where it remains until cool enough for removal and subsequent milling or homogenizing. This method is somewhat laborious and handling costs are high. New methods of cooling these greases have therefore, been developed. In one such method the mould the molten greases is fed on to moving belt in the thin layer. By this methods the greases can be cooled in a continuous way. In another methods the hot greases is fed into a series of horizontal tubes where it remain until greases is complete. A fresh charge of hot greases then forces out the cooled material, which is ready for plasticizing of milling treatment. In modern plants pan cooling is eliminated and other newer methods such as decried above are used.

The homogenizing by means of a variety of suitable devices is the final step in the manufacture of these greases prior to packing in order to achieve smooth structure. The appearance of some greases can be improved by desertion by means of vacuum treatment which removes fine bubbles of air of other volatile materials which interfere with transparent appearance.

Stearate, oleate and palmitate are the most commonly used soaps for the manufacture of lithium and aluminum base greases although soaps of other fatty acid may also be used.

Details of manufacture of lithium and aluminum soap base greases discussed below.

Aluminum base greases

Aluminum soap greases are generally prepared by dissolving a pre made soap in lubricating oil at about 70-150 °C depending upon the type of soap, followed by cooling to transition temperature (50-80 °C) where it is permitted to rest and undergo a sort of phase transformation. The grease is then further cooled and homogenized.

Aluminum soaps are prepared by double decomposition of a soda soap with aluminum sulphate or alum. The precipitated aluminum stearate or oleate is used as the grease below.

Aluminum stearate is more commonly used than other soaps. A good grade of chasis lubricant can be prepared by adding *to 8%* of aluminum stearate in a mineral with *500* SUS viscosity at *50°C*. The process of manufacture is as follow:

The desired quality of aluminum stearate powder is weighed into an open type steam jacketed kettle and cold oil is added slowly with agitation. Just sufficient oil is added to form a soft paste. The paste is agitated until smooth and all lumps have been dissolved. At this point heat is applied and the balance of the oil is slowly added with continued stirring.

As the temperature of the batch increase there will be some frothing which slowly decrease as the temperature nears 140 to 150 °C. This temperature and agitation should be maintained until all frothing has ceased and the batch is clear transpired mass. Then the batch is cooled as rapidly as possible by running cold water in the kettle jacket. The temperature is allowed to drop to 95 °C at which point a very slight gell or tack will be noted. Rapid cooling and agitation should be discontinued promptly and the batch drawn into pan about 3 inches deep of into containers of about 45 kgs. Capacity for proper ageing.

The batch should be allowed to cool slowly. If the batch is cooled too rapidly from the gel point to atmospheric temperature the grease will be soft and will show separation. After being maintained at the transition temperature range (50-80 °C) for sufficient time, the grease is further cooled *and* then homogenized. The grease should be maintained at a temperature of 33 °C for at least 12 hours before transferring to packages.

Lithium base greases

The manufacture of lithium base greases is similar to aluminum base grease. There are two methods of preparing lithium soaps the fire kettle or high temperature method and the steam kettle or lower temperature method.

In the fire kettle method of suspension of pre made lithium stearate soaps (or some other fatty acid soap) in the lubricating fluid is heated to about 205v until the soap is dissolved. To avoid oxidation and dire hazard, the fluid is then chilled rapidly to form an elastic gel. The gel is maintained at the transition to temperature and then mechanically worked by extrusion or milling process to the smooth, buttery texture or a cup of greases.

In the steam kettle method the fatty matter is reacted with alkali (lithium hydroxide monohydrate) in the presence of some of the mineral oil and the grease is finished by slowly working or kneading the reining oil into the hot soap and oil paste. The grease is then chilled, maintained at the transition temperature and homogenized.

In a modification of the steam kettle method the soap is formed *in* a pressure vessel or autoclave and further processing is done in a mixing kettle.

Lithium base greases are generally prepared with 5 to 10 per cent lithium soap though other composition may also be used, a particularly stable lubricating greases can be prepared according to the following formula:

Capric acid	8.7kg.
Stearic acid	5.4 kg.
Acetic acid	1.6 kg.
Lithium hydroxide	4.2 kg.
Glucein	2.2 kg.
Paraffin oil (100 SUS viscosity at 55 °C)	72.77 kg.

This grease has a unworked penetration (*at* 77 °C) of *358* and worked penetration of 339 and the dropping point of the grease is 235 °C.

Manufacture of cold sett greases

The grease so far discussed are manufactured at high temperature and called boiled greases. Another type of greases are made at temperature slightly above the normal temperature and are called cold sett grease. The se greases are usually made from rosin oil, alkali and mineral oil and, in general, are inferior in performance compared to boiled greases. Cold sett greases are cheap lubricant suitable for the lubricating of open type bearing such as fitted with railway, tramcar or other carriage axles.

In the manufacture of cold sell greases the alkali usually lime hydrate an apart of mineral oil are mixed in one container and this mixture is called sett.

The rosin oil and the remainder of mineral oil are mixed in a separate container and this mixture is called oil mix. The greases is then prepared by leading the sett and oil mix, slightly warmed or without warming, through separate lines to a high speed mixing device where the grease is formed in the form of a gel.

Many variations can be made in the above procedure. A part of rosin oil may be mixed with the alkali and mineral oil in helping the oil and lime in suspension by forming and rosin soap. Fillers such as calcium sulphate gypsum etc may also be incorporated in the greases. The greases may also be coloured by adding dye or pigments.

Various formulae and method of manufacturing cold sett carriage greases are given below:

Carriage greases unfilled

Yellow

Rosin oil	27 kg.
Mineral oil	40 kg.
Lime hydrate	9 kg.
Mineral oil, pale	24 kg.

Rosin oil is dissolved in 40 kg. Mineral oil with heat and stirring. Lime hydrate and mineral oil (24kg.) are mixed separately until smooth. And the thin paste of lime to rosin oil mix with thorough agitation. A very heavy gel is formed.

Non soap base greases

Non soap base greases are made by dispersion of the gelling agent in the lubricating oil in colloid mill or homogenizer. The manufacture of non soap base grease *is* simple compared to the manufacture of soap base greases. Many of the clay or silica thickened greases are readily manufactured by simple mixing without the high temperature cooking which is necessary with soap thickeners.

Since these greases are made by simple mixing of the gelling agent into the oil good agitation and fine particle size of the gelling agent is important to give uniform product. Non soap gelling agent are used in the form of fine product.

Finely divided silica (*50* micron max.) will disperse readily in the lubricating oil to give a grease but such a product way be very unstable owing to the hygroscope nature of the greases. Therefore, silica is treated with a water proofing surface active agent e.g. butyl alcohol unless silicones which are themselves highly water repellent form the liquid phase. Clay thickeners also require water proofing with organic compounds such as quaternary ammonium compounds or fatty acid amides.

Silica base greases can be manufactured by dispersing the silica powder *in* the lubricating oil with addition of water proofing compound. In another process sodium silicate, which is acidified and washed, is treated with an alkyl ethoxysiloxane; the ethoxy group react with the silica to provide water proofing.

Inorganic thickeners like silica or clay need dispersing aids such as polar organic compounds of low molecular weight for efficient mixing of gelling agent into the oil. Methanol and acetone are the most popular dispersing aid because they can be easily removed by evaporation in the final stages. Propylene glycol has been used as dispersing aid.

16

Lubricant and Their Environmental Impact

Introduction

The total percentage of lubricant that is successfully disposed of it major lubricant enters the environment in one way or another, the result of this consumption can be seen in motorways and car parks as a black coating of oil on the road.

Some lubricant are intended for use in such a way that they are lost to the environment. Examples are two stroke oils, greases and oils used in tyres, many white railways, chainsaw bar lubricant rubber oils used in tyres, many white oils and so on. Conversely providing efficient management systems are in place, many industrial oils should be largely contained and should not escape into the environment. Accident however, inevitably occur and cause the environmental release of almost any and all types of lubricant.

Three major aspect of the environmental impact of lubricant can be addressed

(i) control via engineering to minimise losses

(ii) minimising the impact of these losses ; and

(iii) efficient collection and treatment of waste material.

In terms of the lubricant aspect

(i) is largely a matter for the equipment designer and builder. The specialist lubricant company is affected by aspect

(ii) and can affect aspect

(iii) The collection and treatment of waste lubricant will now be described, and will be followed by consideration of the environment impact of lubricant.

Collection of waste lubricant

Waste lubricant that is collected is usually disposed off either by burning as fuel or incineration as waste, or is reclaimed. Some lubricant such as industrial oils, can be treated easily and recycled whereas motive engine oil requires more sophisticated treatment to provide reusable base fluids of acceptable quality.

Used industrial lubricants

There are many potential sources of used industrial products but reprocessing is not an option for a large number of these synthetic and fatty oil based product, some product such as transformer oils and hydraulic oils, can be readily collected from large industrial concern and segregated. Consequently contamination can be avoided. These oils may be regenerated to a recognize standard and returned to the original source.

Used automotive lubricant

These will include mono and multi-grade crankcase oils from petrol and diesel engines, together with gear oils and transmission fluids. Used industrial lubricant that have been inadequately segregated will also be included. Apart from the degradation product from the in service use of the oil a wide range of contamination is possible. This includes:

- Water - combustion product, rain water/ salt water ingress
- Fuels ~ residual components of gasoline and diesel fuel
- Solid - soot, additive and wear metals, rust, dirt, etc.
- Chemical- used oil can be used as an unauthorised means of hazardous waste disposal
- Industrial oils- inadequate segregation of oil types can allow contamination by fatty or naphthentic products.

Good management of a used oil collection system is paramount to minimise both the variability of the material supplied to a re refining plant and the problem of contamination by toxic or hazardous materials.

Treatment of collected lubricant

Production of fuel oil blending component

Used lubricant is an excellent source of energy, but contains which when burnt, can create environmental pollution and operational problems. The control of emissions is the central factor governing the use of used oil as a fuel component. Providing strict limit on emissions are met, the content of thc fuel is immaterial. Simple processing (e.g. settling and filtration/ centrifugation) is sufficient to remove coarse solids and water, and a mild chemical treatment (e.g. caustic soda solution) may also be used to reduce concentration of other contaminants. Disposal of waste product may be a problem.

Reclamation of lubricating oils.

Some specific types of industrial oils can be readily segregated and are suitable for relatively simple reprocessing before being returned to their original service. Typical processing methods involve filtration and removal of water or volatile decomposition product under vacuum.

Large industrial customers can arrange for on site reprocessing (e.g. reconditioning of transformer oil at power generation plant), or can collect specific drain oils for site reprocessing and return (e.g. reclamation or railway diesel engine oils). These types of customer specific reprocessing can be cost effective compared to the expense of new oils.

Production of re-refined lubricant base oils

When dealing with oils from multiple sources, complex processes are needed to remove the wide range of contaminants an additives that will be present. The objective is to produce base oil that can then be used as substitutes or alternatives to virigin mineral base oil. Most of these are continuous rather than batch processes and rely on receiving a reasonably homogeneous used oil feedstock if the products are to be consistent. One means of achieving consistency is to mix a complete months supply of used oil and to use that to feed a continuous process appropriate to the characteristics of the resultant mixture. There is a risk that contamination will spoil a large batch, however, and quality checks on the feedstock are very important.

Acid/clay treatment

This has been the principal re-refining process in commercial use (e.g. Meinke process) but has the disadvantage that it generate large amounts of hazardous waste and cannot effectively remove the high concentration of additives used in modern engine oils. It is now being superseded by other newer technologies.

In the acid/ clay process, the used oil is first treated with 98% sulphuric acid; the resulting acid sludge is then separated and the remaining oil is clay treated, neutralized and filtered. Process yield from modern used engine oils are low (50-60% of lube boiling range materials) and large quantities of acid sludge and oil soaked clay are generated. These wastes are difficult and costly to dispose of in an environmentally acceptable manner. Sometimes a thermal pre treatment is used to degrade some of the additives and reduce the work load on the acid treatment stage. Base oils produced by the acid/ clay process are usually dark in colour, have a noticeable odour and are somewhat inferior in quality to virgin mineral oils.

Solvent extraction

Propane or other solvent can be used to selectively extract the base lube material from the used oil. A high boiling asphaltic residue which contains most of the additives and other impurities, is recovered as a separate stream, (note that this is not the same process as refinery furfural or phenol extraction, which uses solvent to selectively remove aromatics from lubricant fractions). A further finishing treatment of the lube material is normally required and may involve low severity acid/clay treatment, clay treatment alone, or hydrofinishing. Solvent extraction plants are expensive to build and operate, and generate significant amount of waste materials and hazardous by products. Overall base oil yield are 70-80%.

Distillation/ clay treatment

Thin film distillation under high vacuum (e.g. Luwa evaporators) allows the separation of gas oil, lube oil and an asphaltic residue containing most of the additives and contaminants from the used oil. The lube oil stream is finished by clay treatment. Overall base oil yield are again 70-*80%* and significant amount of spent clay must be disposed oil.

Distillation/ hydrotreatment

This technology is the most recent (e.g. KTI and ModawK processes). After pre treatment and the thin film distillation, the base oil fraction is hydrotreated under moderate conditions. A final distillation step yield a range of base oil streams of different viscosity. Process yields of base oil are high at 90-95%. By product are a low boiling distillate (used as fuel in the re refining plant) gas oil and a non hazardous asphaltic residue. Emissions and waste stream are limited, therefore this process is capable of meeting very strict environmental controls. Base oils produced by this route tend to be of superior quality compared to the older technologies, The hydrotreatment process is comparatively sophisticated capital-intensive and requires skilled operation, although operating costs are not exceptionally high.

Re refined base oil quality

Lubricant base oil must meet specified minimum performance characteristics, viscosity , viscosity index, pour point and volatility must all meet the requires standards. When dealing with re refined oils, additional characteristics such as colour and odour must also be taken into account. Darkistics such as colour or unusual odour are readily perceived by the customer as representing deficiencies in quality. Many re refined oils, for example, have a definite characteristic cracked or oxidised odour, which may be totally unacceptable in some countries and marked. Table provides quality guidelines for re-refined oil acceptance.

Due to the variety of potential sources of used lubricants, their differing histories of use, and their subsequent levels of possible contaminants, assessment of the quality of the resulting re-refined base oil is a major concern. Quality assurance must be applied, both to the used oil feedstock and more particularly, to the products of the re-refining process. Limits for the concentration of various contaminants in the finished base oil must be set and strictly adhered to,

Possible contaminants in re refined base oils

Fuel and solvent residues These can be present in varying amounts depending on the efficiency of the re-refining of processes employed.

Polycyclic aromatics hydrocarbons (PAHs). These are primarily present as result of the combustion process during previous use of the lubricant, prior to re refining. PAHs are found at varying concentrations in used oil, determined by factors such as drain interval, fuel types and sumps size. Some FAHs are know to be carcinogenic, and the concentration of total PAHs in base fluids must be controlled.

Metals. Metals should not be present in re refined Base oil, either as wear metals or form previous use of additives or as clay or catalyst fines. Metals - can be measured by determining the total sulphated ash content, or individually, by atomiac absorption spectroscopy.

Non metal impurities. Viscosity index (VI) improvers of polychlorinated biphenyls (PCBs) can be determined by dialysis or chlorine analysis, respectively. Indication of the presence of VI improver is given by unusually high viscosity index.

Water and untreated acid. These may be carried over from some processes. Total acid number and copper corrosion tests will indicate the presence of such contaminants in the re-refined oil.

Sulphur content, In virgin base oil this is seen as an index of inherent antioxidant capacity, With re refined oils, those hydrocarbons that were inherently oxidatively unstable will have been oxidised during previous use. The function of the sulphur content of re-refined base oil is not clear; more work is required to determine the need or concentration of sulphur required to meet minimum performance standards.

Health and safety aspects of re-refined oil

Used engine oil is recongnised as posing a carcinogenic risk to man. However providing sensible precaution, such as good personal hygiene, are taken the actual risk to health can be essentially eliminated. This is borne out by epidemiological studies on groups of mechanics where there has been no evidence of an increase in skin cancer.

The main carcinogenic agents in used oil are polycylic aromatic hydrocarbons (FAHs) with 3-7 rings such as benzo(a) pyrene, benz(a) anthracene and chrysene. These chemicals and many others like them, are found in used lubricant, having been formed during the combustion cycle in the engine. FAHs are also present in crude oil, and can be present in unused base fluid leaving the refinery. Refinery techno'ogy is, however, able to remove these harmful PAHs by hydrogenation and solvent extraction. Strict limit of 3% on the DMSO extract of virgin base oil have been introduced by the oil industry; these limits are based on animals studies, which have shown that there is no evidence of carcinogenic activity at DMSO extract levels below 3%. It must be emphsised that the use of this method is only valid for virgin base oils produced from crude oil using 'conventional' refining techniques. Application of the 3% limit to refined oils cannot be relied upon as a demostration of safety.

Environmental consideration of waste lubricant

It is important to consider the total environmental cost and benefits of dealing with used lubricant. The previous sections have indicated that the quality of the re-refined product is determined by the nature of the feedstock, and by the treatment process. The total amount of energy consumed in the collection and re-refining of used oil to an acceptable standard must be balanced against the energy to be gained from utilising the used oil as a fuel.

Of the three base methods of disposal of used oil, the most efficient in terms of energy conservation, in that it displaces in equivalent amount of oils, is the use of the materials as a fuel or fuel supplement. In heating oil, is the use of the material as a fuel is supplied through a burner, some limited pretreatment of the waste oil and blending with conventional fuels are necessary. Pre treatment can range from simple settling and filtration, to heating, emulsion breaking, chemical treatment and centrifugation- the amount of treatment will depend on the nature of the used oil the required fuels specifications and any requirements regarding emissions. The flue gas components of principal environmental concerns are PCBs, FAHs, dioxins and heavy metals. Some treatment of the oil will be required to ensure that emission standard for these materials are not exceeded when waste oil is used as fuel. Should this not be possible, the oil must be considered a hazardous waste and treated accordingly. Waste oils can successfully be burnt in boiler, ranging in size from electricity generating plant and industrial boilers to specially produced small furnace and boiler installations.

Disposal of waste oil as hazardous waste requires that it be incinerated at high temperature to ensure complete oxidation of PAHs, PCBs and PCT (polychlorinated terphenyls), such disposal is mandatory in many countries if the content of some contaminant in the used off exceeds predetermined concentrations e.g. 20ppm of PCB in Germany.

With regard to re refining, providing the used oil is of suitable quality and the process is able to generate a product of sufficiently high quality, the principal environmental consideration concerns the disposal of the by product of the refinery process. The effluent / waste products from some refining processes can be highly toxic and/ or potentially carcinogenic. If these wastes are not disposed or correctly, they represent a potential hazard to the environment, which is at least as severs as that of untreated used oil. The cost of safe disposal of these wastes *is* usually high.

The use of re-refined base oil in the production of lubricants is being increasingly considered on a worldwide basis. The driving force behind this is the concept of recycling of resources thus minimising environmental impact. These consideration while commendable in principle, appear to ignor the environmental cost of collection and transport. A modern plant producing a top quality re-refined base oil is expensive to construct, and is not common. In consequence, a comprehensive collection and transport system to keep it supplied with used oil feedstock it needed. Local solutions such as fuel use in correctly designed system obviate the need for the large scale transport systems. The benefit to be gained from conserving crude oil (the non renewable resource) by re refining less than 1% of refinery output must be weighed against the fuel and energy (90% of refinery output) used in transport and processing. It is also important that perceived environmental benefit must not take precedence over the quality of the resulting lubricant. Full life cycle analysis is require in each market to determine the true picture with regard to environmental impact. If lubricant quality is compromised, the result in term of engine failure and loss of performance could lead to an overall environmental deficit when the cost of replacement parts and decreased efficiency are taken into account. The health consequences of increased PAH concentration are also unknown, and must be considered it re-refined oil are used.

Quality control and process should be able to produce a product of known and consistent quality, suitable for use as a lubricant basestock. In practice, however, oils that can meet the required performance characteristics tend not to be readily available and have historically been expensive. For these reasons, the use or re-refined oil as lubricant base fluid is not considered to represent a viable alternative to virgin base oils of consistent quality when these are readily available. In these circumstance, the most appropriate means of recycling used engine oil is as a where alternative base oil are available. In such cases, the use of re-refined oil in the production of lubricant represent the only viably alternative. Care must be taken to ensure that the re-refining process can produce an oil of acceptable quality.

Biodegradation tests of oils

The concept of biodegradation is at least superficially, a simple one. A compound is degraded by biological mechanism, and so is removed from the environment. The practical assessment of biodegradability is less certain, however, as evidenced by the number and variation of the tests available. The relationship between test results and actual environmental persistence is well established for some classes of compounds. For the majority of other materials, however, no such link has been established.

All the test methods currently employed were designed mainly for use with single chemical species that have a demonstrable water solubility. Oils and oil products are mixtures of hundreds (sometimes thousands) of different chemicals, which are generally of poor water solubility. Whilst some existing methods can be used with materials of poor solubility, such applications, are at best compromise. In the following some of the main terms used in biodegradation tests are described. The differences between the commonly used test methods, and the difficulties of applying these methods to oil products are then outlined. Finally, an indicating of the current applicability of test result to oil products is given.

Current status and applicability

The only oil product for which there are comprehensive data on environmental persistence is crude oil. These real environmental data have been generated as a result of the various oil spills that have occurred over the years. Such incident have shown that oils does degrade. More recently, in Alaska have shown that the addition of essential nutrients PO4, SO4, NO3 etc- can promote rapid degradation by indigenous microorganisms in a short time and at low temperature.

Given that the existing standard tests were developed to correlate with the actual environmental situation for particular types of materials (surfactants), it can be seen that the application of existing test methods (where oil products invariably fail) to lubricants is not always appropriate. There is one test method, developed by the CEC for use with two stroke outboard oils that does correlate with the environmental situation. Although a 67% pass level has been applied to this test which authorities require 70% to be in the line with other methods measuring DOC. The CEC test was, for many years, a tentative test method and not an of acceptance as a general test for oils. The reasons that test took so to the CEC, organisation mainly concerned with engineering type testing of fuels and lubricants. The deficiencies were eventually controlled to the satisfaction of the CEC such that the methods was formally adopted for the evaluation of two stroke out board engine oils only in 1994.

There is a major problem with the CEC test in terms of its long terms future. This is because the method of measurement relies on extracting hydrocarbons form the test system using trichlortifluroethane. This materials is now subject to the provisions of the Montreal protocol concerning ozone depleting substance and it sale have been prohibited after January 1995. Although it may be possible to obtain a licence to continue to use this solvent if it is deemed essential, the security of long term supplies of a compounds that can no longer be generally sold must be doubtful. On a logical basis, it is also difficult to justify the use of environmental damaging procedure in the development of less environmental damaging product.

There is need, therefore, for an internationally recongised test for the biodegradation of oil products that will reflect the true environmental situation, i.e., give an adequate supply of nutrient and oxygen, microbiological degradation of oil can and does occur. The European oil companies working through CONCAWE have a set up a task force of biodegradation expert to develop just such a test. The CONCAWE test method is still under development and it is not expected that a published method will be available until late 1996. However, it is worth describing the salient points as it is possible that this method will become universally accepted for assessing the biodegradation potential oil and oil related product.

The method is based on the sturm test, a significant difference being that it is performed in sealed serum vials, mixing being achieved by shaking. The volume of the vital is approximately one third test material/ medium and inoculum and two thirds air. As the system is sealed, each vessel is sacrificed in order to make a measurement. This is achieved by additing alkali to the mixture, which converts carbon dioxide into dissolved equipment. A major different in the CONCAWE method is the use of a pre-exposed inoculum. The current standard tests (apart from the MITI) all specify an inoculum from a sewage works treating primarily domestic sewage. As these tests were developed from use with surfactants, this means that they effectively used a pre adapted inoculum. This goes a long way to explaining the characteristically poor result obtained for oil in such test. Work by the CONCAWE groups has found that if the inoculum is pre-exposed for a period of two weeks then the degradation obtained is better than with a non adapted inoculum. More importantly, the variability of source but also from the same source over time is greatly diminished, the new test method holds great promise for use with all poorly soluble mixtures such as oils and lubricant. It is to be hoped that the final method, when published, will provide the biodegradation assessment tool that is currently lacking for oils and associated materials.

Until internationally recognised and accepted test method that accurately reflect the environmental impact of oil and oil products are available, the oil industrial will be obligated to work with current, limited test methods. The inapplicability of these methods to complex mixtures of poorly soluble compounds must be understood in order for the apparent failure of oil products in biodegradation tests to be placed in their correct environmental perspective.

Future trends

The largest proportion of lubricant enters the environment by virtue of its being used. Legislation can reduce unauthorised disposal, but this is a minor problem in terms of the overall situation. Engineering can minimise leaks and also increase the dependence on authorised waste disposal specilists to eliminate dumping for example by using dry sump lubrication in car engines, with the lubricant in a replaceable canister than can be changed only at a service station. Modern vehicles are becoming increasingly complex, requiring computer assisted diagnostics as routine elements of servicing. This tend will eventually diminish the ability of the individual motorist by work on the vehicle, and further increase the reliance on specialist workshops.

The largest factor in minimising environmental impact, however, will depends on the lubricant itself- Vegetable oil base fluids are being used in some applications, while readily biodegradable synthetic esters are used in outboard two stroke engines. The choice of a biodegradable base fluid can aid the search for environmental friendliness.

The additives are present in the formulation to perform a specific job. As engineering and fuel change, so does the need for additives. Does a low sulphur fuel (which is becoming the norm due to legislative pressure on acid emissions) need a lubricant with a good a dispersand additives as a high sulphur fuel? The metallic and halogenated components of additives many eventually be replaced by easily biodegradable compounds that perform as effectively as, if not better, than those currently in use.

Identification of the most environmentally acceptable product is becoming increasingly desirable. The identification of the environmental friendly option to the consumer has resulted in some dubious it not misleading marketing claims. In order to circumvent, such practices, many countries have developed ecolabelling schemes that gives an official seal of approval to the best environmental options in many product groups. The best known of these system in the German 'Blue Angle" scheme started in 1970. Other scheme now exist in the USA, Canada, Japan, Scandinavia and the European Union in addition to individual European national schemes.

The development of criteria appropriate for engine oils is not a simple procedure, A scheme has been proposed that recongnise that environmental benefits can be achieved by an automotive engine oil in several ways. Any saving in fuel consumption will have significant benefit in terms of conservation of natural resources (crude oil) and a reduction of emissions. Environmental benefits can also result from a reduction in the toxic effects of any lost lubricant (although as mentioned earlier, such effects are surprisingly small), which can be achieved by reducing the content of the more potentially harmful additives. A removal of the nuisances posed by the promotion of a more biodegradable product is also a potential environmental benefit. Any measures that leads to a reduction of oil consumption will also have environmental option must recognize is the some of the potential benefits may be mutually exclusive and that there is no right answer, to the best means of achieving an benefit. A highly fuel efficient lubricant for example, may not be highly biodegradable an oil that has a low additive treat leaves may not have a low oil consumption.

There are two traditional methods for determining whether a product is environmentally friendly; the establishment of a series of hurdles that must be overcomes, to the awarding of weighted scores in some specified characteristics. The scheme proposed for automotive engine lubricants combines these two approaches. The purpose is to established a level of performance that does not represent a deterioration in standard (environmental benefit must be in addition to and not instead of lubricant performance) and to develop a flexible means of discriminating between product. The scheme is summarised in table. The scheme is based on the assumption that the major environmental impacts of lubricant will form an integral part of the development of product group criteria when these are finished by the relevant authorities.

Suggested product group criteria for an ecolabel for engine oil

Criterion	Baseline of performance	Increment	Factor	Maximum point	Total (%)
Lubricant classification	API SH ACEA TG2 or similar				
Oil consumption	Noack volatility <13%	1%	10	130	24.5
Composition	Zn<0.14%	0.01 %	3	42	8
	P<0.12%	0.01%	3	36	7
	S<1.5%				
	Cl<50ppm	lppm	1	50	9.5
	Heavy metal (Ba,Pb,Cr, Sn,Ni) not detectable				
Fuel efficiency	CEC Ml 1 1 or API sequence VI or equivalent	Tier	75	150	28
Biodegradability	Recongnised test ready biodegradation (e.g sturm test) giving >40% degradation	1%	2	120	23
Exotoxicity	EC or LC50 >200ppm				
PCA content of base	< lOppm by the grimmer method for individual caracinogenic PCAs				
PCB content	Not detectable				

It is said that conflict is one of the most effective stimuli to scientific research and new technology. Mankind has always been in conflict with the environment; it is only now that this realisation has set in, and that acid rain, CFCs, pesticides, etc. are recongnised as a major threat to the environment. The consequent need to minimise mankind effect on the environment has entered the consciousness of regulators all around the globe. Legislation is now being formulated ahead of current technology, with the stated aim of driving technology forward at a pace undreamt of even a few years ago.

17

Jatropha (Bio Diesel) Cultivation & Extraction

Process of Manufacture

Jatropha oilseed is having 35% to 40% oil. This can be extracted by screw press method or solvent extraction method. In the transesterification process extracted oils is allowed to react with methanol (or) ethanol with presence of NaOH/KOH catalyst for producing methyl ester (Bio-diesel, equal weight of Jatropha oil, 240 kg of methanol and 25kg of catalyst (NaOH or KOH) is required. 260 kg of glycerin, by-product of this process can be used to make ethanol which is re-used to make more bio-diesel, or it can be burned as a heating fuel. Oil cake which is the waste of oil extraction process can be used to produce animal feed or fertilizer.

The term biodiesel refers to the ethyl or methyl esters of vegetable oils. Chemically biodiesel is described as mono alkyl esters. Biodiesel is produced from any organic vegetable oils or animal fats which contain triglycerides, by a process of trans esterification. Biodiesel contain oxygen in their molecular structure. This is significantly advantageous to the burning process in an internal combustion engine, not only in improving the efficiency of the fuel but also in turning noxious oxides into less harmful dioxides (carbon and nitrogen) and thus avoids greenhouse gas accumulation. The presence of toxic substances render the oil non-edible and through recent technologies it could be converted into edible oil. In general, the oil is reported to be mixed with ground nut oil for adulteration. This indicates the possibilities of obtaining edible oil from jatropha oil base. The oil is being extensively used in wool spinning, cosmetics, soap, varnishes and candles making. The oil is used as an illuminant because it burns without emitting smoke and is being used as a lubricant also. At present, the Jatropha oil is being imported to meet the demand of the cosmetic industry. The protein content in Jatropha oil cake may be used as raw material for plastics and synthetic fibres. The oil cake contains rich source of nitrogen (3.2 to 4.4%), phosphorous (1.4 to 2.09%) and potassium (1.2 to 1.68%) and valued as organic manure. Though the cake contains 38 percent proteins, it is non-edible due to the presence of toxic substances and could be converted into cattle feed through latest technologies. Jatropha oil cake can, hopefully replace synthetic fertilizers.

Plant Economics of
Jatropha (Bio-Diesel) Cultivation & Extraction

Rated Plant Capacity	=	1 MT/Day
LAND & BUILDING (Land Area 1 Acre)	=	Rs. 13,80,000.00

PLANT & MACHINERY

1. Oil extraction plant
2. Bio-diesel plant
3. Erection & Electricals

FIXED CAPITAL

1. LAND & BUILDING	Rs.	13,80,000.00
2. PLANT & MACHINERY	Rs.	49,00,000.00
3. OTHER FIXED ASSETS	Rs.	4,85,000.00
TOTAL	Rs.	67,65,000.00

RAW MATERIALS

1. Barrels
2. Jatropha seeds
3. Methanol ink
4. Sodium hydroxide

TOTAL WORKING CAPITAL/MONTH

1. RAW MATERIAL	Rs.	4,15,000.00
2. SALARY & WAGES	Rs.	1,21,250.00
3. UTILITIES & OVERHEADS	Rs.	51,500.00
TOTAL	Rs.	5,87,750.00

TOTAL CAPITAL INVESTMENT

TOTAL FIXED CAPITAL	Rs.	67,65,000.00
TOTAL WORKING CAPITAL FOR 3 MONTHS	Rs.	17,63,250.00
TOTAL	Rs.	85,28,250.00

TURN OVER/ANNUM

1. By sale of 300 Mt of Bio-diesel
2. By sale of 70 Mt of Glycerin
3. By sale of 620 Mt. of oilcake

TOTAL Rs. 1,16,26,000.00

PROFIT SALES RATIO = Profit / Sales x 100 = 19%

RATE OF RETURN = Operating profit / T.C.I x 100 = 25%

BREAK EVEN POINT (B.E.P) = 60%

18

Crude Oil Bleaching for Petroleum Jelly

Techniques of Manufacturing Process

The basic raw material for white oil is obtained from petroleum refineries. In petroleum refineries the crude oil is distilled in two stages. In the first stage distillation is done at atmospheric pressure. From the first stage kerosene oil, diesel, etc, are distilled. All the distillates obtained from this atmospheric distillation have less dielectric constant and high viscosity. For this reason these are not suitable for manufacturing white oil. In the second stage the distillation in conducted under reduced pressure. By this distillation, the distillates obtained have higher dielectric constant and lower viscosity.

The heavy neutral cut obtained from the second stage distillation is well suitable for manufacturing the white oil. Heavy neutral cut contain's some higher acid, wax materials, sulfur and their compounds etc. So to convert this cut in to white oil all the above impurities have to be removed. This is done in three steps as discussed below:

Speciality oils are those oils which are used in applications generally not directly connected with lubrication. With the increasing special needs and complexity of modern industry, more and more of special fuction oriented petroleum products are assuming increasing importance.

In the manufacture of most of the speciality oil, the main process is to react a carefully selected base stock of appropriate viscosity with either concentrated sulphuric acid or oleum depending upon the degree of refinement required, and then treating the acid refined oil with clay.

Acid Treatment:-

The acid treatment process consist essentially of treating the base - stock with concentrated sulphuric acid or oleum. The sludge formed is allowed to settle and removed. The acidic oil is then neutralized with alkali usually soda ash. The neutralized oil is either washed with water to remove sodium sulphate, oil-soluble sulphonates and other impurities or, if the oil-soluble sulphonates are to be recovered as a by-product, the oil is extracted with solvent such as ethyl alcohol, isopropyl alcohol or acetone. The solvent, usually isopropyl alcohol, removes sodium petroleum sulphonates, sodium sulphate and other impurities. Sodium salts of oil-soluble sulphonates may be recovered by evaporating the solvent. The solvent is condensed and reused. The washed or solvent extracted oil is then given a finishing treatment with clay.

Reaction and Purpose:-

The reaction of concentrated sulphuric acid or oleum with petroleum constituents is an exothermic and irreversible reaction. Oleum or acid acts like an acidic sulphonating, polymerizing, alkylating precipitating, oxydizing and solvent refining agent. Petroleum products are acid treated for the following reasons.

1. To remove straight chain unsaturated compounds.
2. To remove aromatic compounds.
3. To remove sulphur, nitrogen and oxygen containing compounds.
4. To remove wax.
5. To remove asphaltic and resinous products.

Temperature:-

It has been mentioned that sulphonation is an exothermic and irreversible reaction. The rate of reaction doubles approximately for each rise of temperature by 10°C. Higher temperature favours the formation of oversulphonated materials and products of side reactions and hence the quality is affected.

If maximum decolourization is desired, the lowest practical temperature should be used. It is impossible to produce good colour if the temperature exceeds approximately 60°C because the colouring substances which are formed by oxidation are soluble in the oil and will darken it. If on the other hand the principle objective is the separation of usaturated and asphaltic substance higher temperatures should be used.

The viscosity and pour point will determine the minimum operating temperature. The oil should be brought to the desired temperature at the time of settling and washing is generally kept higher (20-25°C higher) than at the start of rection for better settling and washing.

Plant Economics of Crude Oil Bleaching for Petroleum Jelly

Rated Plant Capacity	= 2 MT/Day
LAND & BUILDING (Land Area 1500 sq.mt.)	= Rs. 22,90,000.00

PLANT & MACHINERY

1. Acid treatment tank
2. Clay treatment kettle.
3. Fraction receiving still
4. Acid neutralizing and washing kettle

5. Condenser
6. Acid settling kettle
7. Alkali settling kettle
8. Oil Cooling kettle
9. Crude oil storage tank
10. Acid storage tank
11. Heating furnace
12. White oil storage tank
13. Vacuum pump
14. Filtering unit
15. D.G.Set
16. Motor-pumps & piping
17. Effluent treatment unit

Fixed Capital

1. LAND & BUILDING	Rs.	22,90,000.00
2. PLANT & MACHINERY	Rs.	14,20,000.00
3. OTHER FIXED ASSETS	Rs.	9,70,000.00
TOTAL	Rs.	46,80,000.00

Raw Materials

1. Petroleum crude oil
2. Fumming sulphuric acid
3. Fuller Earth
4. Activated Carbon
5. Alkali
6. Misc. Chemicals & Additives.

Total Working Capital/Month

1. RAW MATERIAL	Rs.	5,15,500.00
2. SALARY & WAGES	Rs.	88,800.00
3. UTILITIES & OVERHEADS	Rs.	72,500.00
TOTAL	Rs.	6,76,800.00

Total Capital Investment

TOTAL FIXED CAPITAL	Rs.	46,80,000.00
TOTAL WORKING CAPITAL FOR 1 MONTH	Rs.	6,76,800.00
TOTAL	Rs.	53,56,800.00

Turn Over/Annum

By sales of 600 MT. of white oil	Rs.	1,20,00,000.00

PROFIT SALES RATIO = Profit / Sales x 100 = 22%

RATE OF RETURN = Operating profit / T.C.I x 100 = 50%

BREAK EVEN POINT (B.E.P) = 42%

19

Soluble Cutting Oil

FORMULATIONS OF SOLUBLE CUTTING OIL

FORMULATION NO-1

	Parts/Wt	Parts/Wt	%age
1. Sodium Petroleum Sulphonate	15-30	23	27.38
2. Fatty acid Viz; Stearic Acid etc.	20-30	25	29.77
3. Potassium rosinate/ Glycerol Monostearate	15	15	17.87
4. Potassium Hydroxide	5	5	5.93
5. Mineral Oil (Turpentine Oil)	15	15	17.86
6. Water	1	1	1.19
Total		84	100.00

FORMULATION NO-2

	Parts/Wt
1. Sodium Petroleum Sulphonate or Sodium Mohogany Sulphonate	15-30
2. Potassium Rosinate	15
3. Mineral lubricating oil	20-00
4. Potassium Hydroxide	0.01 -0.5
5. Hexylene Glyco	12.5 - 3.5
6. Sulfurized Alkyl Ester of Fatty Acid	20-30
7. Water	0.01- 0.5

FORMULATION -NO- 3

	% age
1. Mineral Oil	88
2. Oleic Acid	8
3. Triethanolamine	3.9
4. Water	Variable

FORMULATION- NO-4

Sulfonated base soluble cutting oil

Sulfonated oil (caster oil and Corn oil)	12.5 kg
Paraffin oil (80 SUS at 100°F)	17.0 kg
Caustic soda (10° be)	4.5 kg
Sulfonated caster oil	25.0 kg
Water	32.0 kg

FORMULATION NO-5

	Parts/Wt
1. Paraffin Oil	250
2. Lard Oil	15
3. Oleic Acid	40
4. Alcohol	10
5. Caustic Soda	4
6. Water	12

FORMULATION NO-6

	Parts/Wt
1. Chlorinated Paraffin Wax	3.5
2. Chlorinated dibenzyl disulphide	4.6
3. Sulphurized Oil	3.5-5.0
4. Mineral Oil	Small Quantity

Other Formulations of Soluble Cutting Oil

Sulfonated Based Soluble Cutting Oil

Cutting oil	:	12.5 Kgs
Paraffin oil	:	17.0 Kgs
Caustic soda	:	4.5 Kgs
Sulfonated castor oil	:	25.0 Kgs
Water	:	32.0 Kgs

The mineral oil and sulfonated castor oil (25 Kgs) are stirred together in a kettle. The caustic solution is then added and the temperature brought to 210°C. The batch is allowed to stand overnight. The sulfonated castor and corn oil (12.5 Kgs) are then mixed in. A sample may then be tested to determine whether the oil is perfectly soluble or not. If not, more caustic soda may be added. If a sample on chilling does not show cloudiness or separation, the final water may be mixed in, completing the process.

Formulations of Other Soluble Oil

1.	Naphthene sulfuric acid	:	15 g
	Olein	:	5 - 7 g
	Spindle oil, refined, (60°C)	:	75 g
	Caustic Potash : until neutralise		
	Hexalin & tetralin (1:1)	:	3 - 4 g.
2.	Spindle oil	:	100 Kgs
	Oleic acid	:	12 Kgs.
	Butanol	:	7 Kgs.
	Triethanolamine	:	0.5 Kgs
	Caustic Potash (38° Be')	:	4.5 Kgs

Heat the oil to about 70°C, add the butanol, and to this add triethanolamine. Add the lye and leave standing hot to clarify.

3.	Alcohol	:	15
	Diglycol lamate	:	85
	Mineral oil	:	400
4.	Mineral oil	:	32
	Oleic acid	:	10
	Alcohol	:	3
	Trigamine	:	5

The above are thoroughly mixed cold and forms a clear transparent oil which readily emulsify on pouring in to water with slight stirring.

5. Spindle oil, refined (20°C)	:	50 Kgs
Oleic acid distilled	:	20 Kgs
Sodium hydroxide (29° Be')	:	About 12.5 Kgs
Alcohol to make clear	:	About 12.5 Kgs
6. a. Mineral oil (spindle oil)	:	80 g
Tall oil	:	20 g
b. Caustic potash (40° Be')	:	6 g
c. Methyl hexalin	:	1-2 g

'a' is saponified with 'b', the resulting contains creamy mass which is cleared with 'c'.

7. Paraffin oil (26 to 30° Be)	:	250 g
Rosin	:	22 g
Oleic acid	:	22 g
Caustic soda	:	3 g
Water	:	10 g
Alcohol	:	7 g

Oil-in-Water Based Cutting Oil Emulsifier

(Oil in Water Emulsion)

Sodium corn oil soap	:	14 %
Water	:	6 %
Mineral oil	:	64
Rosin	:	10
Carbitol	:	2
Diethylene glycol	:	4

Aqueous emulsions of this oil are stable even at 95°C stable aqueous emulsions are prepared by using 1-35 % of the oil. The oil is clear and will not become cloudy when cooled to a temperature of 15°C. It will not be covered by a solid film after standing exposed to the air at a temperature of 30°C over a long period of time or at 95°C for one day. It will readily emulsify with water even after standing exposed to the air at 95°C for two days. Aqueous emulsifier containing this oil are stable even at a temperature of 200°F.

Cutting and Cooling Oil Emulsifier :-

Mineral oil	:	50-60 %
Sulfurized lard oil	:	1-20

Diethalylene glycol	:	0.5-3
Water	:	1-3
Mahogany soaps	:	1-30
Rosin	:	0.5-10
Caustic soda	:	0.6

Soluble Cutting oil No. 1 :-

Mineral oil	:	94
Emulsifier "Ethomen" S/15 & S/12 (Ethoxylated aliphatic amines)		6

Soluble Cutting Oil No. 2 :-

Mineral oil	:	95.0
"Ethomen" S/12	:	2.0
"Arquad" 2 C (Quanternary ammonium salt)	:	2.5

Chlorinated Cutting Oil :-

Coconut oil	:	5 gallons
Light Paraffin oil	:	3.5"
Aqua ammonia (28 %)	:	1"
Chloronaphthalene	:	0.25 Kgs
Caustic soda (40° Be)	:	3.0 Kgs

Five gallons of commercial mixed coconut fatty acids, 3.5 gallons of a paraffin oil, 3 Kgs of caustic soda (40° Be) and 0.25 Kgs. of chloro naphthalene are mixed thoroughly at room temperature or slightly above and then one gallon of aqua ammonia is gradually stirred into the above mixture. The ammonia forms soaps with coconut oil fatty acids. After all ammonia has been stirred in, stirring may be continued for few minutes and the product is then ready for use as a cutting oil base.

Sulfurized Cutting Oil

(U.S. Patent 1,604,068)

Sulfur monochloride	:	7
Mineral spindle oil	:	100
Caustic soda (35° Be)	:	10

7 % of sulfur monochloride is added to mineral spindle oil followed by addition of 10 % caustic soda 135° Be and the temperature is raised to 170°F.

The mixture is agitated by air until all gases are removed. The resultant cutting oil emulsifier compound is superior to lard oil for cutting and threading iron & steel.

The formulations given above are just for illustration. Various other formulations can be developed along these limes by changing the constituents and by a little bit for experimentations.

Formulation of Cutting Oil Base

	Parts/Wt.
Ammonium laurate (commercial) (in paste form)	183
Mineral turpentine oil	366
Pine oil	183

183 parts of commercial ammonium laurate in paste form are dissolved in 366 parts of mineral turpentine oil and 183 parts of pine oil, all parts being by weight and the mixture is warmed slightly until the ammonium laurate dissolves. 1 1/2 lb. of resulting emulsifier base are incorporated into 16 gallons of sulfurized cutting oil to produce finished cutting oil emulsifier ready for use.

Other Formulations of Cutting Oil

	Parts by Wt.
1. Tall oil	32
Caustic potash (45 %)	8
Tertiary butyl alcohol	8
Mineral oil	192
2. Potassium rosin soap	45 lb.
Glyceryl monoleate	35 lb.
Red oil soap	5 lb.
Water	7 1/2 lb.

Stable Aqueous Cutting Oil

In general, stable aqueous emulsion are prepared by using 1 % to 35 % of this oil, although stable aqueous emulsion can be prepared by using proportions of the oil outside these limits.

	Parts
1. Potash soap	30
Olein	7
Paraffin oil	32
Cyclohexanol	2

2.	Potash soap	32
	Turpentine	60
	Olein	6
	Methyl hexalin	2
3.	Aerosol OT	2 Oz.
	Diglycol laurate	28 Oz.
	Mineral oil	170 Oz.
4.	Naphthenic acid	14 lb.
	Oleic acid	11 lb.
	Spindle oil or refined gas oil	50 lb.
	Caustic soda (24° Be') about	12-5 lb.
	Alcohol, Denature	12-5 lb.
5.	Machine oil	70 lb.
	Naphthenic acid	20 lb.
	Caustic soda (d-1.3)	6 lb.
	Glyceryl	4 lb.
6.	Naphthenic acid	20 lb.
	Caustic potash (d 1045)	18 lb.
	Water	12 lb.
	Machine oil	50 lb.
7.	Naphthenic acid	20 lb.
	Caustic soda (d-1.30)	10 lb.
	Machine oil	40 lb.
	Water	30 lb.
8.	Oleic acid	6 1/2
	Polyethylene glycol	
	600 dioleate	12 1/2
	Caustic soda (25 % soln.)	2
	Diethylene glycol	2
	Isopropyl alcohol	3

Add and mix in the given order. 85 % of mineral oil is mixed with 15 % of the above mixer.

Soluble Cutting Oil for Cutting Edges, Drills etc.

1.	Olein	16 g
	Spindle oil, refined	73 g
	Caustic soda (36° Be')	6 g
	Alcohol, denatural	5 g
2.	Olein	20 g
	Spindle oil, refined	72 g
	Caustic potash (40° Be')	8 g
3.	Tall oil refined	20 g
	Spindle oil refined	70 g
	Caustic potash (36° Be')	10 g
4.	Tall oil, refined	20 g
	Spindle oil refined	72 g
	Caustic soda (36° Be)	8 g
5.	Naphthenic or hydroxy fatty acid	12 g
	Spindle oil, refined	80 g
	Caustic soda (36° Be')	6 g
	Benzoline	2 g.
6.	Turkey red oil	15 g
	Olein	10 g
	Spindle oil refined	65 g
	Caustic potash (40° Be')	10 g
7.	Olein	18 g
	Spindle oil refined	45 g
	Caustic potash (40° Be)	7 g
	Water	30 g

The amount of caustic must be varied since the saponificable materials are not constant in acidity.

For formulae 1 to 6 the following procedure is applied.

Put the saponificable raw materials in the kettle, together with 50 - 70 % of the spindle oil. Heat upto 90 - 100°C, and stir in the alkali thoroughly.

Boil with good continuous stirring. The saponification can be considered finished, when the oils look homogeneous and do not thicken any further.

Then add the remainder of the spindle oil, which may be heated previously to about 60°C.

Carry on heating and stirring until homogeneous.

If addition of alcohol is interaded, it should be done together with alkali, because it helps the saponification. However, most of the alcohol is evaporated in this way and does not form a component of the formula.

If alcohol, benzoline, hexalin are wanted in oil, they ought to be added to the finished, cooled oil. It should be kept in mind that a part of the water of the lye evaporates during the manufacture. Thus it might happen that the finished products gelatinize and of course, there is less yield. The evaporated water, therefore ought to be substituted either by adding enough water to the lye, or by introducing small portions of hot water during the manufacture. About 50 % water (on the base of amount of lye) are sufficient in most cases, depending, however, upon the method of manufacture.

If too much water can be eliminated by boiling. There should be only so much water left in the finished product that no cloudiness can be observed. Otherwise, the finished oil may separate into layers. However, the addition of alcohols, hexalin are tends to counter act such a separation.

Formula 7 is manufactured in the same, but hot way.

8. Glyceryl monostearate	75 g
Sperm oil	150 g
Sodium salt or sulphonated	
oleyl alcohol	50 g
Water	1200 c.c.

The above are warmed and mixed vigorously.

Hard Water Stable Soluble Cutting Oil

These are stirred while heating until saponification is completed.

1. Red oil	6 parts
Rozolin	8 parts
Caustic soda (35° Be')	4 parts
Cellosolve	4 parts
Mineral oil	78 parts
2. Rosin 5 parts	
Caustic soda (35° Be')	3.6 parts
Butyl cellosolve	3.4 parts
Mineral oil	78 parts

3.	Rozolin	12 parts
	Paraffin oil (28° Be')	81 parts
	Caustic soda (35° Be')	3.6 parts
	Alcohol	3.4 parts
4.	Castor oil	10 parts
	Rozolin	6 parts
	Mineral oil	45.4"
	Degras	1.7"
	Water	45.4"
	Caustic potash (35° Be')	9.5"

The above are mixed with 3 to 10 times as much water before using. They are stable in presence of HARD WATER.

Rosin Soluble Cutting Oil

Rosin	7.5 lb
100 Vis spindle oil	2.5 gal.
Oleic acid	6.0 lb.
100 Vis. spindle oil	5.5 gal.
Caustic soda (32° Be)	4.0 lb.
Alcohol	2.1 lb.
Yield	10 gal.

Heat the rosin with the first portion of the spindle oil at a temperature of about 212°F. until former is melted, then add the other ingredients in the order listed. The alcohol should be added when the batch has been cooled to room temperature.

Mineral Oil Emulsion Using Trihydroxyl Ethylamine Stearate (T.S.)

T.S. is melted with oil and this added to water (preferably warm water) slowly while stirring vigorously with an electric mixer. Warm water and very rapid stirring produce uniformly stable emulsions.

Mineral oil	75 parts
Water	185 parts
T.S.	15 parts

Mineral oil Emulsion Using Diglycol Stearate (D.S.)

D.S.	10 parts
Mineral oil	50"
Water	500"

Oil is melted with D.S. The water is heated above at 65°C and added slowly while stirring vigorously. Continue stirring until cool. By varying the amounts of water, emulsions of varying consistency are obtained. They are white in colour and stable.

Emulsion Using Lubricating Oil/Fuel Oil

1. Fuel or lubricating oil	88
Triethanolamine oleate	6
Oleic acid	5 1/2
Water	90
2. Lubricating oil	89
Triethanolamine	2.1
Oleic acid	7
Water	100
3. Lubricating oil	89
Monoethanolamine	0.8
Oleic acid	7
Water	100

Other Cutting Oil Emulsions

1. Non Corrosive Cutting Oil:

Mineral oil	71-74 lb.
Castor oil	8 1/4 - 9 1/2 lb.
Rapseed oil	8 1/4 - 9 1/2 lb.
Caustic potash	8 1/4 - 9 1/2 lb.
Soda ash	0.6 - 1 1/4 lb.

The above are mixed and diluted with water.

2. Mineral oil	54.08
Palmoil fatty acid	7.28
Triethanolamine	3.64
Water	35.00

3. Cutting Oil Concentrated:

Pine oil	2.5
Red oil	12.0
Caustic potash	4
Alcohol anhydrous	5
Potassium oleo abietate	16 Oz.

The above possesses excellent self emulsifying properties:

4. Amino stearin	10
Mineral oil	75

This emulsion is stable to hard water and weal acids.

5. Non-Foaming Oil Emulsion:

Stearic acid	1 g
Oil soluble mahogamy sulfonate	99 g
Mineral oil	500 g
Water	5000 c.c.

Warm and mix first these ingredients until clear. Then, add water slowly with vigorous mining.

6. Mineral oil	75
Naphthanic acid sludge	25
7. Mineral oil	75
Naphthenic soap	25
8. Toll oil refined	20
Spindle oil refined	72
Caustic soda (38° Be')	8
Alcohol	to clear
Fatty acid a little	to clear

9.	No.1	No. 2	No. 3	No.4
Dresinate 81	3.76	—	—	—
Dresinate 91	—	5.91	4.05	—
Dresinate 95	—	—	—	11.00
Petroleum sulfonate	11.28	8.86	6.07	7.00
Diethylene glycol				
(coupling agent)	—	1.97	1.42	—
Hexylene glycol				

(coupling agent)	1.44	—	—	—
Water	0.8	—	0.5	—
KOH (45 %)	0.40	0.49	0.25	—
Mineral oil	80.00	80.8	86.05	82
Oleic acid	2.26	1.97	1.65	—

Weigh the dresinate and petroleum sulfonate into a weighed beaker of appropriate size. Add coupling agent and water and alkali as indicated. Swirl the breaker using heat (90°-110°F) if necessary. It is necessary this cloudy mixture is to be made uniform. Then drop in oleic acid from burette. As it clears, end point being approached.

Manufacturing Process of Emulsifiers for Cutting Oils

Chief amongst the emulsifiers used in soluble cutting oils are anionic like sodium petroleum sulphonates and sulfonated fatty oils such as sulfonated castor oil (Turkey red oil) and coconut oil. Other anionic emulsifiers used are sodium, potassium and amine soaps of fatty acids, alkyl sulphates, sulphated fatty oils and alkyl phosphates.

Manufacture of Turkey Red Oils :-

The name "Turkey Red Oil" has since been applied to sulphonated castor oil, which was first used in 1870.

These oils should contain the minimum of free SO_3. If the oil is not properly washed and settled after sulphonation, considerable amounts of ammonium or sodium sulphate will be present. The salts are determined as uncombined SO_3.

The reaction between any oil and sulphuric acid takes place in several ways, depending on the temperature, the intimacy with which the materials are brought into contact, and the time the major reaction results in a sulphated rather than a sulfonated product. With ordinary oils, sulfonation occurs at the double bonds of the fatty acids, resulting in triolein hydrogen sulphate. Further changes yield hydroxy compounds and lactones.

General Method :-

The sulphonation process consists of charging the oil into the sulphonator, which may be a steel jacketed, lead lined tank with an agitator, or a monel, lined tank which is found to be superior. The tank may be single sheel type, equipped with a non-corrodible cooling coil. The oil is agitated and cooled to room temperature or even lower. Concentrated sulfuric acid, 25 % on the weight of the oil, is added slowly. The temperature of the mixture is maintained below 100°F. Experience has shown that oils containing about 4 % of combined SO3 can be used for blending with either vegetable or mineral oil, whereas those that are more highly sulphonated do not blend.

If a blending oil is to be produced the entire amount of acid is added to the oil within 15-30 minutes, but for higher sulphonation the mixing will require a longer period.

Sometimes, after the reaction has taken place the mixture is allowed to stand for several hours for overnight. It is then into wash tank, which may be similar to the sulphonator tank. Here it is mixed with an equal volume of water and allowed to stand until the bath has separated into an oily top layer and a bottom layer consisting of an aqueous acid solution, which is drawn off. one or two washes with brine (1.5 lb. salt to a gallon) or glauber salt solution follow. Each time, the brine is simultaneously mixed with the oil and allowed to settle. The object is to wash out as much of the uncombined sulphuric acid as possible.

At this point manufacturers differ as to the mode of procedure, some neutralize with aqua ammonia, while others use 24 Be' solution of caustic soda, which is added with constant stirring, until a clear transparent oil results. The pH of this oil should be between 5 and 7. The finished oil should be allowed to stand several days before drawing off, in order to allow any water containing sulphates to settle out. The finished product usually contains about 35 % water.

Examples :-

Material Required:

Castor oil	1600 Kgs
Sulphuric acid (1.84 sq. gr.)	380 Kgs
Caustic soda (48° Be')	860 Kgs.

Method :-

200 Kgs of concentrated sulphuric acid is slowly added to castor oil (1600 Kgs.) with continuous stirring in about four and a half hour. The temperature of the mixture as maintained between 25-30°C by circulating water in cooling coils and/or jacket. After stirring 1 1/2 hours. Further, 130 Kgs. of sulphuric acid is added slowly and with continuous stirring in over 3 hours and the batch is allowed to stand for 13 hours without stirring. Finally a further quantity (50 Kgs) of sulfuric acid is added in about 1 hour and stirring is continued for another hour. The batch is then neutralized as quickly as possible by stirring with 40° Be' caustic soda (860 kgs). The temperature rise to 90 to 100°C. The batch should now show an acid reaction to phenolphthaline. Live steam is now passed in for 1/2 an hour. After standing overnight the aqueous salt layer is run off. The product is settle for 2 weeks, the aqueous layer is run off and it is then standardized by addition of requisite quantity of water.

Example 2 :-

Castor oil 2	70 Kgs
Sulfuric acid (1.84 sq.gr.)	60 Kgs
Soda ash	12.5 to 13.5 Kgs.

Method :-

Castor oil sulphonated with the usual precaution and after washing with cold water, it is treated with 12.5 to 13.5 Kgs. of soda ash dissolved in water until the product neutral. It is then heated with indirect steam to remove moisture. A viscous oil soluble in water is obtained.

Process Flow Sheet

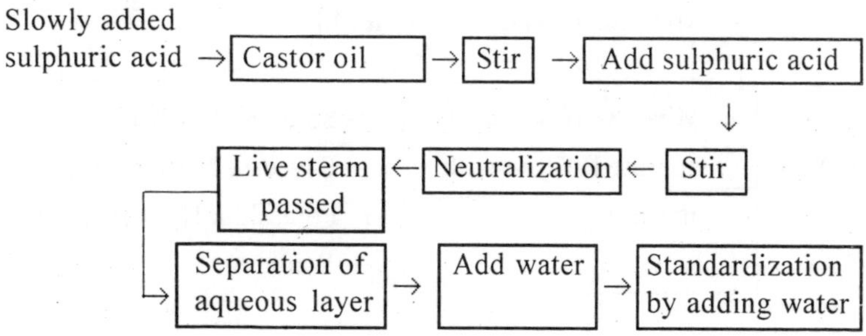

Manufacturing Process of Soluble Cutting Oil

As per Formulation: No-1

		%age
1.	Sodium Petroleum Sulphonate	27.38
2.	Fatty Acid Viz; Stearic Acid	29.77
3.	Glycerol Monostearate/ Potassium Rosinate	17.87
4.	Potassium Hydroxide	5.93
5.	Mineral Oil Viz; Turpentine oil	17.86
6.	Water	1.19

As per above formulation fatty acid viz stearic acid and mineral turpentine oil (Three fourth) in requisite quantities are introduced into a mixing kettle made of stainless steel (electrically operated) equipped with agitator of motor and the contents of the mixer are well stirred by means of the agitator till the mass is well homogenized to form a uniform of mass.

This is followed by addition of requisite quantitity of Sodium Petroleum Sulphonate.

Glycerol Monostearate and Potassium Hydroxide into the mixer and again the contents are well stirred until a homogenous solution is obtained. Water is then added .

This soluble oil base so obtained is then diluted with the remainder of mineral turpentine oil and stir this into the soluble oil base.

The contents are once again well stirred for about 1/2 hour, then finally the product is tested for quality, packed in suitable containers & stored/despatched for marketing.

Process Flow Diagram for the Manufacture of Soluble Cutting Oil

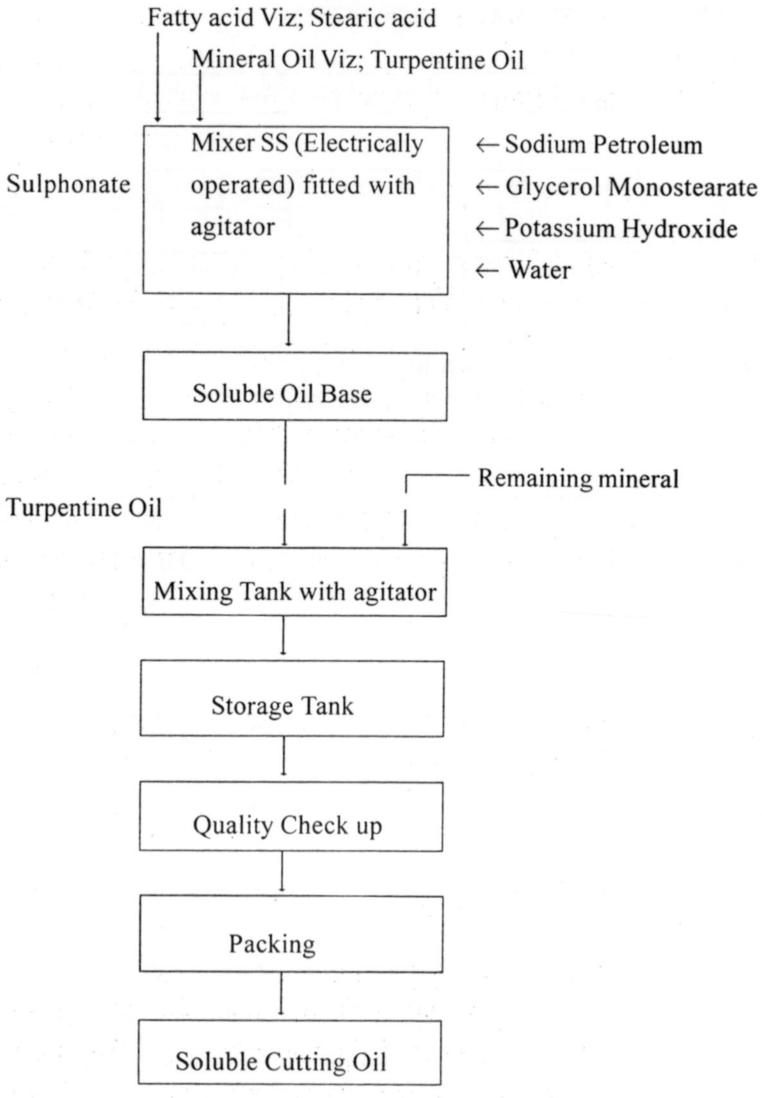

Plant Economics of Soluble Cutting Oil

Rated Plant Capacity	=	10 MT/Day
LAND & BUILDING (Land Area 5000 sq.mt)	=	Rs. 1,64,00,000.00

PLANT & MACHINERY

1. Mixing Kettle (SS)
2. Storage Tanks
3. Automatic Drum Filling Machine
4. Lab Testing Equipments
5. D.G.. Set
6. Material Handling Equipments
7. Instrumentation and Process Control Equipments
8. Miscellancous equipments viz. pipe fittings, valves, motors etc.

Fixed Capital

1.	LAND & BUILDING	Rs.	1,64,00,000.00
2.	PLANT & MACHINERY	Rs.	94,00,000.00
3.	OTHER FIXED ASSETS	Rs.	20,70,000.00
	TOTAL	Rs.	2,78,70,000.00

Raw Materials

1. Sodium Potassum Sulphonate
2. Fatty Acid viz; Stearic acid
3. Glycerol Monostearate
4. Potassium Hydroxide
5. Mineral Oil viz; Turpentine Oil
6. Packing Material

Total Working Capital/Month

1.	RAW MATERIAL	Rs.	1,42,29,240.00
2.	SALARY & WAGES	Rs.	3,37,820.00
3.	UTILITIES & OVERHEADS	Rs.	1,52,000.00
	TOTAL	Rs.	1,47,19,060.00

Total Capital Investment

TOTAL FIXED CAPITAL	Rs. 2,78,70,000.00
TOTAL WORKING CAPITAL FOR 1 MONTH	Rs. 1,47,19,060.00
TOTAL	Rs. 4,25,89,060.00

Turn Over/Annum

By sale of 3000 MT of Soluble Cutting oil	Rs. 21,00,00,000.00

PROFIT SALES RATIO = Profit / Sales x 100 = 12%

RATE OF RETURN = Operating profit / T.C.I x 100 = 58%

BREAK EVEN POINT (B.E.P) = 31%

20

Emulsifiers for Cutting Oils

Manufacturing Process for Cutting Oil Emulsifiers

Basis: 500 Kgs/day of cutting oil emulsifiers

Introduce requisite quantity of oleic acid (400 Kgs) and mineral turpentine oil (40 Kgs) into a mixing vessel made of stainless steel (electrically operated) equipped with agitator & motor.

The contents of the mixer are well stirred together by means of the agitator so as to obtain a uniform solution.

After a uniform and homogeneous mass is achieved, as per the formulation, triethanolamine in calculated quantity (20 Kgs) is added into the mixer and again the contents are well stirred until a clean solution is obtained.

However, some warning of the solution results during the reaction of the acid and other ingredients water in quantity sufficient may be added. This soluble oil base so obtained, is dilutable with the remainder of the mineral turpentine oil (440-40 = 400 Kgs) at any time. Simply stir the remaining 400 Kgs of mineral turpentine oil into the base.

The finally the cutting oil emulsifier is stored in a storage tank, and subsequently filled in suitable containers by means of filling machine and despatched for marketing.

Process Flow Diagram for the Manufacture of Cutting Oil Emulsifier

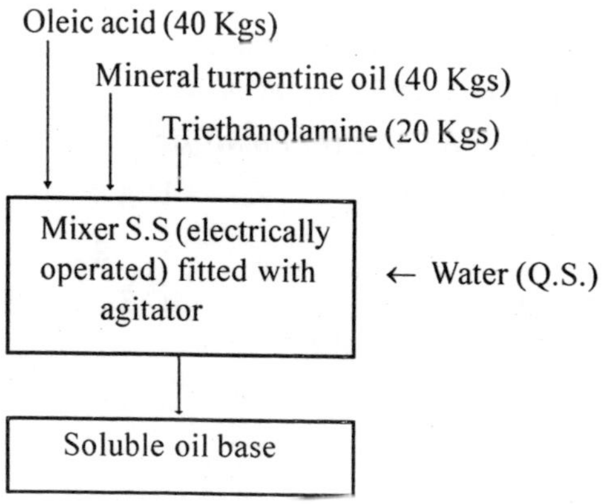

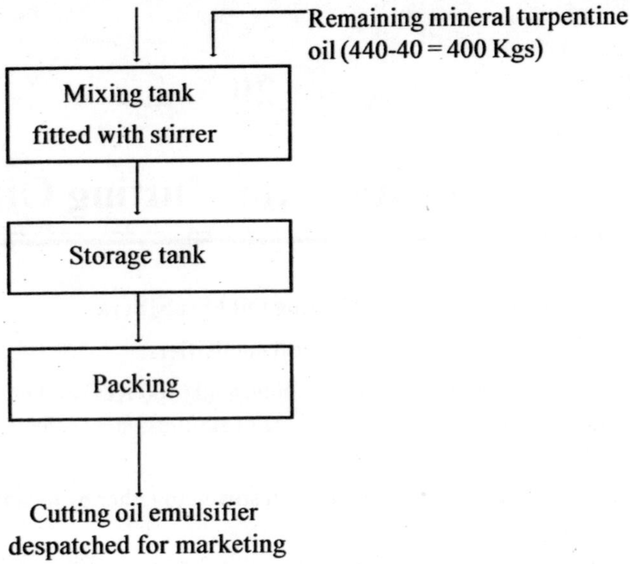

Sulfonated Based Soluble Cutting Oil Emulsifiers

Cutting oil	:	12.5 Kgs
Paraffin oil	:	17.0 Kgs
Caustic soda	:	4.5 Kgs
Sulfonated castor oil	:	25.0 Kgs
Water	:	32.0 Kgs

The mineral oil and sulfonated castor oil (25 Kgs) are stirred together in a kettle. The caustic solution is then added and the temperature brought to 210oC. The batch is allowed to stand overnight. The sulfonated castor and corn oil (12.5 Kgs) are then mixed in. A sample may then be tested to determine whether the oil is perfectly soluble or not. If not, more caustic soda may be added. If a sample on chilling does not show cloudiness or separation, the final water may be mixed in, completing the process.

Formulations of Other Soluble Oil Emulsifiers

1.	Naphthene sulfuric acid	:	15 g
	Olein	:	5 - 7 g
	Spindle oil, refined, (60°C)	:	75 g
	Caustic Potash : until neutralise		
	Hexalin & tetralin (1:1)	:	3 - 4 g.

2. Spindle oil	:	100 Kgs
Oleic acid	:	12 Kgs.
Butanol	:	7 Kgs.
Triethanolamine	:	0.5 Kgs
Caustic Potash (38° Be')	:	4.5 Kgs

Heat the oil to about 70°C, add the butanol, and to this add triethanolamine. Add the lye and leave standing hot to clarify.

3. Alcohol	:	15
Diglycol lamate	:	85
Mineral oil	:	400
4. Mineral oil	:	32
Oleic acid	:	10
Alcohol	:	3
Trigamine	:	5

The above are thoroughly mixed cold and forms a clear transparent oil which readily emulsify on pouring in to water with slight stirring.

5. Spindle oil, refined (20°C)	:	50 Kgs
Oleic acid distilled	:	20 Kgs
Sodium hydroxide (29° Be')	:	About 12.5 Kgs
Alcohol to make clear	:	About 12.5 Kgs

Formulation of Cutting Oil Emulsifier Base

	Parts/Wt.
Ammonium laurate (commercial) (in paste form)	183
Mineral turpentine oil	366
Pine oil	183

183 parts of commercial ammonium laurate in paste form are dissolved in 366 parts of mineral turpentine oil and 183 parts of pine oil, all parts being by weight and the mixture is warmed slightly until the ammonium laurate dissolves. 1 1/2 lbs of resulting emulsifier base are incorporated into 16 gallons of sulfurized cutting oil to produce finished cutting oil emulsifier ready for use.

Manufacturing Process of Emulsifiers for Cutting Oils

Chief amongst the emulsifiers used in soluble cutting oils are anionic like sodium petroleum sulphonates and sulfonated fatty oils such as sulfonated castor oil (Turkey red oil) and coconut oil. Other anionic emulsifiers used are sodium, potassium and amine soaps of fatty acids, alkyl sulphates, sulphated fatty oils and alkyl phosphates.

Manufacture of Turkey Red Oils :-

The name "Turkey Red Oil" has since been applied to sulphonated castor oil, which was first used in 1870.

These oils should contain the minimum of free SO_3. If the oil is not properly washed and settled after sulphonation, considerable amounts of ammonium or sodium sulphate will be present. The salts are determined as uncombined SO_3.

The reaction between any oil and sulphuric acid takes place in several ways, depending on the temperature, the intimacy with which the materials are brought into contact, and the time the major reaction results in a sulphated rather than a sulfonated product. With ordinary oils, sulfonation occurs at the double bonds of the fatty acids, resulting in triolein hydrogen sulphate. Further changes yield hydroxy compounds and lactones.

General Method :-

The sulphonation process consists of charging the oil into the sulphonator, which may be a steel jacketed, lead lined tank with an agitator, or a monel, lined tank which is found to be superior. The tank may be single sheel type, equipped with a non-corrodible cooling coil. The oil is agitated and cooled to room temperature or even lower. Concentrated sulfuric acid, 25 % on the weight of the oil, is added slowly. The temperature of the mixture is maintained below 100°F. Experience has shown that oils containing about 4 % of combined SO_3 can be used for blending with either vegetable or mineral oil, whereas those that are more highly sulphonated do not blend.

If a blending oil is to be produced the entire amount of acid is added to the oil within 15-30 minutes, but for higher sulphonation the mixing will require a longer period.

Sometimes, after the reaction has taken place the mixture is allowed to stand for several hours for overnight. It is then into wash tank, which may be similar to the sulphonator tank. Here it is mixed with an equal volume of water and allowed to stand until the bath has separated into an oily top layer and a bottom layer consisting of an aqueous acid solution, which is drawn off. one or two washes with brine (1.5 lb. salt to a gallon) or glauber salt solution follow. Each time, the brine is simultaneously mixed with the oil and allowed to settle. The object is to wash out as much of the uncombined sulphuric acid as possible.

At this point manufacturers differ as to the mode of procedure, some neutralize with aqua ammonia, while others use 24 Be' solution of caustic soda, which is added with constant stirring, until a clear transparent oil results. The pH of this oil should be between 5 and 7. The finished oil should be allowed to stand several days before drawing off, in order to allow any water containing sulphates to settle out. The finished product usually contains about 35 % water.

Examples :-

Material Required:

Castor oil	1600 Kgs
Sulphuric acid (1.84 sq. gr.)	380 Kgs
Caustic soda (48° Be')	860 Kgs.

Plant Economics of Emulsifier for Cutting Oil

Rated Plant Capacity	=	500 KGS/Day
LAND & BUILDING (Land Area 250 Sq.Mt.)	=	Rs. 7,67,500.00

PLANT & MACHINERY

1. Mixing vessel
2. Storage tanks
3. Mixing tank
4. Drum filling machine
5. Miscellaneous lab equipment
6. Instrumentation & process control
7. Miscellaneous viz. pipe fittings, valves, motors, etc.

Fixed Capital

1.	LAND & BUILDING	Rs.	7,67,500.00
2.	PLANT & MACHINERY	Rs.	4,75,000.00
3.	OTHER FIXED ASSETS	Rs.	1,71,000.00
	TOTAL	Rs.	14,13,500.00

Raw Materials

1. Mineral oil (turpentine oil)
2. Oleic acid
3. Triethanolamine
4. Packaging drums (polyethylene)

Total Working Capital/Month

1.	RAW MATERIAL	Rs.	3,15,500.00
2.	SALARY & WAGES	Rs.	63,973.00
3.	UTILITIES & OVERHEADS	Rs.	50,500.00
	TOTAL	Rs.	4,29,973.00

Total Capital Investment

TOTAL FIXED CAPITAL	Rs.	14,13,500.00
TOTAL WORKING CAPITAL FOR 3 MONTHS	Rs.	12,89,919.00
TOTAL	Rs.	27,03,419.00

Turn Over/Annum

By sale of cutting oil emulsifier

1,50,000 Kgs.	Rs.	75,00,000.00

PROFIT SALES RATIO = Profit / Sales x 100 = 22%

RATE OF RETURN = Operating profit / T.C.I x 100 x 61%

BREAK EVEN POINT (B.E.P) = 43%

21

Peroleum Jelly

Formulations

Synthetic petrolatum can be obtained by any one composition of following formulations :

1. Kella Brand Petroleum Jelly	
Pale Oil	72 %
Micro Crystalline Wax	17 %
Paraffin Wax chlorinated	14 %
2. Savite Chemical	
Oil	65 - 70 %
Micro crystalline Wax	10 - 15 %
Paraffin Wax	20 - 25 %
3. Bharat Petroleum Products	
Pale/white oil	70 %
Micro Crystalline Wax	20 %
Paraffin Wax	10 %
4. Petro Products Industries	
Mineral oil	79.7 %
Microcrystalline Wax	13.6 %
To cofferol (slabilit)	0.4 %
Paraffin Wax	6.3 %
5. Pan Industries	
Mineral Industrics	60 %
Microcrystalline Wax	10 %
Paraffin Wax	30 %
6. White Oil Pale Oil	300 kg
Micro crystalline Wax	100 kg
Paraffin Wax	50 kg
Clay	50 kg

The above formula is for 500 kg of petroleum jelly.

Process of Manufacture

The natural petrolatum is produced by fractional distillation of still residues from the steam distillation of paraffin base petroleum or from steam reduced crude oils from which the light fraction have been removed.

Manufacturing Process of Synthetic Petrolatum

Petrolatum or petroleum jelly can also be made synthetically by blending mineral oil and microcrystalline wax. Paraffin wax is also incorporated. The mineral oil used should be highly refined medicinal white oil (liquid paraffin) if the petroleum jelly is to be used in pharmaceuticals and cosmetics. For less critical application technical white oil or even less retained mineral oils can be used. The waxes should of food grade if the petroleum jelly is to be used in pharmaceuticals. Stabilizers are also added to keep the wax-oil blend from separating or deteriorating other wise.

Manufacture of synthetic jelly consists of mainly blending the direct constituents proper mixing of the constituents is very important to ensure proper stability of the wax-oil system. If the mixing is not proper the oil mill separate from the wax and render the petroleum jelly grainy. For proper mixing the mixing vessel may be rotated or agitation may be done with the help of a turbing.

The blending is done in a kettle provided with electrical heating device, steam heating coils or steam jacket. Microcrystalline wax and paraffin wax is melted and a temperature of 120 to 130°C is maintained, oil is added and the vessel is agitated at a speed of 150-200 r.p.m. to get the whole mass thoroughly mixed. The mixing is continued for 1-2 hours, if the oil is not fully refined white oil and the waxes are of high quality the petrolatum is directly packed.

The formulation adopted here for the production of synthetic petrolatum is :

Basis :	***500 kg***
White Oil/Pale oil	300 kg
Micro Crystalline Wax	100 kg
Paraffin Wax	50 kg
Clay	50 kg
Total	**500 kg**

Plant Economics of Petroleum Jelly

Rated Plant Capacity	=	500 Kg/Day
LAND & BUILDING (Land Area 300 sq. mt.)	=	Rs. 3,25,000.00

PLANT & MACHINERY

1. Pale/white oil storage tank
2. Steam jacketed vessels with stirring arrangement

3. Finished product storage tank
4. Other misc. including electrificati on installation office furniture and equipment technical know how

Fixed Capital

1.	LAND & BUILDING	Rs.	3,25,000.00
2.	PLANT & MACHINERY	Rs.	1,90,000.00
3.	OTHER FIXED ASSETS	Rs.	20,000.00
	TOTAL	Rs.	5,35,000.00

Raw Materials

1. White oil/pale oil
2. Microcrystalline wax
3. Paraffin wax
4. Clay

Total Working Capital/Month

1.	RAW MATERIAL	Rs.	2,73,500.00
2.	SALARY & WAGES	Rs.	30,191.00
3.	UTILITIES & OVERHEADS	Rs.	60,000.00
	TOTAL	Rs.	3,63,691.00

Total Capital Investment

TOTAL FIXED CAPITAL	Rs.	5,35,000.00
TOTAL WORKING CAPITAL FOR 1 MONTH	Rs.	3,63,691.00
TOTAL	Rs.	8,98,691.00

Turn Over/Annum

Sales of 150 M.T of jelly Rs. 52,50,000.00

PROFIT SALES RATIO = Profit / Sales x 100 = 13%

RATE OF RETURN = Operating profit / T.C.I x 100 = 76%

BREAK EVEN POINT (B.E.P) = 48%

22

Toluene and SBP from Crude Naphtha

Process of Manufacturing of Toluene

Toluene is produced from specially selected fractions of petroleum, rich in naphthenes, by catalytic reforming (also known as hydroforming). This involves catalytic dehydrogenation in the presence of hydrogen (which reduces coke formation) to yield a mixture of aromatic hydrocarbons, chiefly toluene.

The feed stock (a selected naphtha fraction) is preheated in heat exchangers and is then totally vaporized at 1,050°F in a furnace.

The reaction gases pass through heat exchangers (preheating the feed stock) to a gas-liquid condenser and separator. The remaining gas and liwuid pass to conventional absorption and stabilizing columns (fractionators), which produce fuel gas (butanes, etc.), gasoline, and hydroformate.

Two or more reactors are necessary for continuous operation. Generally, air is blend into an inert gas (mostly nitrogen and carbon dioxide) so that the mixture contains about 1.5 percent oxygen. The latter combines with the coke, forming carbon dioxide and water, while the inert gas removes the heat of combustion. As this mixture passes through the catalyst bed, the temperature is raised from 700° (inlet) to 1100°F.

The two-pass hydroformate (38 percent toluene) is fed to the toluene recovery plant, where it is distilled. The ketone-free toluene is then charged into a mixer, where it is washed with 98 percent sulfuric acid (about 5 lb per bbl), settled, water-washed, and caustic-washed to remove small amounts of olefins. The washed toluene is run to a refining column, where it is redistilled to produce nitration-grade toluene.

The methyl ethyl ketone recovery plant separates the ketone and non-aromatic hydrocarbons by countercurrent extraction with water.

Chemical Reaction:-

$$C_6H_{11}CH_3 \longrightarrow C_6H_5CH_3 + 3H_2$$

Methyl Cyclohexane Toluene - 80 - 90% Conversion.

Plant Economics of Toluene and SBP from Crude Naphtha

Rated Plant Capacity	=	250 MT/Day
LAND & BUILDING (Land Area 12000 sq. yd.)	=	Rs. 2,52,80,000.00

PLANT & MACHINERY

1. Crude Naphtha storage tank
2. Pump with motor
3. Fractional Distillation Column
4. Condenser
5. Solvent Collection tank
6. SBP solvent storage tank
7. Pump with motor
8. Pre-Heater or heat exchanger
9. Furnace (for complete vaporization)
10. Reactor
11. Condenser
12. Compressor operating pressure
13. Fractionations tower
14. Fuel gas compressor
15. Fuel gas holder
16. Gasoline storage tank
17. Distillation tower
18. Condenser for crude Benzene vapour condensation
19. Storage tank for crude benzene
20. Storage tank for crude Xylene
21. M.E.K. solvent storage tank
22. Water storage tank
23. Azeotrope Distillation tower
24. Azeotrope Distillation Tower for Ketone recovery
25. Storage tank
26. Pump with motor
27. Flash Tower
29. Mixing Tank
30. Sulphuric Acid storage tank
31. Caustic Soda solution preparation tank
32. Distillation and refining column
33. Effluent storage tank
34. Toluene storage tank
35. Pipes, Pumps, Valves, tanks,
    fittings, structures & miscellaneous equipments.

36. Instrumentations & Process control equipments, electrical fittings.
37. Laboratory Testing equipments
38. Boiler

Fixed Capital

1.	LAND & BUILDING	Rs.	2,52,80,000.00
2.	PLANT & MACHINERY	Rs.	6,77,60,000.00
3.	OTHER FIXED ASSETS	Rs.	2,05,00,000.00
	TOTAL	Rs.	11,35,40,000.00

Raw Materials

1. Crude Naphtha
2. Methyl Ethyl Ketone
3. Sulfuric acid
4. Caustic soda
5. Potassium Phosphate solution
6. Catalysts

Total Working Capital/Month

1.	RAW MATERIAL	Rs.	5,86,12,000.00
2.	SALARY & WAGES	Rs.	10,26,750.00
3.	UTILITIES & OVERHEADS	Rs.	89,10,000.00
	TOTAL	Rs.	6,85,48,750.00

Total Capital Investment

TOTAL FIXED CAPITAL	Rs.	11,35,40,000.00
TOTAL WORKING CAPITAL FOR 1 MONTH	Rs.	6,85,48,750.00
TOTAL	Rs.	18,20,88,750.00

Turn Over/Annum

1. By sale of SBP solvent 9000 MT.
2. By sale of Crude mix gasoline 13500 MT.
3. By sale of Fuel gas compressed 6300 Kl.

4. By sale of Crude Benzene 15500 Kl.
5. By sale of Crude Xylene 4500 Kl.
6. By sale of Crude Non-aromatics 28300 Kl.
7. By sale of toluene 12900 Kl.

TOTAL Rs. 11,19,00,000.00

PROFIT SALES RATIO = Profit / Sales x 100 = 22%

RATE OF RETURN = Operating profit / T.C.I x 100 = 136%

BREAK EVEN POINT (B.E.P) = 26%

23

White Oil from Kerosene Oil

Manufacturing Process

White oils are now prepared from paraffinic mixed case, or naphthenic fractions, the choice depending upon the final use; However, for many years, much of the production of white oils came from Russia, Chiefly because of the availability of suitable naphthenic stocks. American oils have been found to be entirely suitable for this purpose.

Naphthenic crudes give products of high specific gravity & viscosity, properties desired in pharmaceutical use, paraffinic stocks produce oils of lighter gravity and lower viscosity suitable for lubrication purposes. White oils should be free of odor and taste & should also be free of hydrocarbons unstable enough to develop them in storage. These properties are attained by the removal of oxygen, nitrogen & sulphur compounds and reactive hydrocarbons by drastic refining, almost universely by sulphuric acid.

The raw material, i.e. paraffinic oil, Kerosine oil is treated with sulphuric acid. Two main products are obtained. The lower layer consists of sulphuric acid and asphalt lake material or tar (sludge). It contains a group of water soluble sulphuric acids which are known as " green acids".

The upper oil layer contains, in addition to a certain amount of sulphur dioxide, the oil soluble sulphuric acids together us the water soluble sulphuric acids and a little far & asphalt like component in dispersed form.

The reaction sludge is drawn off promptly to limit oxidation reduction reactions. The oil layer is neutralized with 20 percent caustic soda solution and washed with ethyl or 150 propyl alcohol or acetone to remove the oil soluble sulfonic acids. The water soluble "green" acids are recovered from the alkali washings. The refined & decolorized by adsorption, either by percolation or connecting with fuller's earth, bentonite etc.

As a by-product, mahagony sulphonates are extracted with alcohol. Since, the asphaltic components remain mainly in the sulphonate, this is coloured a deep red brown. the mayegany sulphonates are used as additives, corrosion inhibitors, detergents for lubricating oils & heating oils etc. In recent times, the demand for such sulphonates has been growing continuously. Hence, it may also be fromed benificial apart to white oils.

Plant Economics of White Oil from Kerosene Oil

Rated Plant Capacity	= 800 Lits/Day
LAND & BUILDING (Land Area 1000 sq. mt.)	= Rs. 17,15,000.00

PLANT & MACHINERY

1. Storage tank
2. Mixing tank
3. Neutralization tank
4. Filters
5. Clay Treatment Unit
6. Lab. Equipments
7. Miscellaneous (pump, pipe fitting etc.)

Fixed Capital

1. LAND & BUILDING	Rs.	17,15,000.00
2. PLANT & MACHINERY	Rs.	9,05,000.00
3. OTHER FIXED ASSETS	Rs.	2,60,000.00
TOTAL	Rs.	28,80,000.00

Raw Materials

1. Kerosene oil
2. Miscellaneous (Sulphuric acid, Caustic Soda, fullers earth and other chemicals and packaging materials)

Total Working Capital/Month

1. RAW MATERIAL	Rs.	1,57,000.00
2. SALARY & WAGES	Rs.	94,297.00
3. UTILITIES & OVERHEADS	Rs.	1,03,750.00
TOTAL	Rs.	3,55,047.00

Total Capital Investment

TOTAL FIXED CAPITAL	Rs.	28,80,000.00
TOTAL WORKING CAPITAL FOR 1 MONTH	Rs.	3,55,047.00
TOTAL	Rs.	32,35,047.00

Turn Over/Annum

By Sales of white oil 240 Tons Rs. 60,00,000.00

PROFIT SALES RATIO = Profit / Sales x 100 = 15%

RATE OF RETURN = Operating profit / T.C.I x 100 = 29%

BREAK EVEN POINT (B.E.P) = 66%

24

Transformer Oil

Manufacturing Process of Transformer Oil

(A) For Transformer Oil Blending

Base oils and requisite additives in requisite quantities as per the following formulation are introduced into the blender or blending kettle (ms, glass fibre lining) fitted with agitator.

Formulation :-

Base oil 88%, Additives 12%.

The entire mass in the blender is well stirred till a thorough blending operation has been accomplished. However, samples are withdrawn from the blender for quality control check up.

The product is transferred to the finished product storage tanks (ms). Subsequently, the blended Transformer oil is transferred to the automatic filling unit and is then ready for despatch.

Transformer oils are used in transformers to dissipate heat and also to act as insulant. The electrical propely required of such an oil is high electric strength and from this point of view, refining of the mineral oil is not as important as that the oil should be free of insoluble impurities such as water and fibre, the combined effect of which is far greater than either alon. For transformer oil a typical minimum electric strength of 100 KV/CM is normal with 50 cycle AC. A simple test for water is the "Crackle" test in wich about 10 ml. of oil is placed in a dry test tube and heated in a silent flame, absence of crackle indicates less than about 50 p.p.m. Water.Specific heat of all mineral oils is similar, about 0.45, so that this factor can be neglected in the choice of an oil to meet the heat dissipation requirement. Cooling is effected by convection, the efficiency being mainly governed by viscosity of the oil. Although only a maximum is laid dowr for most specifications, for safety reasons, of a minimum flash point. Furthe requirements of a transformer oil are low pour point, to cover the contingencie of climatic variations, and freedom from corrosive sulphur compounds.

Compliance with the latter is readily checked by inspecting for stains a piece of polished copper strip which has been immersed in the oil at an elevatec temperature, the British Specification stipulates 3 hours at 1000C.

Life of an oil in service depends on its quality and the operating conditions Normally fifteen years or more is expected, during which time it is subjected t conditions conducive to deterioration, namely, temperatures in the region of 70 to 900C., sometimes contact with atmospheric oxygen, although this is largely avoided in well-designed larger tranformers, and contact with copper and iron , which are oxidation catalysts. Products of oils oxidation range from water and volatile aldehydes, ketones and the lower organic acids, to high molecular weight condensation and polymerization products ,some of which are oil-insoluble . The volatile compounds tend to condense on metal surfaces above the level of the oil and cause corrosion,water, acids and peroxides attack the insulation and protective materials such as cellulose, varnish, paint,paper etc. the polar compounds, water in particular,together with fibres from deteriorated insulating material decrease the electric strength, reduced heat transfer results from accumulation of oil-insoluble, sludge in the cooling ducts and on the core and winding. Reduction of heat transfer leads to overheating of the core and windings which, even if it does not cause complete failure of the transformer, raises the temperature of the oil further accelerates the oxidation process. Oxidation stability of a new oil is usually quoted in terms of acidity developed and sludge which can be precipitated after an accelerated laboratory oxidation procedure which involves heating the oil for a specified period in the presence of air or oxygen, with or without catalyst.

Development of acidity equivalent to 1 mg. KOH/g is usually taken as indicative of the end of the useful life of an oil.

Transformer oils are most readily refined from wax-free naphthenic type petroleum distillates, wax-free because of the low pour point requirement and naphthenic because this type is most amenable to solvent refining. This latter is more usual, as oxidation stability requirements can be readily met by this treament whereas sulphuric acid refining directed to give an oil with a low sludging value can produce an oil provc to high acidity development. Raffinate obtained from the solvent extraction process is given a light contacting with activated clay before final dehydration treatment which may be by further filtration or by use of vacuum. The letter is usually considered preferable since it remove, in addition to suspended water, much of the dissolved water. A typical figure for water solubility in transformer oil is 40 p.p.m. at 200C. It is essential to prevent the ingress of moisture to bulk storage and transport vessels by the fitting of silica gel or similar type breathers. Extension of life of a transformer oil can be effected in a number of ways,such as reduction in access of air to transformer, reduction in catalystic effects, reclamation of used oils, and use of oxidation inhibitors. Contact of the oil with atmospheric oxygen can be minimized by the fitting of a conservator tank so that the expansion and contraction which takes place during load cycles occurs in a confined space i,e. in the auxilliary tank containing relatively cold oil. Only the small surface are of oil in the latter tank is in contact with the atmosphere. Alternatively, complete nitrogen blanketing can be resorted to Improved service can be obtained by protection of constraction material with paints varnishes etc. Which are resistant to the action of oil and its oxidation products. In this way catalystic effects can be reduced.

Reclamation of used transformer oil has been given considerable attention by some of the largest users. Procedures used. Consist essentially of a preliminary removal of suspended material, followed by removal or attempted removal of oxidation products and finally, dehydration and degassing. Suspended matter and free water can be removed by filtration and centrifuging. Sulphuric acid and other chemical treatments have been used for re-refining but generally, either percolation or contacting with an activated clay or alumina is used. The extra lease of life given to the oil depends on its initial condition and expense of the treatment given (two-stage contacting gives better results than one-stage), but the most that can be expected is an increase equivalent to half that of the original newly refined oil. Inhibitors which have been found acceptable include phenyl-@ and phenyl-b-naphthylamine.

IS : 335. Insulating oil for Transformer.

IS : 12819. Transformer oils feed Stock/Base Stock.

Plant Economics of Transformer Oil

Rated Plant Capacity = 5 KLS/Day

LAND & BUILDING (Land Area 1500 sq.mt.) = Rs. 29,00,000.00

PLANT & MACHINERY

1. Dehydrator with coil and agitator
2. Storage Vessel
3. Acid treatment tank
4. Neutralizer/water wash tanks
5. Deparaffinator with agitator
6. Clay treatment tank
7. Filter press
8. Blending tank
9. Compressor
10. Heating equipments
11. Lab equipments
12. Miscellaneous

Fixed Capital

1. LAND & BUILDING	Rs. 29,00,000.00
2. PLANT & MACHINERY	Rs. 12,55,000.00
3. OTHER FIXED ASSETS	Rs. 7,00,000.00
TOTAL	Rs. 48,55,000.00

Raw Materials

1. Base Strock
2. Sulphuric Acid
3. Caustic soda
4. Clay
5. Solvent
6. Miscellaneous

Total Working Capital/Month

1. RAW MATERIAL	Rs.	15,42,500.00
2. SALARY & WAGES	Rs.	1,36,990.00
3. UTILITIES & OVERHEADS	Rs.	2,96,000.00
TOTAL	Rs.	19,75,490.00

Total Capital Investment

TOTAL FIXED CAPITAL	Rs.	48,55,000.00
TOTAL WORKING CAPITAL FOR 1 MONTH	Rs.	19,75,490.00
TOTAL	Rs.	68,30,490.00

Turn Over/Annum

By sale of 1500 KL of Transformer oil per annum Rs. 3,75,00,000.00

PROFIT SALES RATIO = Profit / Sales x 100 = 33%

RATE OF RETURN = Operating profit / T.C.I x 100 = 182%

BREAK EVEN POINT (B.E.P) = 22%

25

Biodiesel Project Report

Product Description and Uses

Biodiesel is a domestically produced, renewable fuel that can be manufactured from vegetable oils, or recycled restaurant oils. Biodiesel is safe, biodegradable, and reduces serious air pollutants such as participate, carbon monoxide, hydrocarbons, and air toxic. Blends of 20% biodiesel with 80% petroleum diesel (B-20) can generally be used in unmodified diesel engines. Biodiesel can also be used in its pure form (B-100), but it too may require certain engine modifications to avoid maintenance and performance problems.

Biodiesel (fatty acid alkyl esters) is a cleaner-burning diesel replacement fuel made from natural, renewable sources such as new and used vegetable oils and animal fats. Just like petroleum diesel, biodiesel operates in compression-ignition engines. Blends of up to 20% biodiesel (mixed with petroleum diesel fuels) can be used in nearly all diesel equipment and are compatible with most storage and distribution equipment. These low level blends (20% and less) generally do not require any engine modifications. Biodiesel can provide the same payload capacity and as diesel.

Using biodiesel in a conventional diesel engine substantially reduces emissions of unburned hydrocarbons, carbon monoxide, sulfates, polycyclic aromatic hydrocarbons, nitrated polycyclic aromatic hydrocarbons, and particulate matter. These reductions increase as the amount of biodiesel blended into diesel fuel increases. The test emissions reductions are seen with B-100.

The use of biodiesel decreases the solid carbon fraction of particulate matter (since the oxygen in biodiesel enables more complete combustion to CO_2) and reduces the sulfate fraction (biodiesel contains less than 24 ppm sulfur), while the soluble, or hydrocarbon, fraction stays the same or increases. Therefore, biodiesel works well with new technologies such as diesel oxidation catalysts (which reduce the soluble fraction of diesel particulate but not the solid carbon fraction).

Emissions of nitrogen oxides increase with the concentration of biodiesel in the fuel. Some biodiesel produces more nitrogen oxides than others, and some additives have shown promise in modifying the increases. More R & D is needed to resolve this issue.

Biodiesel has physical properties very similar to conventional diesel.

Biodiesel's Physical Characteristics

Specific gravity	0.87 to 0.89
Kinematic viscosity @ 40°C	3.7 to 5.8
Cetane number	46 to 70
Higher heating value (btu/lb)	16,928 to 17,996
Sulfur, wt %	0.0 to 0.0024
Cloud point °C	-11 to 16
Pour point °C	-15 to 13
Iodine number	60 to 135
Lower heating value (btu/lb)	15,700 to 16,735

Biodiesel is packed in 35 kg carboys, 225 kg MS Barrels and Bulk in Tankers.

How is Biodiesel Made.—Biodiesel fuel can be made from new or used vegetable oils, which are non-toxic, biodegradable, renewable resources. Fats and oils are chemically reacted with an alcohol (methanol is the usual choice) to produce chemical compounds known as fatty acid methyl esters. Biodiesel is the name given to these esters when they are intended for use as fuel. Glycerol (used in Pharmaceuticals and cosmetics, among other markets) is produced as a co-product.

Biodiesel can be produced by a variety of esterification technologies. The oils and fats are filtered and preprocessed to remove water and contaminants. If free fatty acids are present, they can be removed or transformed into biodiesel using special pretreatment technologies. The pretreated oils and fats are then mixed with an alcohol (usually methanol) and a catalyst (usually sodium or potassium hydroxide). The oil molecules (triglycerides) are broken apart and reformed into esters and glycerol, which are then separated from each other and purified. Approximately 55% of the biodiesel industry can use any fat or oil feedstock, including recycled cooking oils. The other half of the industry is limited to vegetable oils, the least expensive of which is *Jatropha* oil. The *Jatropha* oil industry has been the driving force behind biodiesel commercialization because of large production capacity, product surpluses, and declining prices. Similar issues apply to the recycled oils and animal fats industry, even though these feedstock are less expensive than *Jatropha* oils.

Biodiesel Benefits.—Biodiesel is a substitute or extender for traditional petroleum diesel and you don't need special pumps or high pressure equipment for fueling. In addition, it can be used in conventional diesel engines, so you don't need to buy special vehicles or engines to run biodiesel.

Scientists believe carbon dioxide is one of the main greenhouse gases contributing to global warming. Neat biodiesel (100 per cent biodiesel) reduces carbon dioxide emissions by more than 75 per cent over petroleum diesel. Using a blend of 20 per cent biodiesel reduces carbon dioxide emissions by 15 per cent.

Biodiesel also produces fewer particulate, carbon monoxide, and sulfur dioxide emissions, all targeted as public health risks by the Environmental Protection Agency.

Since biodiesel can be used in conventional diesel engines, the renewable fuel can directly replace petroleum products; reducing the country's dependence on imported oil.

Biodiesel offers safety benefits over petroleum diesel because it is much less combustible, with a flash point greater than 150°C, compared to 77°C for petroleum diesel. It is safe to handle, store, and transport.

Biodiesel can help reduce our dependence on foreign oil and help us leverage our fossil fuel supplies. It can also help reduce greenhouse gas emissions, as well as public health risks associated with air pollution. It is nontoxic and biodegradable. Biodiesel contains only trace amounts of sulfur, typically less than the new EPA standards that will go into effect in 2006 for diesel fuel. It is safe to handle, transport, and store, and has a higher flash point than petroleum diesel. It can also be stored in diesel tanks and pumped with regular equipment except in colder weather, where tank heaters or agitators may be required. Biodiesel mixes readily with petroleum diesel at any blend level, making it a very flexible fuel additive.

Biodiesel is an oxygenated fuel, so it contributes to a more complete fuel burn and a greatly improved emissions profile. The more biodiesel used in a blend, the higher the emission reductions. One of the unique benefits of biodiesel is that it significantly reduces air toxic that are associated with petroleum diesel exhaust and are suspected of causing cancer and other human health problems. NO_x emissions are an exception to the rule, since biodiesel tends to increase NO_x emissions. Recent research has shown a number of ways to mitigate this problem. You can use pure biodiesel in most engines made after 1994 with some limitations. Engine performance (fuel economy, torque, and power) can be less than that of diesel by 8% to 15%, because of the lower energy content of the biodiesel (about 93%). Consumers should be aware of potential cold weather problems during vehicle operation and fuel storage. Consumers should also watch for obvious signs of damage around seals and gaskets. You can use pure biodiesel in older engines, but the seals and gaskets are more likely to be damaged by biodiesel. Also, it helps to start out with a clean storage tank if pure biodiesel is used.

Most people use a blend of 20% biodiesel with petroleum diesel (B-20) to avoid the problems listed above. Engine performance with B-20 is virtually the same as with petroleum diesel. Problems associated with storage, seals and gaskets, and cold weather are minimal. Even very low amounts of biodiesel (1% to 2%) can provide substantial lubricity benefits to premium diesel fuels.

Every liter of biodiesel displaces 0.95 liter of petroleum-based diesel over its life cycle. It is also very energy efficient. For every unit of fossil energy used to produce biodiesel, 3.37 units of biodiesel energy are created. Additionally, biodiesel reduces the amount of carbon dioxide (CO_2) being released into the atmosphere. It releases less fossil CO_2 than does conventional diesel, and the crops used to produce biodiesel absorb large amounts of CO_2 as they grow. And because biodiesel is nontoxic and biodegradable, it is an excellent fuel for use in fragile environments such as estuaries, lakes, rivers, and national parks.

Description.—Biodiesel is a manufactured product, slightly yellow in colour, oily liquid with a slight aromatic odor and a bitter taste.

Applications.—It is commonly used as fuel for stationary diesel engine like pump sets and other agricultural implements and also in Diesel cars.

Standards.—Specifications for Biodiesel (B100): provided by the National Biodiesel Board.

- Standard Specification for Biodiesel Fuel (B100) Blend Stock for Distillate Fuels — provided by ASTM International.
- *Biodiesel Production and Quality:* provided by the National Biodiesel Board.
- Biodiesel Handling and Use Guidelines.
- Biodiesel Handling and Use Guidelines - Japanese version.
- Pure biodiesel (B-100 needs to meet the requirements of ASTM D-6751 to avoid engine operational problems. To obtain a copy of ASTM's Standard Specification for Biodicsel Fuel (B-100) Blend Stock for Distillate Fuels, visit the ASTM International Web site. This table summarizes the requirements for B-100.

Keep up with the latest biodiesel activities by reading the National Biodiesel Board's newsletter, Biodiesel Bulletin.

Transport information.—Hazardous for air, sea and road freight.

Personal protection.—Safety glasses, adequate ventilation.

Consumer Safety.—Biodiesel is used as substitute for Diesel and all safety precautions are same as that of petroleum diesel.

Market Survey and Demand Supply Position

Recent trends are indicative of tremendous increase in the production of Commercial Vehicles and the consumption of Diesel. The import bill is mounting and the availability is going down. New sources will have to be developed and new units have to be put up in the next decade to manufacture Biodiesel which will substitute imported diesel in large quantities to meet the domestic demand where by causing smaller drain of our limited sources of foreign exchange.

The growth of Automotive Industry, particularly in the last 15 years, has been spectacular. It is not the magnitude of volume only, but also the diversity of products (commercial vehicle, cars, two/three wheelers), which have been impressive. The proposed product, i.e. Biodiesel also shows a good potential growth for demand.

Existing Manufacturers.—Presently there are no manufacturers and a number of small scale units manufacturing this product will be set up, all over the country in next few years.

Installed Capacity And Production.—This product is manufactured depending on availability of local raw material supply and local demand to substitute petroleum diesel. The production of last few years is given below :

Year	Production Kilo liters/year
2004-05	Nil*
2005-06	500*

* Estimated.

So the present total production in India, of Biodiesel is estimated to be 500 Kilo liters per year.

Future Demand.—The major user of Biodiesel will be small farmers as well as for blending with diesel in petroleum refinery. The demand for the product will grow with the increase in production of Oil Engines. Due to shortage and irregular supply of electrical power, the growth rate for oil engines, is expected to be very high in coming years for states where electrical power is not easily available. Looking at the tremendous growth in Automotive and Stationary Oil Engines, which is projected to be 10% pa in terms of number of new engines, large quantities of diesel oil will be required. Taking into account the potential for Biodiesel units, the total capacity of these Biodiesel plants will substitute only a tiny fraction of the total diesel requirement.

Conclusion.—From the demand and supply position, it appears that there should be a good scope for a number of new venture with a capacity of 1 to 30 Kilo liters per day.

MANUFACTURING PROCESS DESCRIPTION

Raw Materials.—To manufacture 1 Kilo liters of Biodiesel, consumption of raw materials is as follows:

Methyl Alcohol (98 %)	150 liters.
Vegetable Oil	1,050 liters.
Caustic Potash	3.8 Kgs.

Input Materials Preparation.—*Jatropha* or Physic Nut Oil is the input material oil can be crude but should be filtered first if recently obtained from oil press. The feedstock should be free of water and other foreign materials. In case the temperature causes the vegetable oil to gel up or become solid, the material should be liquefied by heating up to 40°C in the reactor tank. (Oilseed Crushing Plant is an Optional Activities for input requirements).

Methanol, MeOH - Anhydrous and at least 98% pure, and container grounded to protect from sparks.

Potassium Hydroxide, KOH - At least 85% in purity in flakes, powder or pellets. It is very sensitive to atmospheric moisture and must be stored in air-tight containers. It can be purchased in 20 kg plastic bags.

First, an acid value test is run then a bench-scale batch (50 ml to 200 ml input oil) should be conducted to determine optimum amount of MeOH and KOH for successful operation for every batch of incoming vegetable oil or animal fat (30 minutes esterification or mixing).

Chemical Reaction.—The chemical reaction involved in the manufacture is as follows :

$$(C_nH_{n+2})COOH + CH_3OH \xrightarrow{\text{Catalyst}} H_3C\text{-}OOC(C_nH_{n+2}) + H_2O.$$

Brief Process Description

Trans-esterification (for a series of batches or semi-continuous process).—Required amount of MeOH and KOH are mixed in catalyst reactor (takes about 10 minutes), until KOH has completely dissolved, (the solution becomes potassium methoxide). Vegetable oil is then poured or transferred to main reactor having desired amount of vegetable oil or animal fat. (Reactor tank is calibrated to allow faster determination of volume).

The methoxide is then poured into the reactor and mixing is started immediately. It is mixed for 60 minutes (esterrfication process). The ester material is then transferred (by pump or gravity) into the settling tank(s). In semi-continuous process, mixing of MeOH and KOH can be simultaneously done during the esterification step.

Settling/Phase Separation.—The mixture is settled for 6—18 hours. Two phases or layers will be observed. (Settling tank has a viewing mechanism, either a clear hose, sight glass or window strip). The bottom phase (crude glycerin) is drained, or pumped out into the glycerin container for purification or removal of excess MeOH. The upper phase (Biodiesel) is transferred into a washing tank for washing.

Biodiesel Sweetening/Refining.—Excess MeOH in the Biodiesel is removed using either vacuum or by heating. The Biodiesel may be washed with acidified water. This can be accomplished by mixing acetic acid (tannic or acetic acid) with water. Volume of water is about 40% that of Biodiesel. The acidified water is stirred into the Biodiesel as aeration stones near the bottom of the tank bubble water and air up through the fuel. After settling overnight the water is drained off the bottom. If necessary the fuel is then dried with heat, stirring and aeration. This step toay me omitted if settling time is over 18 hours, or KOH in the Biodiesel is below 50 ppm or 0.005% and filtered using at least 2 microns. The Biodiesel is pumped into the storage or packaging container. The pump should be equipped with at least 2 microns filter.

Optional Activities.—Methanol Recovery: Methanol recovered from Biodiesel and crude glycerin may be used back in the esterification process. Recovered methanol must be anhydrous and 98% pure, for effective use.

Crude Glycerin Purification/Disposal.—MeOH is removed from crude glycerin by vacuum or heating. Glycerin may be purified using ion-exchange method (Bulgarian Process) or tower distillation method (High heat traditional method). Glycerin may be shipped to a glycerin purification plant nearby.

Oilseed Crushing Plant.—For a 500 liter per day Biodiesel plant (with 21 days per month or 250 days operation per year), the crushing plant should be able to provide at least 125,000 liter per year. This requires at least 72 hectares of area planted with *Jatropha.* For *Jatropha* at 80% oil expelling efficiency and 30% oil content, the crushing plant needs 1150 kg of *Jatropha* seeds per day (200kg/hr expeller is needed), at 8 hours/day operation. For semi-continuous 4 batch/day these amounts will increase by four times.

BIODIESEL PROCESS IN DETAIL

Ingredients

Reaction Raw Materials.—*Jatropha* Oil, Methanol (CH_3OH) 99%+ pure, Potassium hydroxide (must be dry).

Titration.—Isopropyl alcohol 99%+ pure, Distilled water, Phenolphthalein solution (not more than a year old, kept protected from strong light).

Washing.—Vinegar, Water.

Procedure

Filter oil to remove any solid particles. Heat oil to remove any water content (optional). Perform titration to determine how much catalyst is needed. Prepare potassium methoxide. Heat oil if required, mix in the potassium methoxide while stirring. Allow to settle, remove the glycerine. Wash and dry. Check quality.

This procedure is called trans-esterification, similar to soap making. (To make soap you take a transfatty acid or triglyceride oil and blend it with a solution of potassium hydroxide and water. This reaction causes the ester chains to separate from the glycerine. These ester chains are what becomes the soap. They are also called lipids. Their unique characteristic of being attracted to polar molecules such as water on one end and to non-polar olecules like oil on the other end is what makes them effective as soap).

In trans-esterification, KOH and methanol are mixed to create potassium methoxide ($K^+ CH_3O^-$). When mixed in with the oil this strong polar-bonded chemical breaks the transfatty acid into glycerine and also ester chains (biodiesel), along with some soap if you are not careful. The esters become methyl esters. They would be ethyl esters if reacted with ethanol instead of methanol.

1. **Filtering.**—Filter the oil to remove solid particles. You may have to warm it up a bit first to get it to run freely, 35°C should be enough. Use a double layer of cheesecloth in a funnel, or a restaurant or canteen-type coffee filter.
2. **Removing the Water.**—Heat the oil first to remove any water content. Waste oil will probably contain water, which can slow down the reaction and cause saponification (soap formation). The less water in the oil the better. Raise the temperature to 100°C, hold it there and allow any water to boil off. Use a mixer to avoid steam pockets forming below the oil and exploding, splashing hot oil out of the container. Or drain water puddles out from the bottom as they form, you can save any oil that comes out with the water later. When boiling slows, raise the temperature to 130°C for 10 minutes. Remove heat and allow to cool. Regular source of oil does not need to have the water boiled off, in which case do not do it, boiling means extra energy and time.
3. **Basic Titration.**—Dissolve 1 gram of KOH in 1 liter of distilled or de-ionized water (0.1% KOH solution). An electronic pH meter is best, but you can also use pH test strips (or litmus paper), or henolphthalein solution to get end point. In a smaller beaker, dissolve 1 ml of dewatered oil in 10 ml of pure isopropyl alcohol. Warm the beaker gently by standing it in some hot water, stir until all the oil dissolves in the alcohol and the mixture turns clear. Add 2 drops of phenolphthalein solution.

Using a burette, add 0.1% KOH solution drop by drop to the oil alcohol phenolphthalein solution, stirring all the time, until the solution stays pink (magenta) for 10 seconds. Take the number of mis of 0.1% KOH solution you used and add 5.0. This is the number of grams of KOH you will need per liter of oil.

With a pH meter or test strips, use the same procedure without adding the phenolphthalein. Add the 0.1% KOH solution drop by drop as before until the pH reaches 8.5.

4. **Test Batches.**—The first few times you do this process, it is a good practice to first try out your KOH amounts on a 1 liter batch. This works really well and you do not need to heat up the oil too much, just enough so it will spin well. Start by mixing up the KOH and methanol. First make sure that vessels used are dry. Forming the exothermal potassium methoxide polar molecule will heat up the vessel a bit. Keep mixing until all the KOH has been dissolved.

   Once the potassium methoxide is prepared, add to 1 liter of oil. Make certain all your weights and volumes are precise. If you are unsure of the titration result then use 5.0 grams of KOH per liter of oil. Smaller batches need only be run for about 15—20 minutes for separation to be completed before switching off. The settling takes sometime to complete. The solution can be poured from the vessel into another container right after switching off the agitator. It is good to do a few batches with varying amounts of KOH recorded, so later when checking results one can choose the KOH quantity that did the best job. When too much KOH is used the result can be a troublesome gel that is tough to do anything with. When not enough KOH is used the reaction does not go far enough so some unreacted oil will be mixed with the biodiesel and glycerine. This will form three levels with biodiesel on top above unreacted oil with glycerine on the bottom. If there is too much water in the oil it will form soaps and settle right above the glycerine forming a fourth level in the container. This layer is not too easy to separate from the unreacted oil and glycerine layers.

5. **Preparing the Potassium Methoxide.**—Generally the amount of methanol needed is 20% of the oil by mass. The densities of these two liquids are fairly close, so 20% of methanol by volume should be about right. To be completely sure, measure out a half-liter of both fluids, weigh, and calculate exactly what 20% by mass is. Different oils can have different densities depending on what type of oil it originally was.

   Example.—When trans-esterifying 100 liters of oil, use 20 liters of methanol. The methanol is mixed into a solution with the KOH, creating potassium methoxide in an exothermic reaction (it gets warm from bonds forming). Keep all utensils the KOH comes in contact with as dry as possible.

CAUTION.—Treat potassium methoxide with extreme caution! Do not inhale any vapours! If any potassium methoxide gets splashed on your skin, it will burn you without your feeling it (killing the nerves). Wash immediately with lots of water. Always have a hose running when working with potassium methoxide. Potassium methoxide is also very corrosive to paints. KOH reacts with aluminum, tin and zinc. Use glass, enamel or stainless steel containers, stainless steel is best.

6. **Heating and Mixing.**—Pre-heat waste vegetable oil 48—54 °C. A propeller coupled to a electric motor works fine as a mixer. Too much agitation causes splashing and bubbles through vortexing and reduces mix efficiency. There should be a vortex just appearing on the surface. Adjust the speed, or the pitch or size of the stirrer to get the right effect. Alternately an electric pump plumbed to form a mixing loop for stirring the oil would do a nice job. Mount the pump above the level that glycerine will gel at, to prevent clogging up the pump.

   Add the potassium methoxide to the oil while stirring, stir the mixture for 50 minutes to an hour. The reaction is often complete in 30 minutes, but longer is better. The trans-esterification process separates the methyl esters from the glycerine. The CH_3O of the methanol then caps off the ester chains and OH from the KOH stabilizes the glycerine.

7. **Settling and Separation.**—Allow the solution to settle and cool for at least eight hours, preferably longer. The methyl esters (biodiesel) will be floating on top while the denser glycerine will have congealed on the bottom of the container forming a hard gelatinous mass (the mixing pump must be mounted above this level). An alternative method is to allow the reactants to settle for at least an hour after mixing while keeping the mixture above 38°C, which keeps the glycerine semi-liquid (it solidifies below 38°C). Then carefully decant the biodiesel. This can be done by draining the reactants out of the bottom of the container through a transparent hose. The semi-liquid glycerine has a dark brown colour and the biodiesel is honey-coloured. Keep a watch on what flows through the sight tube. When the lighter-coloured biodiesel appears divert it to a separate container. If any biodiesel stays with the glycerine it is easy to retrieve it later once the glycerine has solidified. If you left the mixture in the tank until the glycerine gelled, reheat the tank just enough to liquify the glycerine again. Do not stir it! Then decant it out as above.

8. **Glycerine.**—The glycerine from oil is brown and usually turns to a solid below about 38°C. Glycerine from fresh oil often stays a liquid at lower temperatures. Reclaimed glycerine is composted after being

vented for three weeks to allow residual methanol to evaporate off or after heating it to 66°C to boil off any methanol content (the boiling point of methanol is 64.7°C). The excess methanol can be recovered for re-use when boiled off if you run the vapours through a condenser. Another way of disposing of the glycerine, though a great bit more complicated, would be to separate its components, mostly methanol, pure glycerine (a valuable product for medicines, tinctures, hand lotions, dried plant arrangements and many other uses) and wax. This is often accomplished by distilling it, but glycerine has a high boiling point even under high vacuum so this method is difficult. Other idea for disposing of the glycerine is breaking it down to usable methane gas, with a Bio Gas methane digester.

9. **Soap Residue.**—Suspended in the biodiesel will also be some soapy ' residues. These are the result of K^+ ions from the KOH reacting with water created when the methanol bonds with the ester chains along with any other water that was suspended in the oil. If the reaction produces more than the usual amount of soap, this happens when KOH comes into contact with water before it has a chance to react with the oil. In this case the excess water should have been boiled off first.

   The part of the process where it is vital to keep all water out of the reaction is when making the potassium methoxide. Keep the vessels KOH comes in contact with as dry as possible. The chances of a good clean splitting of ester from glycerine with little soap by-product are much better on a warm dry summer day than on a damp winter day.

10. **Washing and Drying.**—The biodiesel from this stage can be used to the fuel tanks of vehicles. It is to let it settle for a while (about 2 days), allowing the majority of the soap residues to settle before running the biodiesel through a filtration system then into the vehicle fuel tank. Another method is to wash the soaps out of the fuel with water, one or more times. When washing biodiesel the first time it is best to add a small amount of dilute acetic acid before adding the water. The acetic acid brings the pH of the solution closer to neutral because it neutralizes and drops out any KOH suspended in the biodiesel.

    A simple way of washing is using a PVC container with a valve 3-4 inches from bottom. Fill with water until it is halfway between the container's bottom and the valve, then fill up with the biodiesel to be washed. After a gentle stirring (keep it gentle, do not agitate up soaps) followed by 12—24 hours of settling, the oil and water will separate, the cleaned oil can be decanted out the valve, leaving the denser soapy water to be drained out the bottom. This process might have to be repeated two or three times to remove close to 100% of soaps. The

Production of Biodiesel using Jatropha as Feedstock

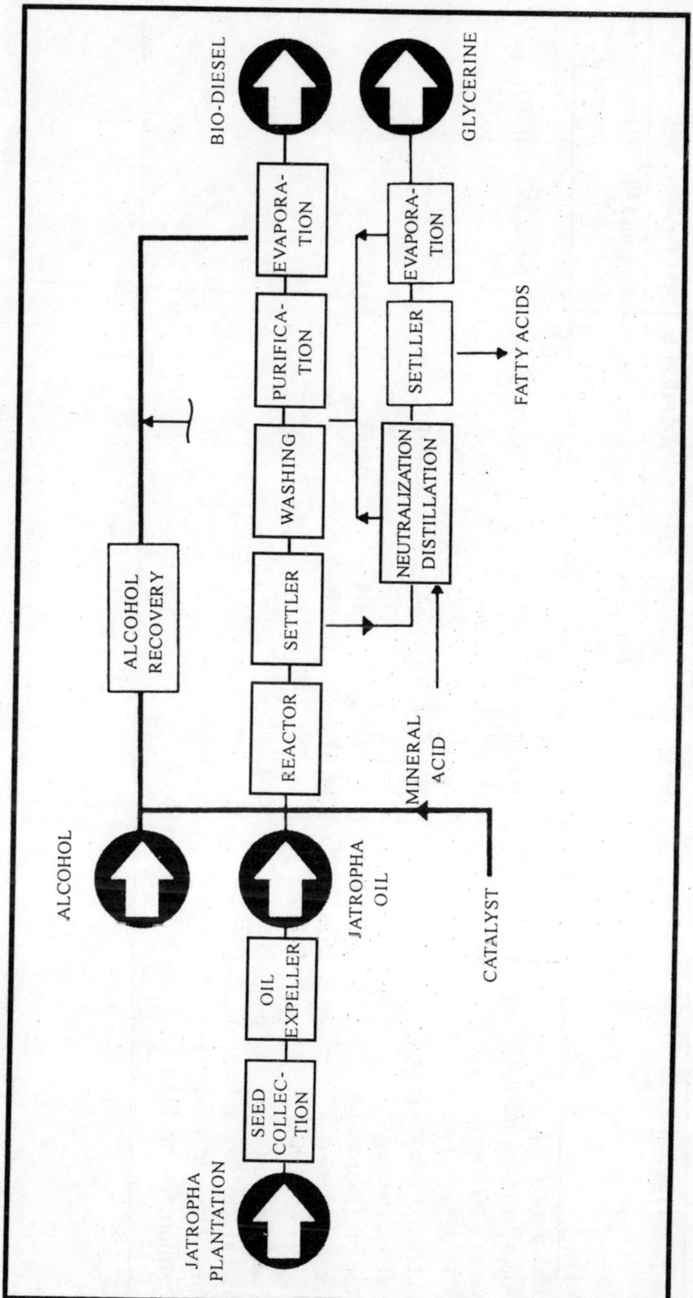

Biodiesel Specifications and Testing Results

Property (units)	ASTM D-6751	Limits	Methyl Esters of oils			
			Sunflower Oil	Palm Oil	Jatropha Oil	*Pongamia pinnata*
Flash point (°C)	D-93	Min. 130	73	127	163	92
Phosphorus (% mass)	D-4951	Max.0.001	<0.oo1	<o.oo1	<0.oo1	0.001
Water & sediment (% vol)	D-2709	Max. 0.050	0.04	0.01	0.05	0.03
CCR100% (% mass)	D-4530	Max. 0.050	0.01	<o.o1	<o.o1	<o.o1
Sulphated ash (% mass)	D-874	Max. 0.020	0.001	n.d	n.d.	0.002
Viscosity at 40° C (cst)	D-445	1.9—6.0	4.103	4.506	4.440	4.16
Sulphur (% mass)	D-5453	Max. 0.05	0.04	0.038	O.020	0.003
Cetane number	D-613	Min. 47	55.6	54.6	57.1	55.1
Copper corrosion	D-130	Max. 3	1	1b	1b	1b
Neutralization value	D-664	Max. 0.80	0.20	0.24	0.48	0.10
Free glycerin (% mass)	D-6584	Max. 0.020	0.02	0.01	0.01	0.01
Total glycerin (% mass)	D-6584	Max. 0.240	0.02	0.01	0.02	0.01
Distillation temp. (360°C)	D-1160	90%	90%	90%	90%	90%

second and third washings can be done with water alone. After the third washing any remaining water gets removed by reheating the oil slowly, the water and other impurities sink to bottom. The finished product should have a pH of 7, checked with litmus paper or with a digital pH tester.

The water from the third wash can be used for the first or second washes for the next batch. The impurities can be left in the re-heater for the next batch and removed when it accumulates. Transesterified and washed biodiesel will become clearer over time as any remaining soaps drop out of the solution.

Quantity of Methanol to be Used

The stoichiometric quantity of methanol is the amount needed to convert triclycerides (oils) into esters (biodiesel), the methyl portion of methyl esters. You also need an excess of methanol to push the conversion process towards completion, without the excess the process runs out (reaches equilibrium) before all the triglycerides are converted to esters, resulting in poor fuel that does not combust well and can be corrosive. The excess methanol acts more like a catalyst. It encourages the process but does not become a part of the final product and can be recovered afterwards.

1. **Stoichiometric quantity.**—The stoichiometric quantity is usually said to be 12.5% methanol by volume, that is, 125 ml of methanol per litre of oil. In fact it depends on the amounts of the various fatty acids in the oil, and varies from one oil to another. Calculate the average proportions of the different fatty acids in each of the more common oils, calculate their total molecular weights, and from this calculate the stoichiometric amount of methanol required to convert them. The amount varies from 11.3% for rapeseed oil (canola) to 16.3% for coconut oil. These figures are averages, fatty acid quantities vary somewhat when oil crops are grown in different conditions in different parts of the world. But they are close enough for our purposes, and a lot more accurate than the general figure of 12.5%. If you have an analysis of the fatty acid content of your oil, you can calculate the correct stoichiometric ratio.
2. **Excess.**—How much excess is needed depends on several different factors: the type of oil, its condition, the type, size and shape of the processor, the type and duration of agitation, the temperature of the process, and it does not make much sense anyway if the stoichiometric ratio is wrong in the first place. However, excess is usually between 60% and 100% of the stoichiometric amount.

The stoichiometric ratio of *Jatropha* oil is 12.5%, that is 125 ml of methanol per liter of oil, the excess would range between 75 ml and 125 ml, for a total amount of methanol of 200—250 ml per litre of oil. Oils with higher stoichiometric ratios seem to need higher excesses. So, for fresh soya or canola, you can try 60%, though 67% or more would be better. For palm kernel or coconut, closer to 100% excess would be better. If you do not know what kind of oil it is, try using 25% methanol, 250 ml methanol to 1 liter of oil. If you've taken care with the titration, used accurate measurements and followed the instructions carefully, you should get a good, clean split, with esters on top and the glycerine and free fatty acids cleanly separated at the bottom. If you have trouble washing it, with a lot of frothing, that could be because the process did not go far enough and unconverted material is forming emulsions, try using more methanol next time. If everything works well, try using less methanol. You will soon figure out what's best for you.

Treatment of Liquid Effluents

There is only one point from where the effluent is discharged with traces of catalyst. The methanol will be recovered and will be absent in effluent. It is lead to collection tank. It is then allowed to settle. The clear treated water which will be within limits for BOD and COD will be used for gardening purposes.

Power Requirement

The requirement of electrical power will be 20.5 KW of connected load, which is available from local electrical supply agency.

Details of power requirement for the equipments is given below :

SI. No.	Equipments		Quantity	Power HP
1.	Catalyst Reactor Pump		1	1.00
2.	Main Reactor Pump		1	1.00
3.	Washing Vessel Pump		1	2.00
4.	Settling Tank Pump		1	2.00
5.	Heaters		1	15.00
6.	Lighting			0.50
7.	Miscellaneous			2.00
8.	Air Compressor		1	2.00
9.	Cooling Water Pump		1	2.00
			TOTAL H.P.	27-50
Requirement of connected load		=	27.50	x 0.75 KW
		=	20.63	KW
Requirement of Fuel Oil		=	0.2	KL.
Requirement of Water		=	50	cu.m.

Utilities Specifications

Process Water.—Process water should be free of mud and suspended particles. It should be available at a pressure of 3 Kg/sq.cm.

Electricity.—It shall be available at 440 volts, A/C supply at 50 Hz. frequency and 3 phase supply.

Cooling Water.—It should be available at 30°C and a return temperature of 37°C at a pressure of 4/cm^2.

Steam.—It should be available at 10 Kg/sq. cm pressure.

Marment and Selling Arrangements

The item will be manufactured by a few units. This will help in selling product, taking advantage for schemes in remote area. The entrepreneur is well connected with consuming industry. The product will be mostly sold in local area.

The product will be sold directly to bulk customers and in certain cases through agents and suppliers allowing some commission. Competition is proposed to be met by aggressive marketing, maintaining good quality and cheaper rates.

Negotiations are being made with various prospective customers and they are found interested in purchasing the product for their annual requirements.

Production Capacity and Target

Year	I	II	III	IV	V	VI	VII
Capacity	70	80	90	100	100	100	100
	Utilization % BIODIESEL						
Production KL/year	175	200	225	250	250	250	250
	Crude GLYCERINE						
Production tons/year	41	46	52	58	58	58	58

Cost of Project and Means of Finance

A. Cost of Finance	Rs.
1. Land and site	5300
2. Building and Civil Work	98400
3. Plant And Machinery	978652
4. Utilities	340000
5. Knowhow and Engineering Fees	50000
6. Misc. Fixed Assets	171673

PLANT AND MACHINERY

Sl. No.	Equipment	Specifications	Capacity Liters	Qty Nos.	Price Rs.
A. MAIN PLANT					
1.	Catalyst Reactor made of SS-304		340	1	50000
2.	Main Reactor made of SS-304		1500	1	100000
3.	Vapour Condenser of area 1 sq.m. of MS			1	50000
4.	Settling Tank made of SS-304		1500	1	150000
5.	Settling Tank made of SS-304		2000	1	200000
6.	Micron Filters made of SS-304				20000
			Total Rs.		**570000**
B. STORAGE TANKS					
1.	Methyl Alcohol Storage Tank		5000	1	30000
2.	Product Storage Tank		5000	1	30000
3.	Vegetable Oil Storage Tank		5000	1	30000
			Total Rs.		**90000**
C. PUMPS					
1.	Catalyst Reactor Pump			1	5000

SI. No.	Equipment	Specifications	Capacity Liters	Qty Nos.	Price Rs
2.	Main Reactor Pump			1	5000
3.	Washing Vessel Pump			1	10000
4.	Settling Tank Pump			1	10000
			Total Rs.		**30000**

Total P lantco st (A+ B + C)	·690000
Add: C Excise@ 15.75%'	108675
	798675
Add: M.Sales Tax @ 10 96	79868
	878543
Add: Insurance @ 1%	8785
Add: Transportation, Freight,	887328
Packing, Loading, Forwarcing,	
Unloading Charges to Factory Site @ 4%	35493
	922821
Add: Erection and Commissioning charges @ 5%	46141
	968962
Add: Painting/Coating Charges	9690
Grand Total Rs.	**978652**

7.	Prelim, and Preoperative Expences	46980
8.	Contingencies, and Escalation	97700
9.	Margin Money for working Capital	348206
	Total	**2136911**

Land

(a)	Cost of 100 sq. mt. land	@Rs. 40/sq.m.	4000
(b)	Cost of Leveling and Land Development @Rs. 2.0 per sq. m.		200
(c)	Cost of Construction of Roads		500
(d)	Cost of Fencing		500
(e)	Cost of Gate		100
	Total Rs.		5300

Building

		Area sq. m.	**Rate Rs/sq. m.**	**Total Rs.**
(a)	Factory Building with Staircase and Water Tank Office Building	30	2500	75000
(b)	Watchman's Cabin	5	2000	10000
(c)	Equipment Foundations, Sewers, Drains etc.			2500
(d)	Effluent Tanks			5000
(e)	Misc. Civil Work			5000
(f)	Architect and Structural Engineers' fee			900
			Sub Total	98400
	Total of Land and Building			103700

Cost of Utilities

SI.. No.	**Description**	**Capacity**	**Rate Rs.**	**Cost Rs.**
1.	Boiler 100 Kg/hr		5000	300000
2.	Air Compressor		10000	10000

3.	Cooling Tower for Cooling Water	20 USGPM	20000	30000
	Total Rs.			**340000**
	Add: Transport, Erection, Fitting, Insurance etc. @5%			17000
	Total Rs.			**357000**

VARIOUS PROJECT REPORTS IN CD-ROMS

50 ELECTRICAL, ELECTRONIC AND COMPUTER BASED INDUSTRIES Rs. 12000/-

Air conditioners & parts, AAC & ACSR aluminium conductors, business process outsource (B.P.O.), cyber cafe, Call centre (international), Call centre (domestic), Ceiling fan, Chokes & patties, Chokes & starters, Choke of fluorescent tubes, Compact disk, Computer education institute, Computer assembly, Computer continuous stationery, Computer software, Cello tape, Compact fluorescent lamps, Distribution transformer, Domestic transformer, Electrical panel boards, Electrical domestic appliances, Electric energy meters, Electric fans, Electric motors, Electric switches and sockets, Electronic choke (ballast), Electronic toys (E.O.U), Electrical stamping for transformer, Electrical repairing, Epoxy transformers, F.H.P. motors, GLS lamps, GLS lamps & fluorescent tubes, H.T. & l.t. insulator, HT air brake switches d.o. fuse, Lightening arrestor, Integrated circuits, Light emitting diodes (L.E.D.), Miniature circuit breaker, Mixer/grinder (mixi), Medical transcription, printed circuit boards (PCB), PVC wires and cables, power inverters, Power transformer, Portal, Solar cells, Tubular poles for electrical transmission, Telephone (push button & cordless), un interrupted power supply, Servo controlled stabilizer, Voltage stabilizer.

54 PAINT, VARNISH, SOLVENTS, LACQUERS, RESINS, ENAMEL, PIGMENTS THINNER & POWDER COATING PROJECTS Rs. 12000/-

The content cover in cd rom- automobile paints, Aluminium paint , Acrylic copolymer emulsion, Acrylic emulsion paints, Bituminous based corrosion resistant, Cement paint, Clear transparent lacquer for coating on brass bangles to make it weather-resistant, Copper phthalocyanine blue & green , Dry distemper and cement paint, (water based) in liquid form for electrophoretic coating application on metal plates, Enamel removers, Enamelling of copper wire, Epoxy resins, Glass putty, glass coating solution, Hammertone paints, Insulating varnish, insulating varnish, (Poly Vinyl butyral based, ffc grade), Lime colour/cement colour (synthetic- red iron oxide) used for Šflooring , Lacquer emulsion (high shine and medium shine) for leather finishing & N.C.lacquer for leather finishing (formulation & manufacturing processes), Naphtha based thinner, N.C.putty , N.C. thinners used in automobiles , Oil-bound distemper paints, Paint industry paint removers, Paint driers, powder coating paints, Paint and reducer, Primer paints, Enamel paints & distemper, Powder coating primer paints & enamel paints, Poly vinyl acetate emulsion, Pigments binders for textile printing putty and water proofing paint, Phenol formaldehyde resin, Poly amide resin, Refractory paint (graphite based), Red oxide pigments from iron pickling plant waste, Stoving paint, Silicone emulsion for textile, Stainer for paints, Solvents & thinners, Texture paints, thinners,thinners (ethyl alcohol based), Thinners (white spirit based), Urea formaldehyde resin, Unsaturated polyester resins, varnish (clear) for wood (flame-retarding type), Wood primer for paints, Wall putty, Wire enamel.

67 RUBBER AND RUBBER GOODS INDUSTRIES Rs. 12000/-

Auto tyre tubes & flaps, Autorubber moulding parts & steel jacks, Auto tubes, Coir foam (rubberized coir), Crumb rubber, Crumb rubber modified bitumen (crmb), Cycles tyres and tubes, Field rubber converted to the 60% latex rubber, Gaskets, Hawai chappals, hard rubber battery container, Hose pipe Rubber (Radiator),(Rubber Hoses for Automobiles), Latex foam rubber (spong rubber), Latex rubber thread, Latex rubber based adhesive, latex rubber condoms, Latex foam rubber stabilizer, Microcellular sheets(rubber sheets for shoe soles, Oil seals,'o' ringss, Rubber powder, Rubber hose pipe, Rubber auto gaskets, Rubber eraser, rubberised cork sheet, Rubberised foam for manufacture of mattresses, Cushion etc., Rubber auto parts, Rubber goods from waste rubber, Rubber band, Rubber plantation, Rubber process oil, rubber hoses for automobiles, Rubber reclaiming, Rubber ball, rubber beading for automobiles, Rubber epdm auto parts, Rubber transmission belt & v-belt, Rubber stereo, Rubber & plastic sheets, Mats & flaps, Rubber sheet for automobiles, Rubber balloon, Rubber cots and aprons, Rubber roller for textile mills & paper industrie, Rubber flooring, Rubber solutions, rubber adhesive for plywood, Rubber rollers & ebonite rollers, rubberized cloth, Rubber hose pipe & rubber glazing, Rubber moulding & lining of rubber sheeting, Rubber adhesive (all purpose) neoprene & isoprene basedrubber moulding & lining of rubber sheeting, Rubber chappel and rubber sheet, Rubber sheet and allied hospital rubber goods, Rubber caps (closures) for pharmaceutical uses, Rubber plastic stamp & pad (automatic), rubber compound for toys (using plaster of paris), Rubber sheets for shoe soles (eva) (ethylene vinyl acetate sheet for sole), Surgical examination gloves (disposable), Synthetic rubber adhesive, Silicon rubber nipple/teats, Tyres, tubes & flap (moped to truck), Tyre retreading materials (tread rubber, Cushion, gum (compound) rubber solution pre-cured rubber),Tyre & tubes, Tyre retreading by cold process, Vulcanising adhesive formulation vulcanizing rubber solution/cement for automobile tyres, V-belts water based latex adhesives.

52 COSMETICS (HERBAL & SYNTHETICS) TECHNOLOGY PROJECTS (52 PROJECTS REPORTS) Rs. 12000/-

After shave lotion, Antiseptic cream (boro plus type), Ayurvedic dant manjan (red colour - dabur type), Anti-dandruff cream, Aloe vera gel stabilized, Ayurvedic medicines, Body creams and lotions, Baby oil (body oil), Cosmetics industry (modern), Cold creams, Car shampoo, Coconut oil from copra, Detergent cake & powder, Enamel removers, Extraction of essential oil (cardamon, jeera, ajowan, ginger oil etc.) & packing of ground spice,Face mask (liquid form) strawberry flavour (milk mask, Cleansing mask, butter milk mask,paw paw mask & others), Face cream and body cream , Herbal cosmetic , Henna paste making, Hair oils, Hair dye in form of hair oil, Herbal face paste, Herbal shampoo & creams, hair removing cream, Hair fixer (hair gel for afro hair), Hair removing wax, Hair colour mate (formulations and process), Herbal tooth paste & tooth powder, Hair dye liquid, herbal extracts, hair dye powder, Hair colour mate (formulations and process), keshkala tel (vasmol or godrej keshkala tel type), Kali mehandi powder (hair dye powder), Lipsticks , Liquid soap, liquid bindi & sindur, Liquid toilet cleaner (Harpic type), Mustard oil, Nail enamel (nail polish), Rose water, Shampoo, Shaving Cream, scents and perfumes, Spray (perfume), Toilet soap industry (soap from soap stock), Toilet & herbal soap, Tooth powders, Tooth paste gel type (like colgate, close-up etc.),Tooth paste (calcium carbonate base), Toilet soap with glycerine transparent soap, Talcum powder (face & toilet powder).

ENGINEERS INDIA RESEARCH INSTITUTE Mobile : 9811437895

4449, Nai Sarak, Main Road, Delhi - 110 006 (INDIA) Ph./Fax : 91-11- 23918117, 23916431, 23840361